SUCCESS IS A MINDSTATE

The Struggle, Hustle, and Evolution of Shiloh Jones

SUCCESS IS A MINDSTATE

THE STRUGGLE, HUSTLE, AND EVOLUTION OF SHILOH JONES

A Street-preneur's Autobiography
By

Shiloh Jones

Disclaimer: This is the author's recollection of events, relayed according to the best of his knowledge. The names and attributes of people mentioned in this book may have been changed to protect anonymity.

Copyright © 2022 by Shiloh Jones.

All rights reserved. No part of this book may be used or reproduced in any manner whatsoever without prior written consent of the authors, except as provided by the United States of America copyright law.

Published by Best Seller Publishing®, St. Augustine, FL
Best Seller Publishing® is a registered trademark.
Printed in the United States of America.
ISBN:978-1-956649-71-0

This publication is designed to provide accurate and authoritative information with regard to the subject matter covered. It is sold with the understanding that the publisher is not engaged in rendering legal, accounting, or other professional advice. If legal advice or other expert assistance is required, the services of a competent professional should be sought. The opinions expressed by the authors in this book are not endorsed by Best Seller Publishing® and are the sole responsibility of the author rendering the opinion.

For more information, please write:
Best Seller Publishing®
53 Marine Street
St. Augustine, FL 32084
or call 1 (626) 765-9750
Visit us online at: www.BestSellerPublishing.org

Contents

Dedication ix
Prologue xiii

Part I: THEN 1

1. Ages 1 to 7: This Is Where My Story Starts 3
2. Ages 7 to 11: Welcome to the Jungle 17
3. Age 11: The Day That Changed Me Forever................29
4. Age 12: Finding My Rhyme 37
5. Age 13: "By the Way, My Name Is Brother Hakeem"...43
6. Ages 13 to 15: My First Job, Cleaning Porta Potties....53
7. Age 15: Pops Walks Back Into My Life........................63
8. Age 15: Chimborazo Boulevard, Between P Street and M Street 75
9. Age 16: We Ride Together or We Die Together 87
10. Age 17: "This Is the Richmond Police; Open Up" 97
11. Age 17: There Was a Weird Energy about the Place ..107
12. Age 18: "I'm Pregnant, and I'm Keeping It"...............119
13. Age 18: That Soul Connection Was in Her Eyes........127
14. Age 19: Elated, Scared, Empowered, Refueled, and Reborn ...137
15. Age 20: Only Thing I'm Left with Is You, Weed 149
16. Ages 20 to 22: Let's Hear It for New York.................157

17 Age 22: It All Started with a Cough 175
18 Age 22: Money in Motion: Approaching Hustling as a
     Business..181
19 Age 24: Beware the Wounded Ego 193
20 Ages 21 to 25: One of the Lucky Few Who Made It out
     of the Game 205
21 Age 25: We've All Got Demons...223
22 Ages 25 to 38: God Works in Mysterious Ways! 233

Part II: NOW **239**

23 One Mistake Away from Prison to Successful Businessman...241
24 Coming to Terms with My Anger and Finding
     Forgiveness for My Pops 247
25 Evolution...255
26 Making the Transition from
     the Streets to the Corporate World......................................265
27 How to Maintain Success 271
28 Becoming the Best Version of Yourself 281
29 Doing the Right Thing Means Doing Things Right!...............291
30 Use Me but Don't Misuse Me..295
31 Burning the Candle at Both Ends 299
32 What I Learned from the Club...307
33 Advice on a Stick, Wisdom on a Platter...................................313
34 So What about Sheila?..327
35 My Reason Will Always Be My Girls 333
And Then It All Makes Sense..343

Part III: RESPECT **347**

   My Dad: By Ree Jones, My Daughter 349
   The Continuing Success of Shiloh Jones:
      By Bill Jones, My Father 351
   What the Evolution of Shiloh Jones Means to Me:
      By B. J. Moore, My Friend 355
   Shiloh Jones: By Jetaune Bledsoe, My Friend 359
   What I Know about Shiloh Jones: By George Copeland,
      My Friend and Mentee..361
   The Evolution of Shiloh Jones: By Rocstagis............................363

Epilogue 365

Dedication

Thanks for your interest in reading this book about me and my perspective on life. Hopefully, you can pull from a number of things I've talked about and put them to use in your own journey. My goal is to inspire you, motivate you, entertain you, and connect with you. But before we get fully into this shit, I'd like to dedicate, shout out, and give love where it's due.

Gratitude to God and the Universe

Not to sound cliché, but nothing is possible without the help of what I call God and the universe. You may have a different way of thinking about spiritual energy and divine presence, but it's my belief that it's all the same oneness, the same connection, that we have the power to tap into. I owe this energy my first thanks and my highest respect. It is this energy that willed me to write this book and showed me that my story is bigger than myself and should be shared with you.

Love to My Family

To my mother, who has made huge positive changes in her life with incredible discipline and willpower. Through the work of evolution and hard work on both our parts, we have developed a relationship now that is beyond our expectations. She is an amazing human being who has learned to take mental illness and use it to find purpose in her life currently.

To my firstborn and fellow Aquarian, Ree. My greatest hope is that she "unlocks" her powerful inner potential and surpasses my success in life because she has that "it" factor.

To Kai, my second child and one of the most amazing beings I know.

To one of the most beautiful human beings I know, Sheila, you have an incredible soul! I really want to say thank you for always believing in me and sticking by my side, even when I was lost and angry. No matter what happens, I will always have your back as you've had mine.

To Bill Jones, my father and a source of inspiration, especially with his amazing transformation in the last twenty years.

All of you have been very pivotal in my own evolution.

Thanks to My Friends

Especially those who hounded me about writing this book over the past few years: DaVon Wimbush (aka Rocstagis), I appreciate you as a brother.

Angelo, you are also my brother, and I will be there for you through thick and thin.

To my other brothers, B. J. Moore, Cecilio, James, Yah, George, Tarik, and Ish: man, I love all of y'all, and I'm only a phone call away if you ever need me.

Also, very big love to my group of brothers I speak to almost every day: my bro Rio, Kino, Pat, Pope, Mal, Kwame, Wayne, and Lequan. You guys help me stay balanced on a daily and weekly basis. Thanks for being my circle of accountability.

Pride to My Mentees

I also dedicate this book to the people I've mentored. I am grateful for being part of the process that changed their quality of life. I know some of them have grown to be very successful, and I am so proud. In so many ways, you've probably helped me grow more than I've helped you.

Props to My Editor

I'd like to thank my initial editor, Jo Lord, who was wonderful throughout this process. She was truly a pleasure to work with and really took the time to understand me as a person, even though we come from two very different walks of life.

Brotherhood with Those Who've Gone Against the Grain and Persevered

I know firsthand how hard the road is for those who choose to go their own way. A guy told me the other day that he had to get his head right and his confidence up before having a simple meeting with me. He told me that he finds my story very intimidating. I applaud him for working through his own mental barriers, remaining positive, and keeping our meeting despite his fears. But it made me think about the many people built to react in the opposite way.

On the surface, people like me can intimidate others without even knowing it. Others see people like me—people with confidence—and process us as arrogant. Men, especially, are intimidated by the success of other men. While I think this is stupid and unproductive, it's true that this backward way of thinking plagues our society. And sadly, people who surround a successful person often become overwhelmed with emotions like jealousy and envy. It's so strange when the qualities that first attracted a person to you are the same ones they end up hating you for.

When you think about it, what is jealousy but intimidation with rebelliousness attached to it? Jealousy hinders our ability to become successful. Until we can be happy for others when they achieve, we'll never experience real success ourselves.

Those who have walked a different path can relate all too well. It's a heavy burden to carry, especially when you want to be a free and loving individual. To those who deal with this on a regular basis, I would like to say this: stay strong as you find a way to cope with it, as I know this negative energy can impact your life in many ways. Understand that you are a beacon of greatness, and vow to not let this overshadow your pureness to remain a phenomenal influence. Recognize that you are doing something right and don't let it affect your character, change who you are, or alter your godly qualities.

Unapologetically remain you!

> *Our influences greatly influence us.*
> *That's why I think it's so important that we influence.*
> —SHILOH JONES

Rage and Despair with a Side of Street Cheese

It was the morning of October 28, 1997.

I sat at a broken-down kitchen table in the quiet and pondered my existence. I was just eighteen years old, but I'd already gone through more than most people do in a lifetime. Hell, in the past four months alone, I'd lived through my fair share of shit and then some.

I'd graduated from high school one day and gotten an eviction notice from my apartment the next.

Learned that my girlfriend was pregnant.

Battled alcoholics and crackheads for work at the labor pool starting at 5 a.m. every weekday.

Got hit by a car and seriously injured while standing on a fucking sidewalk talking with friends.

Quit work to recover.

Ran out of money.

Dropped out of college.

It was the evening of October 28, 1997.

I'd been living at my sister's place a couple of blocks from the projects in the two weeks since my eviction. With no advance notice, she kicked me out. There were too many people staying there, she said, and I had to be the one to leave.

I had nowhere to go.
No money in my pocket.
No parents in the picture.
Not a soul in this world to help.

It was midnight on October 28, 1997.

Because I didn't know what else to do, I started walking. I walked for hours, as far as my rage and despair would take me. I saw the neighborhood turn into a ghost town. Heard the buzz of the streetlights and screaming in the distance. Inhaled the smell of street cheese, rotten food, and old piss. I slept that night—the first of many I'd spend outside, waiting for daylight to come—on the bench of a bus stop downtown.

I was a month away from fatherhood. I was at my make-or-break moment. And I was determined that I would never again depend on anyone else for my survival. Out there in the cold, I heard a whisper from the universe. It told me there was a power I could tap into that would change everything: the power of me!

That night, I was an eighteen-year-old failure.

It's January 19, 2021.

At the time of writing this, I was a forty-one-year-old multi-preneur with a few companies, earning millions of dollars annually.

I am a father of two daughters, an activist in my community, and a provider of jobs to almost one hundred people.

I have success.
I have security.
I have purpose.
And I have peace.
If I can have those things, you can, too. Here's how.

PART I

I started out on the corners, to
pushing dimes to quarters,
defied mom's orders, SHE STILL TRIED SUPPORTIN' US,
Life was unlawful, she cried when they caught us,
AND MY DAD PUNK ASS, HE BOUNCED
ON ME AND HIS DAUGHTER,
Two years later, now this bitch in California,
That's when I changed up, like Transformers,
Into a Northside nigga, I had to fight for my own,
THEN FIGHT FOR THE THRONE
for a life of my own,
All else fails? I know I can trust mines,
Before I'm fucked by 'em, I know I can bust mines,
Rappers on that bullshit, nigga fuck lyin',
Before I tell stories, Ima have to touch mines.

—Excerpt from hip-hop song by Shiloh Jones

Ages 1 to 7: This Is Where My Story Starts

I started out on a path to find myself until I realized that I was on a path to define myself.
— Shiloh Jones

WE ALL START OFF as equals in life. Innocent and pure, untouched by the world's evil. As our brains learn how to think and comprehend, we start to feel either empowered by our circumstances or disadvantaged by them. We come to realize that it's the families we're given, the environments in which we live, and the cards we're dealt that define us. This is where my story starts.

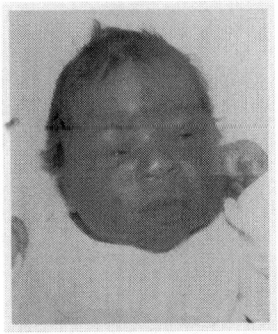

Me, as a little baby, looking quite ugly. LOL.

When you're a little kid, you look at your parents as if they're God. Because at that point, they are. They take care of all your basic needs and provide food, shelter, and clothing. They can do no wrong. You love them unconditionally.

Life is perfect!

You don't have a care in the world.

Until you do.

Me, a little older, looking a little bit cuter. LOL.

SPARKS FLEW, CHEMISTRY BREWED

But let's back up a little. For me, it all started when my mother, Joan, met my father, Bill.

They got together when she was twenty-seven and he was twenty-eight. She was a high school teacher at Peabody Public School in Petersburg, Virginia. He was an insurance agent. They had a mutual acquaintance, Cheryl, who desperately wanted to see my mom in a relationship.

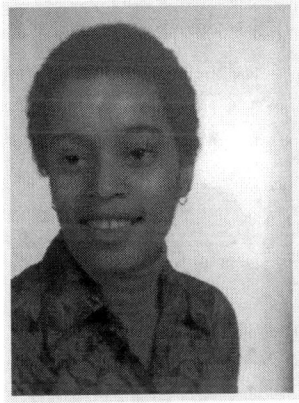

My mom during her college years.   *My mom in her cap and gown.*

"You gotta meet this guy, he's so you!" she told my mom. On the night they finally met at Cheryl's house for dinner, my father couldn't stop playing with my mom's hair. Sparks flew, chemistry brewed. He went home with her and didn't leave. They got married, moved into a new place together, and began life as a unit.

Joan and Bill had their first child, a girl, a couple of years later. They named her Brandi. They had me when Brandi was two years old. As far as marriages go, theirs was planned out pretty perfectly. They thought ahead and actually took the time to strategize to conceive both pregnancies.

My mom's dad, Ralph Richard Bolling, Sr.

My mother's parents hadn't provided much of a stable home life for her or her four siblings. For one thing, they married and divorced each other three times. For another, her father, Ralph, was a Casanova who had plenty of women, a "playa" to the fullest. He was such a player that my mom's last memory of her dad was of him getting stabbed to death by one of his girls after she learned that he was cheating on her.

My mom's mother, Viola Curley.

Mom describes him as a very tall, handsome man who never had time for family, only his women. This is what drove her mother, Viola, to insanity and a mental institution, where she spent much of my mother's childhood. The kids went to live with different family members, from north of Baltimore city to the country in Virginia. From then on, my mother felt like a black sheep, like she had no place to call home.

My great-grandmother on my mom's father's side, Helen Bolling Embry.

My father's mother and aunt (left and center) and his grandmother (right).

My father's parents, in contrast, were very traditional. My grandfather Frederick was one of the first black firefighters in Virginia. (Amazing, right?) My grandmother Willieta was a stay-at-home wife. My father was rowdy as a kid. He got into so much trouble, a judge gave him the option of going to jail or going into the Army. (That choice was typical back in those days, as so many young men were needed to fight in the Vietnam War.)

Pops as a rowdy young boy.

My dad's father, Frederick Robinson, Sr.

A mural made in my grandfather's honor in Jackson Ward in 2021.

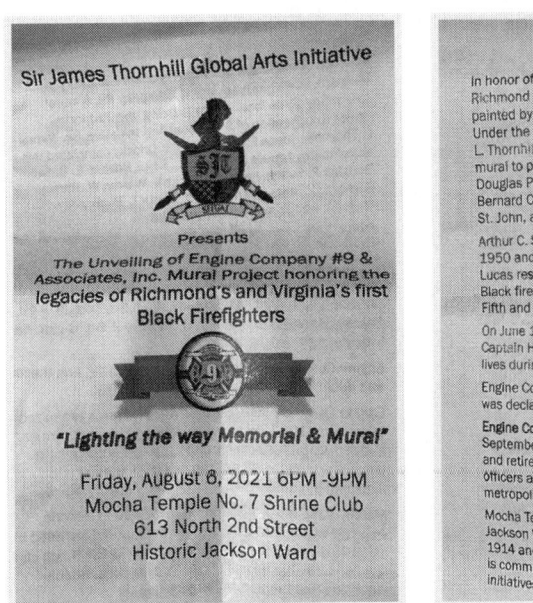

Mural itinerary presented by officials of the city, including the Mayor.

Pops chose the Army and was trained as a Morse code interceptor, which was very stressful work. After getting out of the military, it took a minute for him to settle back in, but when he did, he was back to being Mr. Charisma. My father was a salesman. Natural to the heart. A merchant by trade. Could sell water to a whale, dirt to an ant, sand to a camel, air to a land mammal. He sold everything from insurance to toys, from meat to house alarms.

In the 1970s, he landed on the new concept of multilevel marketing and became a distributor for Amway™, one of the world's biggest companies at the time. He was progressive and an overachiever, and he did really well in this new venture. There weren't many blacks at my dad's level with Amway™, which made him a valuable commodity to the company. He quickly went from selling household products to speaking to crowds of three thousand people or more. Once, he spoke to thirty-five thousand people. These years were the height of my parents' marriage. They made great money, and it came fast. Life was good! Actually, it was great. So what happened, you ask?

My grandfather's funeral.

My Father, the Casanova

My mother, early in marriage.

Like my mother's father, my own father was a bit of a Casanova. The charm and charisma that made him the perfect salesperson also made him very attractive to women. He cheated with the wives of some of his Amway™ sponsors, the people over him in the company's hierarchy. He got caught and was blackballed and banned from the organization. Things went south from there. In my mom's eyes, he was becoming like her father, the very man who'd abandoned her so many years before. The deep anger and hatred she had for her father started to transfer to my father. Tensions rose. My parents started arguing most of the time. When they weren't arguing, they ignored each other. It all happened so fast.

I remember being about seven years old when things really started to get rough. Food got scarce. Sometimes there wasn't any gas for the car.

Once, I came home and found that the power had been turned off. This was hard for me to process. The concept of electricity being "sold," people paying monthly bills to a company for it and having it disconnected when they didn't pay, was a concept I just couldn't grasp.

Through it all, my dad stayed positive, no matter what was going on. Funny as hell, too. He had a joke for every situation and made great light out of even the worst times. With him around, somehow things didn't seem so bad. So we managed.

I remember he used to wow us kids with the stupidest shit. He would pull up to a stoplight, for example, and say, "Watch this, guys. You want to see me magically make this light turn green when I tell it to?" Then he would psychically concentrate on the light and flick his wrist. The light would turn green every time, which was fucking amazing to us at that age. It was only when we got a little older and understood the synchronization of stoplights that we realized he was just looking at the other lights to help with the timing of his "magic." He also liked to pull quarters out of our ears and then hand them to us. Endless quarters. I was astounded by how amazing he was. His amazingness, however, wasn't enough to ease the tension between him and my mom. They hung in there but argued more and more.

Then one day, Pops left.

Butterfly Effect

It's funny how one simple shift in life can cause such a resounding butterfly effect. The day started off like any other in my world. Woke up. Got dressed. Ate breakfast. Packed my book bag. Said a few words to my sister. Headed to school to learn the fundamental bullshit kids learn at that age. Attended after-school program. Waited for Mom to pick me up. It was Tuesday, so we went to Church's Chicken to get the $2 special (two pieces and a biscuit) with orange soda. We got home and my sister and I headed to the kitchen table to eat. It was around the time when my father usually came home, one of the highlights of my day.

"Hey Mommy, where's Daddy?" I asked.

She grunted and said, "Your father probably out and about running 'round somewhere. He'll bring his ass home sooner or later."

Time passed. It was almost bedtime, and I started to get worried. I asked my mom about him a thousand times until she finally snapped at me and told me to go to bed.

"Your father is grown. He knows how to take care of himself! Now go to bed! You have school tomorrow!"

I stayed up half the fucking night hoping he was okay. Did somebody hurt him? Did he get into a car accident? Maybe he was working late? If he did, why didn't he call? Maybe he couldn't? I mindfucked myself until I was so exhausted that I finally passed out.

Next morning. New day. Regular routine. Where was Pops? Oh shit. I almost forgot. I ran to his room, where my mother was getting dressed.

"Mommy, where's Daddy? Did you hear from him?"

"No son," she answered. "Let's get ready for school. You have a big day ahead of you. Go 'head, you already running behind, and I can't afford to be late to work."

"But Mommy ..."

"No buts, let's go," she said with an unnatural calmness and then shooed me off.

All day long, I couldn't focus. Couldn't concentrate. He was all I thought about. Did he die? Was he at a hospital? Whatever was happening, it was all too strange. Why was I the only one worried like this? I mean, sure my sister seemed worried, but I was earth-shatteringly worried. My mother and sister were able to get through their day with a resilience I couldn't understand. I was weaker. More vulnerable. Less evolved. FUCK SCHOOL! Where was he? I stayed in this crisis state for three days before my mother sat me down and spoke the words I'll never forget.

"Son, come here, I have to talk to you," she said. "I don't think your father is coming back home."

"What do you mean 'not coming back home'?"

"I mean he's gone. He packed his stuff and left. I knew this a few days ago but didn't know how to tell you. I thought maybe it was just another argument. But sometimes grown folks have arguments they can't get over."

I was crushed. What the fuck was she saying to me? He wouldn't do this to me. He was my best friend. My buddy. My light. My world. Because he was the only other male in the house, we had an unspeakable bond that nobody else could understand.

On that very day, I evolved. I felt emotions that I'd never felt before. I felt true hurt. I felt anger. I felt hate. I felt disconnected. I had no reason to blame myself, yet I did. I felt hatred toward my mom. I felt hatred toward my dad. I felt hatred toward my sister, even though she, in theory, should have been feeling the same way I was. But she was stronger than me. My most devastating emotions came from the fact that he didn't even give us a reason. He just left.

You were my hero. Why? How can you go from having a family every day to turning your emotional light switch off and abandoning what you love most, who you love most? I had so many questions but nobody who would answer them.

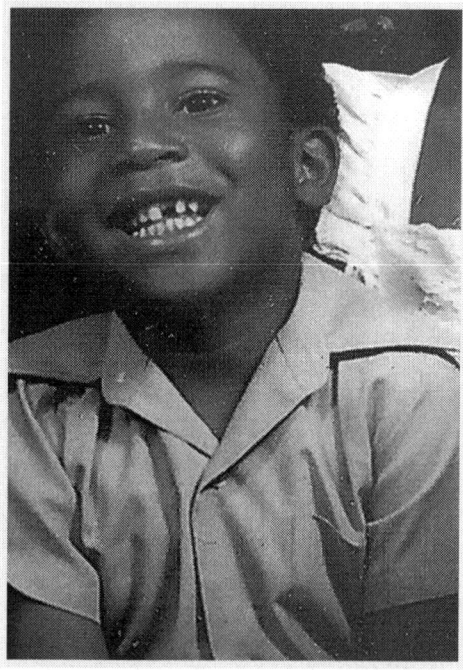

Here is a picture of me super duper youngin.

In the beginning, I looked at you as if you were a god,
To me, you couldn't do wrong cuz
I ain't think you had flaws,
You used to clothe me, feed me,
and even change my diapers,
And when I grew up,
I wanted my life to be just like yours,
I thought things were strange the way
you and Mom used to fuss,
And Mom dukes used to turn around and argue at us,
And it was up until this day, I used to blame myself,
Cuz I ain't understand the way you
just packed up and left,
I remember, one afternoon, I waited for you to come home, Cuz you told me you'll see me later when we spoke on the phone,
8 o'clock rolled around, 9 o'clock, and then 10,
I waited up inside my bed cuz then
you were my best friend,
12 o'clock, 1 o'clock, yo, I ain't sleep that night,
It would have been real comforting just to see you in sight, just to
look in my eyes for you to tell me what's wrong,
Nigga, you made me a statistic in this government song.

—Excerpt from hip-hop song by Shiloh Jones

Ages 7 to 11: Welcome to the Jungle

THE YEARS THAT FOLLOWED were very rough on me. I felt fragile. Without a foundation. Imagine a body without a spine, a body that had always had a spine until one day it was ripped out. Now imagine telling that same body to be everything it was before, to keep functioning as if nothing had changed. Days seemed longer. I felt alone. I started playing alone. Entertaining myself. For some reason, it was harder for me to talk to people. To make friends. To have fun. To be comfortable. I guess mine is the textbook example of abandonment—in this case, by a father—and the issues it can cause.

Speech Impediment

I don't how or when it started, but I developed a really bad speech impediment. Goes to show you how things that affect you psychologically can affect you physiologically as well. I developed a horrible stutter. I couldn't get a sentence out without sounding like a Run-DMC record. Every time I spoke, it sounded as if Jam Master Jay was performing on a set of Technics SL-1200s, trying to get the best DJ scratch possible. I couldn't control it, either. It was crazy! My sister teased me. People looked at me strangely, like I was mentally disabled or something. I hated it. But I couldn't control it. And the fucked-up thing was that the more I tried to control it, the more it happened.

When I was in public, my mind would say, *Take your time, Shiloh. Take your time. All you have to do is concentrate. There are too many people around. Just say the least amount of words possible. You can get through this.* Okay, here it goes, "Th-th-th-th." And I would be back to being stuttering Johnny again. FUCK! FUCKING FUCK! And it didn't just happen some of the time; it happened all of the time. I mean ALL THE TIME! At school, at the grocery store, even at the dinner table. I would try to tell a joke. Here I go, "Th-th-th-th-th." Even my mom and sister would be like, "Spit it out, Shiloh. Fuck, we gon' be here all night." The damn joke wasn't even funny by the time I got to the punchline.

I couldn't help but wonder what was wrong with me. I didn't have the mental capacity to scientifically break down what was going on, nor did I have anyone smart enough in my world to help me understand why this was happening.

THE OVERACHIEVING SISTER

Me and my sister.

My sister was born on July 22, 1977, three days before my pops's twenty-ninth birthday. Brandi is a Cancer, and my dad is a Leo. Growing up, she was a lot like my pops. She was very likable, got along with everyone, and seemed to be good at everything she tried. During her early years, she danced, and I don't mean no bullshit dancing, either. She was on fucking dance teams, on some *So You Think You Can Dance* TV show-type shit and, when she entered competitions, she always placed.

She played the harp. (Like, who plays the harp in the hood? Nigga, she did!) She was on the swim team. She was in the chess club. A fucking mermaid Bobby Fischer harpist! Oh no, it didn't stop there. She also played piano. (I don't know how many of you have tried to acquire this skill, but it's like teaching yourself how to be ambidextrous.) She played sports at our local recreation center, Hotchkiss, and was also a cheerleader. She was a straight-A student and often my tutor. Yo, she was an all-around MVP, you hear me? And she actually stuck up for me when people tried to tease me because of my stuttering and lisp.

Oh, did I forget to mention that I also had a lisp? It was almost as if God gave me a tongue that was too large for my mouth. So when I said words starting with "S," my tongue didn't know what the fuck to do. I sounded like Sly, the slithering snake, every time I spoke. Having a lisp and a stutter was a double whammy. What kind of trick was the universe playing on me? I also had a gap between my two front teeth—a Grand Canyon-sized gap. Like, seriously, you could put a Charms Blow Pop between my teeth.

Sidebar for a minute: I know you're going to think I'm crazy, but bear with me. I was realistic about our financial situation, so I knew braces were far out of the question. So I studied the science behind braces in an encyclopedia (we had our own set) and learned that they work by applying constant pressure on the teeth and gums and slowly manipulating the positioning of the teeth. Every night, I'd take my hands and apply pressure to close the gap in my front teeth. If you see me now, you'd swear I had braces as a kid. All of my front teeth are perfectly aligned! Nigga, I was my own braces! I mean, it did take years, but by the time I was a teenager, my Colgates were straight.

Back to my sister. Like I said, she would stick up for me and would even fight people for disrespecting me—even boys. "You not gon' just fuck with my little brother like that!" she'd say, and she'd windmill the fuck out of them. It's kinda hard to skillfully fight someone who's windmilling you at full speed, arms flailing. I promise you, this won her many fights.

Living in the Murder Capital of the U.S.

The reason the fighting started was that we were forced to move to a rougher neighborhood in Richmond—Northside—when I was about ten or so. This is what my mother could afford. It was during the '80s, and everybody was selling some form of drug on the corners (usually crack, coke, or weed). Crack, in particular, had destroyed the streets. We just stayed away from those corners where so many people gathered. My sister and I would have to take strange paths and weird turns to get where we wanted to go.

Northside was wild! A jungle. At the time, Richmond had one of the highest per capita murder rates in the country. The city was even nicknamed the "Murder Capital." You were at risk of being jumped just walking to the corner store. You could see a dead body, a fight, a shooting, friends tricking, drunks arguing, and drug deals going down, all within a good walk. I know it sounds like I'm exaggerating, but really I'm not being descriptive enough. Anyone who grew up in Northside in the '80s or '90s will know exactly what I'm saying. And I'm sure they have endless stories about how crazy it was. Truthfully, I applaud and respect anybody who grew up in that era and made it out successfully. It was a full-time job for a lot of people to keep from getting hooked on drugs, shot, or locked up in jail.

> I DON'T KNOW WHAT YOU SEE, BUT ALL I SEE IS **THE GHETTO**,
> BROKE PEOPLE HUSTLING, STREET HOES IN STILETTOS,
> MIND FRAMES WE CAN'T LET GO,
> **COPS** HARASS US,
> PAIN AND SUFFERING THE ONLY THINGS
> **MEDIA BLAST** OF US,
> I SEE CRACKHEADS, BEGGING FOR
> QUARTERS, NICKELS, AND DIMES,
> SO THEY CAN PUT IT ALL TOGETHER, AND GO COP DIMES,
> I SEEN THE BROKEST MUFUCKAS SPEND THEIR LAST ON SHINES,
> CUZ THEY WON'T SHIT ALL THEIR LIFE,
> ALL THEY WANT IS TO SHINE
> **WHAT I SEE OUT MY WINDOW**
> IS HUSTLAS DIME-BAGGING,
> NICKEL-NINE PACKING, TRIGGER HAPPY TRYIN' BLAST IT.
>
> —EXCERPT FROM HIP-HOP SONG BY SHILOH JONES

FIGHTS EVERY DAY

Even at the age of ten, this environment affected me greatly, affected my family greatly. Brandi and I had to walk to school. We both attended J. E. B. Stuart Elementary School and, yes, there were fights every day. On the corner, a block away, were all the hustlers at Brookland Park Boulevard and Fendall Avenue. We took a cross street, Crawford, to avoid the busy "boulevard," which was the nickname for the corner. We lived two blocks away from school, so there was no catching the bus. Northside was full of animals and barbarians, to say the least. And it appeared everybody had bigger brothers or cousins who protected them. If they ever got their ass whipped for fucking with someone, their brothers and cousins would retaliate in an endless beef cycle that I could never compete with or stand up against. Who was I?

I didn't have family like that, or that I knew of at the time. I was new to the area, so I didn't fuck with anybody. I stayed to myself. (I take that back, I had one friend: a guy named Rio who lived around the block from me.) But that damn sure didn't stop people from fucking with me. I don't think a day went by that I wasn't fucked with. But my sister stood up for herself. She stood up for me, too. If someone talked shit, she would talk shit back. Even if she got beat up, that wouldn't stop her. I used to think she was crazy. I remember times we'd be walking home and a group of people would come over to fuck with us. She'd immediately talk shit back. I would ignore it, thinking, "Yo, just shut the fuck up, Brandi." But nooooo, there she'd go, mouthing back, and they'd have to prove to each other that they weren't going to just let her pop off like that.

And then it happened. We got beat the fuck up. I cried. She was just mad. That fight aftereffect, bull-breathing mad. An hour later, she acted like nothing happened while I felt like another piece of me had been violated. I went through this hell, summer in and summer out. Winter in, winter out. (Speaking of that, do you know how horrible it is to fight when it's cold? Your hands feel like they're going to break and shatter. It hurts more to hit someone in the cold than it does to get hit.)

Losing My Stutter

Oddly enough, one thing improved when we moved to Northside. Within six months, I lost my stutter. Just like that. Poof! It was gone. It was as if my body had to adjust to dealing with what was the greater evil and determined, "Nigga, fuck yo' stutter. We have to put our energy into just surviving this Northside bullshit!" I believe Northside shocked the stutter out of my ass and from that point on, I never stuttered again.

But I felt displaced, isolated, bullied, picked on, and teased during those earlier years. My fucking sister had to take up for me most of the time. That's right, a girl. This same girl outworked me in everything she did. Had more confidence than me. More heart than me. More skills than me. I was living in her shadow. I was the fuckup in the family. The black sheep. I couldn't get shit right. I did, however, make good grades. Every year, I made honor roll or scholar roll. This was automatic for me.

School was probably the only thing I was good at back then. Around this time, two things started giving me the upper hand: I had an older sister who had taken more advanced classes than I had, and I had time on my side. I used to grab her books when I was finished with my work and study them. Half the time, what I read was over my head. The other half, I grasped the concepts and was able to look into the future work I'd be faced with.

The Chuck Taylors

When we moved to Northside, my mother decided to quit teaching school for a while. She had a friend, Liz, who renovated houses. My mother decided she would start painting and wallpapering (an ancient art, LOL) for her. Liz started outsourcing enough work to my mother that Mom was able to start her own company, Lady's Choice. She wasn't making much money at all, and sometimes none. It all depended on the jobs that came through and, more importantly, on who felt like paying. We were on a super-tight budget, which meant hand-me-down clothes and not looking hip in the least. When it was time to get more clothes, my mother was famous for taking us to thrift shops and secondhand stores for shirts and pants that had been passed through God knows how many hands. I didn't get cool shit like Levi's; I got Bugle Boys and whatever fit me on the clearance rack.

I'll never forget one day when I was about ten or eleven. My mom came home with the biggest smile on her face and said, "Look what I got you from the thrift store. Check out what I picked up for you." She pulled some shoes from a paper bag. A pair of white Chuck Taylors. The classic ones. I was a little confused because I didn't know what the fuck I was looking at. She said, "Boy, you don't know what these are? These are the shit! They will always be in style. Do you know how many muthafuckas would want these? Take 'em upstairs and put 'em away."

I thanked her, then took them upstairs and stared at them for a couple of hours, processing what she said. How could I verify this? I had no friends, no computer, and no internet. Let me first say that what you wore was everything in the hood. It was better to be plain than to wear some wackshit. Trust me, they will tear you the fuck apart. You thought the streets were the jungle? The classroom was worse.

I wondered if I should play it safe by wearing the same thrift-store British Knights that I'd been wearing all along. I mean, shit, at least they were British Knights. They were in style at the time. Or should I trust my mom because my knowledge about fashion was not extensive at all? (Matter of fact, it was very limited.) I didn't have a big brother to school me in fashion. No pops to guide me in setting my own style. Just me mindfucking myself into a very basic style. I figured that way I'd stay "invisible."

Taking My Chances

I slept on it and, by morning, I said to myself, "You know what? Fuck it, I'm going to take my chances." Took the shoes, laced them up, and thought, "Mom, I hope you're fucking right on this one!" Walked to school, nothing. Nobody said shit. I'm good! I got to about 10:30 when the teacher had to leave the room. She was gone for what seemed like forever. The moment she left, the class started with the usual "teacher gone" talk-shit time. I stayed in my book and read ahead.

I swear it wasn't five minutes before one of the class clowns said, "A yooo, what the fuuuuck, dis nigga got Chuck Taylorrrrrs on," with a very sharp, sarcastic emphasis on the "R." The entire class roared like that was the only funny thing they'd ever heard in their lives! The laughter went on for more than ten minutes. Niggas were falling out of their chairs and shit, all extra dramatic. I mean, muthafuckas' ribs was hurting from laughing so hard. I swear I even looked over and saw someone slobbering spit out of his mouth, that's how hard they were laughing.

What was going through my head? Well apparently, jackass, you picked the wrong option. These shoes are not cool! They are not timeless! Fuck you, Mom! You were wrong, and now I have to feel the effects of this shit. I lie to you not, I wanted to take those stupid-ass shoes off right there and throw them in the fucking trash. Throw them in a dump truck. Use them for guts for the nearest landfill. That shit was so embarrassing. Even the cute girls in the class were laughing. It was like slow motion as I turned around and looked at people laughing so hard, I could see 99 percent of their dental work.

The rest of the day felt like an eternity. I felt wack as hell. I couldn't wait to get home to take them damn shoes off. It was worse than a marathon runner after running a 25K. I'm not sure what I learned that day, but I know it affected me both then and in the future. Probably explains why I have over 150 pairs of shoes in my closet as we speak. It's funny how things that affect you psychologically when you're young play out when you're older. And anybody who knows me knows how much of a sneaker head I am to this day. Nowadays, I literally give shoes to people around me who can't afford them, sometimes before I even wear them.

The Big Surprise

Three years had passed since my dad left, and his absence was taking a toll on the whole family. His lack of presence manifested in many ways in the three of us. First of all, it put way too much pressure on my mom, and it wasn't hard to see how the stress was affecting her. Raising two kids alone had to be challenging, to say the least. She started becoming more stressed, shorter with her words, less nurturing, harder. And even though I couldn't understand it back then, as a grown man now, I do. I see her pain now; back then, not so much. I mean, not only did she have daddy issues when she was a child but now yet another man, whom she'd opened herself up to deeply, had abandoned her.

This shaped a very ugly view of men in her world. She started to hate them. Everything about them. How cocky they were, how chauvinistic they were, how they thought they had the right to rule the world. She became a staunch feminist, anti-men, mentally, emotionally, and physically. She sat me and my sister down one evening and told us that she had to talk to us.

"About what, Mommy?" I asked.

"Just go get your sister," she said. "I need to be honest with both of you."

"Okay. BRAAAAANDIIIIIIII!" I yelled at the top of my lungs, same way I always did when my mom told me to get Brandi, like she couldn't do that herself.

When we were all together, our mom told us, "I'm gay. I like women. You know the way I used to be with your father? Well, I feel that way about women now. I just wanted to be honest with both of you and let you know."

My mom, shortly after breaking the news to us that she was coming out of the closet.

After taking a minute to absorb that, I didn't really know what to say. What did that even mean? I was still a virgin. Nobody had taught me about the birds and the bees at that point. I simply had no connection to what the hell she was saying to me. In my brain, I was like, "And? Shit, that's all you wanted?" It didn't bother me at all.

Becoming the Hot Gossip

Once my mother came out of the closet, she was pretty open about her life socially. Being more open about it socially meant our neighbors knew. Neighbors knowing meant their kids knew. The news spread like wildfire. And back then, homosexuality was not widely understood and certainly not widely accepted. (Dammit, another fucking thing I had to deal with. Needless to say, this was just something else that I was going to get teased about. At this point, I was starting to have it up to here with the bullshit.)

Back then, my mother's girlfriend was a lady named Brenda. Classic butch type. My mom loved the masculine side of gay women. Forgive me for saying this, but my mom's choice of a girlfriend only advertised, "Heyyy, I'm gay!" So the entire neighborhood talked about it like it was a disease or some shit.

Today, I'm happy that my mother is living her truth. She recently told me that it took a lot of heartache before she was ready to be honest with herself about her attraction to women and her aversion to men. She says she finally found herself at age thirty-five and knew that she had to make herself happy. As a little boy, I had the same acceptance of my mother's sexual orientation. I loved her and accepted her in any fucking form in which she chose to come. Beyond the negative attention it brought, her coming out didn't really change anything back then. But the struggle was real.

3

Age 11: The Day That Changed Me Forever

FOR EVERY ONE of us, there comes a time when our environment slowly becomes part of us—part of how we think, part of how we act, part of what we are. One lateral shift can make all the difference. Just one event can change everything, or a person, forever. I know when this day came for me. I remember it vividly.

The day started like any other day when I was eleven years old. Woke up, brushed my teeth, put my clothes on, ate breakfast, waited for my sister, grabbed my book bag, and walked to school. It was a Friday. I'd had a long week. At J. E. B. Stuart Elementary School, we had rec time, with one group of kids out on the playground for a while, and then the next group. Bell rang and we had to line up, as this was our time to go out. Fast-forward a little. I was on the playground, just chilling by myself, as always. This dude was talking with a few of his friends and they went to crack on me, telling jokes. I don't know how I became the topic of the conversation. I believe it was because I had some MC Hammer pants on (fuck off, that's when Hammer was cool) and this nigga started going in on me.

I believe I said something smart back like, "Man, leave me the fuck alone." In that moment, the whole atmosphere changed.

"What? The fuck you say to me, nigga?" he said. He and his friends moved closer.

"Man, go 'head," I replied.

"Nah, nigga. Da fuck you say to me? I'll punch yo' ass in yo' face, bitch! Say something!"

Let me first say that, yes, these dudes were older than I was. Fifth graders. I'd seen them fight before. I'd seen them jump people before. They were fighters. So in that moment, I don't know if my little leave-me-the-fuck-alone comment was about to get me jumped or not. All I knew was that the pot was brewing. Brewing like shit! I didn't know what to do as they came closer. So I did some bullshit. I turned and tried to walk away. (This is when I learned that this tactic never works, by the way.)

"Nah, little nigga. Come here," one of them said.

"Hit Dat Nigga, Cuz"

And the famous hood anthem came from one of his boys' lips: "Hit dat nigga, cuz." Suddenly, everything was in slow fucking motion. I tried to walk away—Lord knows I tried. This nigga grabbed my shoulder and tugged to turn me around. POWWWW! The first blow is always a number. It brings you from reality to a surreal dimension that moves all too fast. Adrenaline starts rushing. I took the first punch. Tried to walk away again. My mind was racing. I could not afford to get suspended. My mom would kill me if I told her I got put out for fighting. Besides, even if I did fight back, I'd get my ass jumped by his four friends waiting to stomp me the fuck out.

I felt a tap on the shoulder. "Aye, cuz."

I think my dumbass might have even turned and walked into this one. POWWWW! Another one landed. At this point, everybody in the yard was gathering around. I did my Jesus thing and turned the other cheek. Embarrassed, I proceeded to walk away. Now I was thinking, I just need to get inside the school. Need to escape. I felt another tug on the shoulder. This time, I refused to turn around. BUMMMMMMPPPP. It was the sound of him hitting me in the back of the head.

Thankfully, I made it into the building, but not before hearing all kinds of shit like:

"Damn, he got his ass whipped!"

"Yeeeah, cuz." (That was his homeboy on that one.)

"Wow, he didn't even hit back."

I was embarrassed. Ashamed. I was at my lowest point. Things couldn't get worse. I died out there on that playground that day. A part of me was snatched.

Not One Ounce of Fuck Left

I went home mad. Mad at my mom because on that playground I thought about how pissed she'd be if I got suspended for fighting, and I hesitated for that reason. Mad at my school for allowing this to happen. Mad at those guys for being so evil. Mad at everyone who laughed at me. Those heartless muthafuckas! I realized that nobody gave a fuck about me.

I had a conversation with God that night. I made myself a promise. Made Him a promise that nobody on earth would ever make me feel like that again. Nobody would ever get the pleasure of making a name at my expense. Nobody would ever take a piece of me again. Nobody! Fuck a punishment! Fuck a jumping! Fuck if I got my ass whipped. That was the very last ass whipping I would ever give away, especially for free. You might whip my ass, but bitch you're gonna have to work for it. And Ima give you everything I fucking got! WHAT THE FUCK do I have to lose? What else can a person take from me? I have nothing else!

Truthfully, I didn't do it for the respect. I did it because I didn't have anything else to give. I had NOT ONE OUNCE of fuck left.

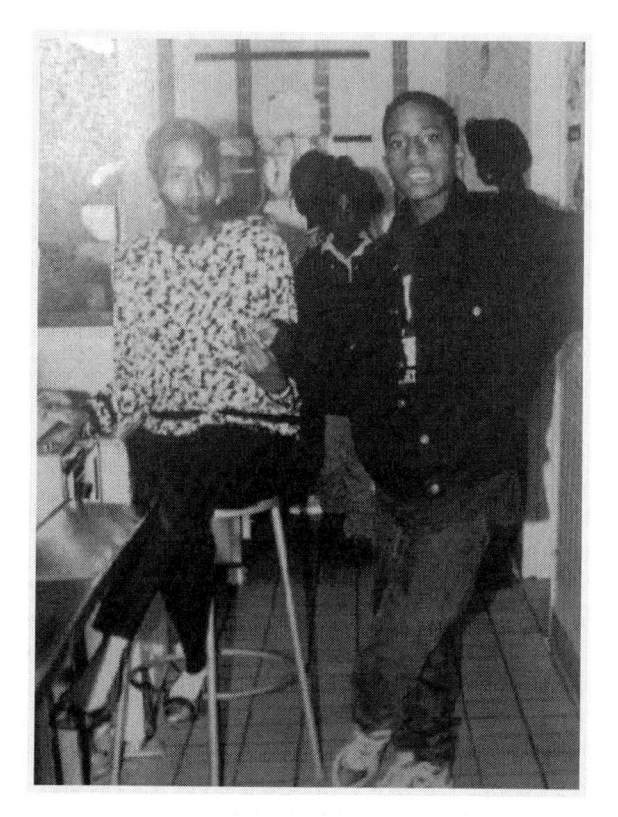

Me in sixth grade, standing in the lunch line.

Enough was enough! Let's get it, Northside!

After I started getting bullied, I decided I wasn't gonna take shit anymore. And taking no shit is exactly what happened. Man, did I fight. I fought damn near every day. For every reason. Someone teased me about my mom's lifestyle choices, they got punched in the face. Someone fucked with me about my outfit, it warranted a punch. Someone asked me what the fuck I was doing walking through their neighborhood, I asked, "What makes this your neighborhood? I'll walk where the fuck I want." I started to develop a new level of confidence. Started taking routes that I wouldn't walk before. No longer did I feel like a victim. I'm not saying I liked fighting, but hey, if I had to get in anyway, I might as well give it my best shot.

I Wasn't Gonna Be a Sheep Running with the Wolves

This is when I learned what works and what doesn't work in a fight. I stopped being so adrenaline-fueled because I realized that's when you have the least amount of control. Those are your worst fights. The calmer you are, the better off you are. The more you can think. You become more combat-intelligent. The more you're caught in adrenaline-fueled, fighting-frenzy mode, the more primitive your response is, making you more vulnerable. This holds true for me, anyway. Maybe not you. I fought for the dumbest reasons. But they didn't feel dumb at the time. It started to be about principle after a while. What made someone think they had the right to fuck with me when I didn't feel like I had the right to fuck with them? My internal response was, "God made you the same way He made me. You eat, sleep, and shit like I do. Bleed like I do. No, you're not going to just violate me like that!"

What I truly learned is that nobody is really looking for a good fight. They want a fight they can dominate. The bully doesn't want the best challenge; he wants an easy kill, an easy target. This knowledge was a game changer. See, you think that the more passive you are to an aggressive adversary, the more inclined they'll be to spare you. NOPE! Total fucking opposite. You have to face your adversaries in life with equal, if not greater, force. If somebody brings you a flame, you bring a forest fire! If someone attacks you with a tidal wave, you respond with a tsunami! There is no middle ground. Any less and you fuck yourself. You can't play sheep in a world full of wolves. You have to refuse to be the prey when surrounded by predators. By any means necessary, become a predator when around predators. When in Rome ...

And sure, I got my ass whipped. But you can bet your ass I gave some ass whippings, too. I remember fighting so much, my mom would simply look at me when I came home and say, "So who you got fighting with today, boy?" as she examined the collar on my T-shirt, stretched out from a recent tussle. Every time, I swore to her that I didn't start it. After a while, she stopped believing me.

Here's What Saved Me

You're probably wondering about school, right? Luckily, that was the thing that saved me. Sure, I got in fights in school, but I got stellar grades, too. When I did fight, my teacher and the principal knew that I never started it. And it was always with the so-called troublemakers. I went from being the quiet kid to Mr. Bully Repellent. At the very worst, I'd get a half day of in-school suspension, where I used the time to do my schoolwork; the person I'd fought with would get an average of five days of out-of-school suspension. I think the school believed in the moral compass that I'd developed.

This experience gave me an innate hate for bullies. In my brain, I was so "You're not going to bully me" that I became a bit passive-aggressive. Eventually, about a quarter of the fights I got into happened when I was standing up for other people because I just couldn't watch them get bullied. It was too painful to watch, simply because I'd been there. I knew what it was to feel helpless, and that's what bullies prey on. Even if it meant taking one on the chin, I stood up for other people because when I saw someone going through it, my body remembered what it felt like, and it was dying all over again. They didn't deserve that shit no more than I did. Even as a grown man, this is still one of my pet peeves. I've put myself in some real dangerous and stupid situations through the years, taking up for other people.

This heart I was gaining rapidly is probably what inspired me to get into sports. That and Rio. So Rio, the friend I mentioned earlier, ended up becoming my best friend. Come to think of it, he was one of only three people I knew growing up who had his original mother and father in the same home and who were still together. I admired and envied him because of his family setup.

As we became cool, his father treated me like a son. His father just so happened to be the neighborhood legend, and he just so happened to be the coach of our local recreational football team. His name was Coach B, and Coach B had a way of recognizing shit in you that you ain't even recognized in yourself. I guess that's what made him such a legend in our hood.

So naturally, this gravitated me to football. I ended up joining the league and earning a position as a halfback. It's what I call the "suicide position." Every practice, I did about a million drills of "running up the hole," which is running straight into (and hopefully through) the defensive line. Naturally, Coach B put the biggest people on the defensive line, so I was literally running up on people twice my size. Even though I still felt like an outsider, football gave me my first perspective on what it felt like to be part of a team. It also gave me my first valuable lessons on being in shape. Sounds crazy, but when you learn to push your body to new limits, your mind starts expanding as well. But as I broke new ground physically, my mind wanted something more.

4

Age 12: Finding My Rhyme

THE YEARS as a single parent and sole breadwinner were very hard on my mom. She was getting more and more stressed as the sheer physical labor started taking a toll on her patience, demeanor, and spirit. She became more irritated. More short-tempered. More secluded. I was going on twelve years old and feeling like we were starting to lose our connection, our bond. And each day, it grew worse. She'd come home from work and I'd be excited to see her.

She'd greet me rudely with "ATTTT! Don't speak to me until I've been home for at least an hour or two and had a Budweiser or two." Of course, this dampened our communication, so much so that I started avoiding her until she came and spoke to me first.

Starting My Writing Therapy

There was no talking about my day, what went on in school, how life was going. Nada. So I came up with an idea. It didn't solve our communication issues entirely, but it worked for me at the time. I decided to start writing. I mean, she said I couldn't talk to her; she didn't say that I couldn't write to her. So my writing began. I don't know if she was actually reading the shit or not. (Half the time she probably wasn't.) But that didn't stop me. I thought there was a possibility she was reading what I wrote, and that was enough for me.

I wrote about my day. I wrote about whatever fight I'd gotten into. Then I started writing poems. Come to think of it now, this was my first journaling and writing therapy system. I wrote about everything, sometimes to release the frustrations of the day and sometimes to mentally escape my reality. As a matter of fact, once I started writing at that age, I never stopped. Writing is what glued the pieces of my psyche together. No matter what happened in life, the pen and paper never judged me, never stereotyped me, never treated me unkindly.

I think my gravitation toward writing came from a need to feed my intellectual yearning for something deeper. Something more meaningful. Writing, combined with reading my favorite books at the time, ignited my thirst even more. My mother's inability to communicate with me, mixed with my insatiable appetite to get my thoughts out, led me to begin writing letters to her about my day. That led to journaling. Then poetry. Until I discovered rap.

Finding the Rhyme

Once I heard rap for the first time and truly grasped the concept of the first song I fell in love with, my poetry morphed into spitting rhymes. I mean, really, what is rap but poetry with rhythmic cadence over beats? Eventually, I found that hip-hop was an even better way to express my thoughts and feelings. Hip-hop not only helped me discover who I was but also provided me with a form of release therapy. It allowed me to express so many different elements in me. From my creative side to my intellectual side, mental lyrical regurgitation, storytelling, my pain, my happiness—anything that was going on in my life or my head.

Sometimes it was my version of journaling. Other times the artistic expression was the same as with fashion and throwing on a dope-ass outfit to define you. Sometimes it was about battling and who was the more talented wordsmith. It undoubtedly gave me pure freedom to express myself. Express the art within me. And art imitates life.

At times, it was about my environment, an analysis of what was going on around me. It was just that, a blank canvas to paint the art of my choosing, no matter what style I wanted to use. And I was adamant about not being locked into any one style. My being was versatile, as were my thoughts. So naturally, my art should be as well.

My First Rhyme

When I first started out, I wrote a few bars here and there before finally committing to making my first real rap verse. It was some simple ABC-123 shit. But hey, every great talent has to start somewhere, right? I memorized it all in like a day. I wrote it to the Smif-N-Wessun's "Sound Bwoy Bureill" from their first album, *Dah Shinin'*, the most fire beat ever at the time! It was 1992, during what most consider the golden age of hip-hop. This was before the World Wide Web connected people from around the world as much as it does now. As a matter of fact, this was before the mass distribution of CDs, when people were still listening to music on audiotapes. And you couldn't order tapes online; you had to go to the record store and hope they had whatever you wanted in stock. Our choices were Sam Goody and BK Music.

Back then, I made music with my friend Ish. We came up with the idea at the same time—we inspired each other. I wrote my rhyme; he wrote his. And then afterward, we'd spit to each other and brag about whose was the dopest. Of course, my shit was. (I'll stick to that to this day.)

Early on, we were out in the neighborhood, bragging about our new rhymes, when one of the guys asked us to spit it. So we did. Needless to say, not many people were impressed. Probably not even one. Did this stop us? Nope! In fact, it may have been the very thing that fueled us. I can't speak for Ish, but I wasn't going to stop until people thought I was as dope as I was in my head. I had to give them some time—they just hadn't caught on yet.

But first, I knew my mission was to gain some more skill. This one little rhyme wasn't going to work for me. Back to the lab, Batman! And that's exactly what I did. I wrote and I wrote and I wrote. I also honed my delivery by practicing freestyling every chance I got. "Off of the Dome" is what we called our freestyling process. We would throw on the beat and then say anything that came into our minds, trying to make as much sense as possible, for as long as possible. This really helped my delivery because it allowed me to go with the flow, versus writing, which is more precise and focused.

"Gaaaooww, He Murdered That Joint!"

Gatherings known as cyphers happened often in our neighborhood. That's where we'd all spit our latest rhymes or freestyle to showboat our skills and get crowd reaction. When I first started with hip-hop, I knew I wasn't ready for one of those yet. I mean, those dudes were pros. Some of the nicest cats to hear, way nicer than what I heard on the radio. My goal was to rip one of those cyphers. When I wrote and practiced freestyling, the only thing on my mind was competing in one of them. Eventually, I got my shit up enough and felt I was ready. I had infinite raps memorized in my mind, and my freestyle was good enough to carry me for a good sixty seconds or so. So with my material prepared, I waited for the next cypher opportunity.

My chance came one day when I was with a few of my buddies. We were walking to the store to get something to roll up with and there it was: a group of dudes standing in a tight huddle, bopping their heads in unison. One dude was beatboxing, while others were taking turns spitting. My crew walked up and engaged amicably by bopping our heads to their unified rhythm. The mic got passed around (metaphorically). My heart started beating fast. This was my chance. After the next guy spit, I told myself I'd jump in and spit whatever rhyme I decided was appropriate for this cypher.

He took his turn and, when it sounded like he was coming to a close, I jumped in and did my thing. By the middle of my verse, everybody was going off. They were shocked because they didn't even know I rapped. (Not only did I rap but I was secretly getting nice on their ass on the low.) I murdered it. And afterward, people were hyped up, pushing me around, pumping their fists, and holding their hands over their mouths, shouting, "That nigga nice as a bitch, cuz," "You ripped that shit, bwoy," and "Gaaaooww, he murdered that joint!"

That was all I needed. My head was in the sky! I'd accomplished what I'd set out to do. I'd developed enough talent to warrant some applause. It was nice. More than nice, really, because it was validation. Damn right! That night, I went home and wrote more raps. I was hooked. Addicted. Now it wasn't just a hobby; it was a culture for me. We spoke our own language. Walked to the beat of a different tune. Now, I thought, being good at it isn't enough; I want to be great at it! A river cuts through rock, not because of its power but because of its persistence.

Kahlil Gibran and The Prophet

Then one day, out of the blue, my mother gave me what I had been missing. She came home from doing her thrift-store shopping and said, "Here, Shiloh, I got you something." She dug into her brown paper bag and handed me a book: *The Prophet* by Kahlil Gibran. When I asked why she got me the book, she said, "It just made me think about you." (To this day, I think the book somehow chose my mother to find its way to me.)

Wow, my first real book! I went upstairs and immediately started reading it. This book stuck to me with every page. Its overall theme was about morals, principles, and God. With my growing interest in exploring the principles I was teaching myself in the world, this joint was really on time. This book started to feed the hunger in my mind. It made me even more curious about life and perspective. It drove me to question everything about my spiritual path and ultimately led me to where I am today.

5

Age 13: "By the Way, My Name Is Brother Hakeem"

ON MY WALK HOME, down Brookland Park Boulevard, one evening, a guy in a black suit stopped me. He was trying to push a newsletter on me. It was named *The Final Call*. I asked how much it cost and he responded, "Any donation is greatly appreciated, my young brother."

"Sorry, I don't have any money on me," I said, turning to leave.

"There's something about you, my brother. I see you all the time. You remind me of myself when I was your age. Take this only if you will read it." I was shocked. Nobody in the neighborhood gave anything away for free without an ulterior motive. But he appeared to be a very straightforward guy. He seemed at peace with himself and confident in the propaganda he handed me. Although I'd passed this place several times, I had no idea what it was, who the people inside were, or what they stood for. So I had no preconceived notions and was a clean slate for the experience that was to come.

When I got home, I took a stab at *The Final Call*. (Shit, why not? I liked reading anyway.) I read that newsletter page after page. The articles in it opened my eyes to things I didn't know existed. Stuff that was going on in places I didn't know anything about. This is when I was first introduced to the idea of oppression and its effects on people. More importantly, it's when I was introduced to the movement that was trying to do something about oppression. The bottom line was that these people stood for a positive cause. I wanted to know more.

The next day, on my walk home, I saw the guy again. "How'd you like the paper, young brother?" he asked.

"You know what? I enjoyed it," I said. "I have a lot of questions, though."

"I tell you what, my young brother. I want you to come to one of our meetings. Just check it out and see if any of those questions get answered before you have to ask them. Fair enough?"

"That's fair!" I told him.

"Okay, good, my brother," he said. "Come in tomorrow night around seven," he said. "By the way, my name is Brother Hakeem."

A Hell of an Experience

I didn't know what to expect when I went to the first meeting, but it was a hell of an experience. First of all, there were only men there. I was the youngest guy by far. The next youngest had to be in his late twenties or more. I arrived a little late and just observed. Brother Hakeem immediately welcomed me and introduced me to the attendees, who were in a classroom setting. The person in charge of the meeting, known as the supreme captain, gave a little speech and then randomly (and aggressively, in my opinion) asked one of the members a question. The member had to answer back swiftly.

If he didn't know the answer or gave one that was incomplete, the supreme captain would tell him, "THAT'S INCORRECT, BROTHER! DROP DOWN AND GIVE ME FIFTY!" And sure 'nough, the member would drop down and bust out fifty pushups. That's not even the amazing part. Dude would drop down and bang them joints out like it was nothing. I'd never seen people do pushups so fast and efficient in my life! I didn't know the human body could move so fast.

"THIS IS THE FRUIT OF ISLAM, BROTHER. KNOW YOUR STUFF!" he commanded.

In short, these guys were exposed to knowledge, expected to study it, and expected to KNOW IT! No excuses. This was a level of discipline that I'd never seen before. Even to this day, the one thing I truly respect about the Nation of Islam (NOI) is how much it focuses on self-discipline and self-mastery. Islam is different from other religions in that there's a very physical component to it. Anyhow, all this at my first meeting was very much over my head. But it intrigued me. I wanted to know what they knew. (The competitive side of me hates when people know something that I don't and I have that "It's over my head" feeling.) They were smart. They were disciplined. They were committed.

After the meeting was over, Brother Hakeem came up to me. He wanted to process it with me and ask me what I thought. He truly valued my opinion, or at least he acted like he did.

The Nation of Islam

Let me say this. At the time, Brother Hakeem was the most sincere person I'd ever met. He said his words with such conviction, and everything seemed like a movement with him because he was so passionate. When he conversed with you, he took all attention off his surroundings and was completely engaged. He just "felt" like he stood for something. Like he was about something. Maybe because I didn't have an active father figure in my life, I gravitated to his personality. Role model type. I honestly thought the hood needed more Brother Hakeems. He cared about the community. He cared about black people. He cared about our forward progression and putting an end to the stereotypes. He wanted our people to be something, do something, be better than the media was portraying us, stronger than the niggas hustling out on the corners.

He explained to me what the NOI was all about. He also said that the meeting had been attended by the Fruit of Islam (FOI) and how the FOI are the stronger men in the organization. They were the warriors. He talked about how powerful the mind is and that being a warrior doesn't mean wielding a sword or a gun but wielding your mind. That's a true warrior.

Brother Hakeem taught me a lot over the next few months. He was my first mentor. He knew about my situation at home without my pops and didn't judge me for it. Instead, he embraced me. He shared his story with me. He taught me that fearing a man is disrespectful to God, or Allah (whichever name you choose to use). As a matter of fact, I was taught that the only thing you should fear is God.

I learned about Elijah Muhammad and about el-Hajj Malik el-Shabazz, also known as Malcolm X. I learned about Wallace Fard Muhammad, the prophet Muhammad, and Minister Louis Farrakhan. I was taught about salat, a ritual prayer performed by Muslims five times a day. I read *How to Eat to Live* by Elijah Muhammad, which went into great detail on how to feed your body. I learned about fasting and Ramadan, the Koran and the Qur'an, and the difference between the two. Islamic and Arabic scholars prefer the spelling Qur'an, but in much of the non-Arabic, Western press, the name of the scripture is commonly spelled Koran.

I came to understand the powerful NOI movement and the involvement of its members in the community. Why they sell *The Final Call* newsletters, why they sell bean pies, why they were for certain things, why they were against certain things. I was a sponge. And I started to learn more about myself and about morals, principles, values, purpose, and perspective. In this period of my life, I defined an important part of myself. In fact, parts of this era will be ingrained in me forever. However, there are parts that weren't meant to live in me for the rest of my life. Things I didn't agree with. But that was alright. Standing on your own value and principle system is part of being your own man. Being your own leader.

Grab a Seat, Here's Where It Gets Interesting

So what did I disagree with, you ask? How could I say so many great things about the FOI and the NOI and not be a practicing Muslim today? Good question. Grab a seat, this is where it gets interesting. For starters, I attended way more FOI meetings than NOI meetings. NOI meetings were more like Sunday church services, geared for those who go once a week. I wasn't really interested in those meetings. I preferred the more intense FOI meetings. They got my blood pumping. Although NOI meetings were boring to me, I was pressured to attend. One day, I finally gave in. When I went, I was unfamiliar with the setup. So I arrived a little late and was careful not to disturb what was going on. Not five minutes after I sat down, one of the brothers tapped me on the shoulder and whispered in my ear. "Brother, you sitting on the wrong side of the room," he said. "Only the women and children sit on this side."

I moved. But shit didn't sit right with me. I looked back and noticed that the other side of the room was filled with women and children. Then I looked back over at "my" side. I felt uncomfortable. I didn't like it. See, this is what I have a problem with. Remember how my dad left me when I was seven years old? My mom took care of me from then on. My mom was my father and mother. I lived in a household with ONLY females. Plus, my mom was at the height of her feminist shit at the time. I truly looked at women as equal to men. I still do! The only thing that separates us as humans is our sex organs, and no one is greater than the other. I couldn't get with this! It shocked me because these guys were the same guys that I thought were soooo intelligent. Why would they allow this? That night, I realized that this was one of the tenets of the religion and that there was a difference between being religious and being spiritual. Religion can be so tradition-bound that the followers will carry on old ways without questioning them or evolving the system.

I Never Attended Another Meeting

You guys talk all this equality shit, this non-oppression shit, and then you segregate your women from men? What message does that send to the women? The children? Then I found out that a NOI man is allowed to have more than one wife, but a wife is not allowed to have more than one husband. As a young Muslim, I wasn't okay with this oppression of women! I didn't agree with it. It contradicted my belief system and what I personally stood for. True equality. So I never attended another NOI meeting again.

Northside Hustlers Versus Muslim Brothers

Up until now, I'd been merely disillusioned with my Muslim brothers and some of their beliefs. But at this point, things with them reached an entirely new level and shit started to get real. My family was still living in Northside when a major event transpired. I can't remember it in full detail, as it was so long ago, but I'll give you the short of it. Something happened between the neighborhood hustlers and the Muslim brothers. It escalated to be a "Muslims versus the neighborhood hustlers" type of situation. The tension went from bad to worse when one of the hustlers beat up one of the Muslims.

Now, the Muslims had a code that they lived by, especially the FOI, and that was to never stand down! The very thing I'd respected them for turned out to be the thing, when taken to the extreme, that sent matters into dangerous territory.

I have to give you this story from two different angles: from mine, and from my homie, Rio, whom I previously mentioned. The reason is because I only knew my side of the story until I was a full-fledged adult. When I was recalling my traumas with Rio, this story came up, and he was shocked because he was on the other side of that story, which means I didn't get the full story until years and years later. (It's so funny how life works.)

Now there are a few things to note. As most close friends do, Rio and I had times when we grew apart, but then life weirdly drew us back together. This story takes place during one of the times when we weren't closely hanging with each other. He had gotten tight with some of the dudes from around the way in the neighborhood. And let's just say that this group of friends weren't angels. They got caught up in hustling, like most of the kids in the neighborhoods get influenced and trapped by. (In my opinion, that's why they call it trappin', 'cause it's literally a trap, but that's a different story.) Anyway, they had some wild moments.

Here is Rio's side:

One afternoon, two guys from the neighborhood, T and Nick, came by Rio's house, like any other day, but that day they were all hype, T-shirts stretched around the collar, like they had just gotten in a fight. T said, "Yo, we just got the brawling, bro!"

"With who?" Rio asked.

"The Muslim preacher dude down at the corner. The nigga usually don't say shit to us and allow us to hustle out there. Today, he tried to bark on us like we pussy. Trying to tell us we can't be out here on this corner no mo'. Fuck outta here, nigga, we jumped that nigga!" Nick said.

"For real, bro?" Rio said.

"Man, we beat the shit out of that nigga. Fuck dat," T said.

Rio thought nothing of it at that point. He just carried about his day with them.

That night, his father, Coach B, came to him and said, "If T and Nick come over here tomorrow, promise me you won't go with them."

"Why?" Rio asked him.

"'Cause I said so!" Coach B warned. "Just promise me you won't go with them!" Then he grabbed Rio's arm and shook him sternly with a belligerent tone, "DO YOU HEAR ME?"

Rio (left) and Coach B (right)

"Yes sir, I hear you," Rio said, a bit shaken. "I promise."

The next day, sure 'nough, Nick came to his house. It was the moment of truth. Even though his dad wasn't home, Rio still respected his wishes. His dad always had a way of just "knowing things."

"Bro, I gotta go get a haircut," Rio said, curving Nick in a nice way so he wouldn't question him further. "I'll catch back up with you."

He left, and Rio got his hair cut an hour or two later. After leaving the barbershop, he cut through his usual shortcut.

Apparently, seconds before Nick hit the corner, a van had pulled up. Two men jumped out, sliced Nick's throat quickly, scrambled back in the van, and pulled away. When Rio hit the corner, he literally saw Nick holding his throat, walking toward him, eyes wide open in sheer terror, gasping for breath. Blood was leaking around Nick's hands as he tried to hold his throat, still gasping, still panicking.

In shock, Rio saw Nick fall to his knees. He hovered over him. The next moments would change his life; the image of life leaving Nick's body would stay with him forever.

"Until you see someone you know die in front of you, you will never know what that feeling does to you," he told me. "I saw the fire truck come. The police come. I saw them cover the lifeless body with a sheet. I even saw when they removed the lifeless corpse from the concrete and dropped him mistakenly as they loaded him into the vehicle. All I could think was, I was supposed to be with him. I might've been laying right beside him, all if it wasn't for … my pops."

Later, he asked his father how he knew to tell him not to go with Nick at that exact time. Rio hadn't told him about the fight that had happened previously.

Coach B simply responded, "God spoke to me. So I had to listen, son."

Northside Story

After that, (this is from my angle now) the neighborhood hustlers stood together, and so did the brothers. It was a real standoff. The tension in Northside was thick.

The day after everyone found out about the murder, the hustlers already knew the brothers had done it. The brothers knew that the hustlers would retaliate. What happened next was gangster as fuck! I remember coming out to the boulevard (the main street in the neighborhood, Brookland Park Boulevard) and the hustlers looking like they were about to do something. Anyone from the hood knows that feeling when something is about to pop off!

The brothers stood firm and marched outside of the mosque, about forty to fifty deep. They were lined in perfect paramilitary formation, surrounding the mosque as if they were protecting it, sticking out their chests, and looking forward in perfect unison. They didn't move for hours. This fucked the hustlers up. Caught them off guard. I swear to this day, if the hustlers were facing any other adversary, that adversary would have got shot the fuck up. But it was the conviction of the brothers, their union, their bravery, and their will that de-escalated the tension that day. And trust me, them hustler dudes were not bitch-ass niggas. Most of them are locked up today for a string of murders, so I believe half of them had already had a body under their belt.

Now I have to sidebar for a moment. At this point, it was becoming abundantly clear to me that most of the brothers had a history. Bigger picture: are you familiar with how Elijah Muhammad grew to have so many followers so fast? It's because he targeted a lot of his recruitment to jails and prisons, reaching out to people who'd lost their way. So, do the math. Many of the brothers had been hustlers, drug dealers, and murderers in their previous lives.

Now I'm not saying that *all* American Black Muslims were recruited like this; I'm just saying that a large number were, and that's a fact. Elijah grew his part of the organization so fast by recruiting and accepting people who'd been rejected by society. Needless to say, just like the hustlers, the brothers weren't bitch-ass niggas either. (Funny, this new knowledge finally explained why them boys were banging them damn pushups out like that.) Do you see how this situation was a recipe for disaster on the Northside with the brothers versus the hustlers?

"Take Care, My Young Brother!"

So here's how I thought about it at the time. At that age, I had to process this situation with the tools I had. For me, there was no excuse for murder! I wasn't down with that. It wasn't cool with me. It stood against the mindset of my mentor, Brother Hakeem. It stood against mine. I couldn't justify it and didn't want to be part of something like that. The very next day, I went and found my mentor and let him know that we had to talk.

I was honest with him and told him how I couldn't compromise the only thing I had, my belief system. Surprisingly, he understood. I could see that he didn't agree with everything that had happened, but his belief system was to be loyal to his religion, and his religion comprised his brothers. I respected that. I looked in his eyes and realized something: the reason that was making me separate from the NOI was the same reason that was making him stay, even though we both knew the beef had gone too far. I told him that I wouldn't be attending any more meetings and that I couldn't consider myself a Muslim anymore. I'll never forget what Brother Hakeem told me.

He said, "Youngblood, to be a Muslim simply means to be a person of peace. My brother, you will always be a Muslim at heart because you have a peaceful soul. Take care, young brother!"

And on that day, we parted ways respectfully.

6

Ages 13 to 15: My First Job, Cleaning Porta Potties

Progress is a process.
— Shiloh Jones

OKAY, SO LET'S jump back just a little bit. When I was about thirteen years old, I started attending Henderson Middle School on the Northside. At this point, things were progressively getting worse at home. My mother was growing more distant. After leaving the temple (which we call the mosque), I had idle time, and you know what they say about idle time. I spent my days chilling with a few neighborhood friends and, truthfully, most of them were up to no good. We did the kind of ignorant shit that young teen boys from the hood do.

For example, we used to go in the alley near the intersecting street, throw rocks at moving cars, and run. Why did we do this stupid shit? Who knows? To this day, I couldn't give you a logical reason if my life depended on it. I remember one time, we hit this car real good, ran to my house, and stood on the porch, breathing hard, with adrenaline rushing. No sooner than a minute later, a guy with a black leather jacket ran up on us with a gun in his hand, looking for revenge.

"Which one of you li'l mufuckas threw a rock at my shit?" he sputtered.

My homie and I looked at each other like, WTF? (Shit just got real!) Luckily, by the grace of God, my mother pulled up, talked to the guy, cussed me the fuck out, and put me on punishment. Skin of my teeth, I swear that dude probably would have pistol-whipped the shit out of one of us. Big Diesel, full-force looking-ass nigga. That boy had come for blood.

My list of thirteen-year-old stupid shit ran deep. But I kept up them good grades, though! I didn't fuck around with that schoolwork. I told you, being smart made me proud of myself. I was in spelling bees, chess club, and SPACE, a program for which only ten gifted and talented students were chosen from the entire school every year. And that was back in the days when it wasn't cool to be smart, so nerds stood out. But I was a different kind of nerd. Not a Steve Urkel type but an "I'm a regular dude just like you, only smarter" type. I wore that shit proudly! But I did continue to fight all the time and do reckless shit for no reason.

Mr. Genius

There was one girl in the neighborhood who'd caught my eye. I don't remember her name, but I had a big crush on her. Like most thirteen-year-old boys, I was pretty immature in my attempts to impress her. Once, we decided to walk to R&S, the neighborhood corner store. When we got there, Mr. Genius came up with the most brilliant dumb idea ever. "Hey, you want some bubble gum?" I asked in my cockiest voice.

"Yeah, you gon' get some?" she replied.

"Yeah, what kind you want?" I asked, still cocky but with no damn money in my pocket.

She said that she liked all flavors, so I came up with a plan and proceeded to act. It was wintertime, so we had long-sleeved jackets on. I grabbed two packs of Bubblicious and quickly slipped them down my sleeve, using my David Blaine sleight-of-hand maneuver. Man, I repeated that process till I had two sleeves full of bubble gum packs. I was so slick, she didn't even know what I'd done.

When we left the store, I started chucking out all of these packs. I had every damn flavor, the multi-flavors, even the ones with the juicy squirt in the middle. All in all, I'd stolen about $15 worth of Bubblicious. And as I stood, proud as a lion after a large game kill, I gave her half of the gum and decided that I would sell the other half at school the next day. (For all those who grew up in my era, you know what I mean. Bubblegum "loosies" were a hot commodity at school. Them joints went for a quarter a pop. You could get $1.25 a pack just by breaking it down.) Man, them shits would be done by lunchtime. What?? I just got cool points in this girl's eyes *and* I got to make some money tomorrow, too? Sheeyyyyyyyt! I was feeling like the man!

"Let Me Go Get My Muthafucking Belt"

I got home no more than three hours later and, as I was chilling on the couch, Mom dukes walked in the room. "Get up!" she said, looking all serious and shit. "What happened when you went to the store today?"

"What happened when I went to the store today?" I repeated. (You know a nigga's guilty when they repeat the same shit you asked them, like they didn't hear you the first time but they heard you perfectly fine.)

"Ima ask you one more time!" she demanded.

"I don't know what you talkin''bout," I tried again.

"Oh, you gon' lie? You not even gon' admit it? I already know what happened. So you Mr. Big Man, huh? You gon' go out here and embarrass me? That's what the fuck we doing now? Matter of fact, let me go get my muthafucking belt."

And man, did she go get that belt. She came back in and whipped fire out of me. She must've unleashed on me all the fury from her stress at work, my father's pain, her father's pain, and whoever had cut her off in traffic that day. You know how when you get a whipping and your parent folds the belt? Well, the fold came loose and she was beating me like she had a slave whip in her hand, only the wrong end released so the side with the metal buckle was on the striking end. I screamed and hollered during this beating, which seemed to last for every bit of ten minutes straight. Honestly, she blacked out on me.

Apparently, the girl told her mom what I did and her mother thought she'd be a good neighbor and tell my mom. That embarrassed my mom, and one thing she hated was embarrassment. This happened on a Thursday night. I had school the next day. FUCK!

THE STRAW THAT BROKE THE CAMEL'S BACK

When I woke up the next morning, I had welts and bruises over my entire body, even my face! I looked like I'd been beaten straight off the *Amistad* slave ship. I laugh now, but the shit wasn't funny at the time. I was, after all, going to have to walk around school all day like that. Well, by the time I got to my Spanish class, which was second period, my teachers started questioning me. I told them it was nothing, which probably raised a whole lot of red flags for them. They kept badgering me and made me stay back after class. I broke down and told them the whole story: how I stole, got caught, and got a whipping. These mufuckas reported me to Child Protective Services (CPS).

Gooooot-damn! I tried everything in my power to defuse the situation, but they said it was their "obligation and duty" to report the incident and have it investigated. On some ol' "mandated reporter" shit. For my relationship with my mother, this was the nail in the coffin, the straw that broke the camel's back. It would forever change from that point on. My mother thought I'd called CPS intentionally to get back at her. I swore I didn't. She didn't believe me, and that was the end of her nurturing relationship toward me, which was already fragile as fuck. Now she hated me. She started putting me in the same box as my father, her father, and all the slimy men in the world who she felt were against her.

Now she really didn't have time for me, even less than before. She'd just gotten out of a bad relationship with the chick named Brenda. They'd had a really bad falling out, big fight and everything. (Side note: I saw my mom beat the brakes off Brenda, which was the defining moment of their final moments.)

VINNIE, MY MOM'S ESCAPE FROM LIFE

After Brenda, my mom started dating someone new. Vinnie was her name. Vinnie came from the projects, and it was no secret that she sold drugs and knew nobody but street people. Vinnie was an answer to my mom's prayers, in a sense. She had money and showered my mom with it. She bought her gifts all the time—diamonds, gold—and even gave her money.

My mom in the days of Vinnie.

And they were always together. Vinnie was my mom's escape from the hell of her job, me, the rat race, a rebound from Brenda, and life in general. I don't know exactly when my mom started using coke recreationally, but this was the first time that it was apparent to me, the first time I knew it for a fact. I mean, she did grow up in the hippie era, when they did all the drug experimenting on the planet. She was not a big weed person, but Vinnie was. Vinnie could smoke weed all day, but my mother's drug of choice was cocaine. Of course, cocaine has its physical and mental side effects. (In the words of Rick James, cocaine is a helluva drug.) Over the next few years, these side effects showed up in my mother more and more.

Vinnie ended up getting a new home in Henrico. I believe my mom may have helped co-sign for it. Once this new home was purchased, my mother immediately started staying there. It started with weekends and slowly moved to weekdays. Eventually, she would only come home to get clothes. Like I said, our relationship was pretty much fucked at this point. We both knew it. I mean, I still loved her and I knew she loved me. But circumstances had brought us to this point in life.

15 Years Old and Basic Needs Going Unmet

Some things started happening that became pretty pivotal in my life. The more my mother was gone, the more my basic needs, like for food and clothes, went unmet. Honestly, I think she was so caught up in what she was doing, she didn't really put too much thought into it. I can say this, though: every summer, when Brandi and I went back-to-school shopping, Mom would allot around $250 for clothes and let us spend the money as we saw fit. My sister would come back with all these outfits, while I would just buy one pair of shoes, maybe two pairs of jeans, and four shirts, MAX! And this shit had to last me all year. A young, active boy wearing the same shoes every day? Yo, my shoes would be stinking like crazy by the time three months went by. Most of the time, they had holes in them, too. Once again, it's funny how the things that affect us when we're young play out when we're older. I really have a clothes fetish now. I have a closet room the size of a baby master suite. But that's just me on my bullshit (how past traumas are linked to current overcompensations).

Anyway, my mother started spending more and more time with Vinnie. And since Brandi and I were essentially living at the house all by ourselves, my other best friend, Ish, was spending a lot of time there. He had the same exact issues with his mom. Her drug was men, though. So we became close. We had this in common, understood each other. When my mom would come home, she'd either welcome Ish or cuss him out, depending on her mood. Coke has a way of making you emotionally imbalanced, and her behavior was becoming more erratic.

It got so bad that she flipped out on me one time and put locks and chains on all of the kitchen cabinets. She truly locked everything she could. I think she was either trying to starve me out or, well, I really don't know what the fuck rationale she had for doing this. She didn't buy any groceries for me for the next six months. I had access to the stove but no food. I was only fifteen years old. What the fuck was I supposed to do with that? How was I supposed to survive?

I examined my options and realized I was old enough to get a job. The legal working age in Virginia was fifteen years and six months, my exact age. I found out about a program that was hiring kids my age, and I'll never forget this. It connected me to a job at a company called Waste Management (WM). I went through the interview process and was hired. It was summer, and they told me to come to work the next day.

It gets hot as fuck in Virginia in the summertime. On my first day at work, the temperature was predicted to be 102 degrees. I got there early, ready to work. I was curious as to what I was going to be doing, since I knew that WM was a company in the business of trash. I didn't care. I just needed money. I needed to eat. I would've taken whatever came my way.

At 8 a.m., they had me fill out paperwork and showed me a short video on safety. Then they gave me some safety glasses and a pair of latex work gloves and told me that they were going to put me on PPS duty. I didn't know what the fuck PPS was, but hey, I was ready. Let's get it! The company was staffed with nothing but white folks, so I was the only black guy there. It felt like some affirmative action bullshit, really. At 11 a.m., they took me outside to a yard covered in asphalt with no fucking shade. The yard was full of portable toilets. So now it's clicking for me that PPS duty means Porta Potty Sanitation.

Making $5.25 an Hour Cleaning Porta Potties

You ever seen commercials for this device used by people who can't bend over to pick things up or for grabbing things in hard-to-reach places? When you squeeze the handle, the tip squeezes like tongs. Okay, so my job was to pick all the large, non-flushable items out of the Porta Potty with this genius of an invention so that it could be flushed out properly. I guess technology wasn't advanced enough back then to do it in a more efficient way. Shitty job? Yes, literally! But fuck it, I'm cool with that. Somebody had to do it. Besides, I needed the money, even though these muthafuckas were only paying me minimum wage, which was $5.25 an hour at the time. (I know, complete bullshit.)

I got busy anyway, despite how disgusting it was. Busting ass, I banged out about seven of them. And it was nasty! I knew which of the Porta Potties came from parties, cause they would have champagne bottles in them. I also knew which ones came from construction sites because they had food thrown in them. And that cheap-ass "handy grip" tool wasn't worth shit. How the hell you gon' pick up a champagne bottle that's slickened with slippery-ass feces and piss slime with one of those? I had to hold my nose, breathe out my mouth, reach in, and grab it with my gloved hand. After throwing up in my mouth twenty times, I started to become dehydrated. Keep in mind that it was 102 degrees out this bitch today and I was sweating like crazy.

I decided to go inside, ask these dudes for some water, and catch a quick breather. The moment I stepped in the door, the manager, a big, burly hillbilly type, said, "BOY, I DIDN'T TELL YOU TO COME IN HERE. GET YOUR ASS BACK OUT THERE AND GET TO CLEANING!"

Shocked as I was, I was highly motivated to keep this job. I responded calmly, "I got you, man. I just need some water. I felt like I was going to pass out."

"YOU DON'T TELL ME WHEN YOU WANT A BREAK; I TELL YOU WHEN YOU GET A BREAK," he yelled. "LIKE I SAID, GIT YOUR ASS OUT THERE AND KEEP WORKING!" Then he looked at his coworker and said, "That's what's wrong with them; they're so lazy."

Cussing That 300-Pound White Boy the Fuck Out

Alright, so I need y'all to follow me on this one. Review everything I wrote, everything I went through, everything I stood for at the time. This muthafucka wasn't going to talk to me like that! FUCK this job! FUCK the money I was going to get from it! FUCK the fact that I was hungry and needed food! I cussed that 300-pound white boy the fuck out. Then I took my gloves and threw them in his face.

The only reason I left was because they said that the cops were on their way. I had too much black power in me and too much self-respect to allow anybody to straight out demean me like he'd just done. I didn't even care if they jumped me in that bitch, those guys were going to know that they couldn't talk to me, or any other black person, like that. That shit ended here! See, this was before people were suing companies for discrimination and it wasn't politically incorrect and unacceptable like it is now to treat employees like that, especially in a southern commonwealth state. These mufuckas were getting away with that shit left and right. And I'm sorry, they were contradicting my belief system. It wasn't going down like that!

As I walked away and started heading home, I realized this was a wasted day and opportunity. I wasn't any closer to getting the dough I needed to eat. But some things were bigger than money. I knew even then that I'd rather starve than have someone treat me with less than the respect I knew I deserved. Back to the drawing board.

I HATED SCHOOL AS A YOUNGIN',
YOU COULDN'T TELL ME NOTHING!
CUSSING, CLASS CUTTING, THEN RETURN BACK FOR THEIR LUNCHES,
I HATED OTHER KIDS, WITH A PASSION LIKE "FUCK 'EM,"
THEY WENT HOME TO THEIR PARENTS,
SHI WENT HOME TO HUSTLING,
NOTHING TO LOOK FORWARD TO BUT CHICKS THAT I WAS CRUSHING,
SPLIFFS AND GETTING BLUNTED, CYPHERS AND SPITTING SOMETHIN',
CONDUCT, OUT-OF-CONTROL,
ALWAYS FIGHTING WITH NIGGAS TUSSLIN',
WAS BULLIED FIRST, UNTIL I KNEW MY WORTH,
IT SWITCHED TO KNUCKLIN'.

—EXCERPT FROM HIP-HOP SONG BY SHILOH JONES

7

AGE 15: POPS WALKS BACK INTO MY LIFE

FIRST JOB DIDN'T even last a day. Now I needed to move on to a new job. I knew a girl from my neighborhood who was cool with me and my friend Ish, the friend who stayed over at my house all the time. She said, "I could get ya on at the joint I work at. Y'all down?"

"You damn skippy we down!" we told her.

One thing that always worked in your boy's favor: I was cool as fuck. So I always had a string or two I could pull from somewhere. The girl said she was dumb cool with her manager (honestly, I think she was banging him) and told us both to come in for an interview. The job was at a pizza joint, Papa John's Pizza. It was about four miles from the crib and, because we were broke as hell, we didn't have a choice but to walk. The manager there was young, in his mid-twenties, and a pretty cool dude. He was new to the area, and I believe he hired us for cool points and because he needed some local dudes from the area to fit in with. He hired us on the spot and told us that we could start training three days later.

Ima tell you why this job was such a sweet one. Remember I told you that my mom was going through her "psycho" thing with all the locks and chains in the kitchen? Well, this job was in the food industry. Check that, the one thing I needed! Bingo! I'm in the money. The manager ended up becoming friends with us, so he'd let me take pizzas home every time I worked. Even when I didn't work, I'd go up there and just make myself one. And the one thing my mom couldn't lock was the stove, so AAAAAAAHAAAAA! Joke's on you, Mom! Give your boy some time, he'll figure out a way. So bam, pizza and an oven I could use. Nigga, I'm good.

Pizza 24/7, Plus a Steady Diet of Weed

I was on a pizza diet 24/7. I ate every type of pizza you could think of. I got bored and started making up pizzas. To this day, I still believe I'm the originator of the Philly steak and cheese pizza. I used Steak-Umm beef, green peppers, onions, mozzarella, and provolone. BANGING! Man, nobody was making them joints! At least not where I was from. All the other employees started getting me to make pizzas for them. We even had a few customers who'd heard about my Philly pizzas and wanted me to make one for them, too. So I would ring it up under "specialty pizza" on the cash register. It's amazing what you can do with limited resources. Fuck you, that's creative!

So what happened this time, you ask? Alright, I started smoking weed. I don't know when exactly. I don't even know why. I could blame it on the fact that every time I saw my mom, she had Vinnie with her and Vinnie always had a joint in her hand, openly smoking in front of us. I could blame it on the fact that I walked by the shit every day on the corner, since the neighborhood hustlers did nothing but smoke weed and sell drugs. I could blame it on the hip-hop culture I was around at that age and how it was perpetuated and glorified. My favorite rapper at the time, for example, was Redman, and he didn't talk about anything but blunts in his songs. Whether it was environment or curiosity (or a combination of the two), I started smoking.

Going from Smoking Weed to Selling It

I'm Mr. Extreme, so I tend to overdo everything. I was smoking heavy. Back then, I could get a dime (about $10 of weed) and roll three blunts out of it. Phillies Blunt was the brand of choice to roll up with. It later moved to Dutches (Dutch Masters Corona Deluxe, to be exact). But just smoking weed wasn't good enough, right? So I started selling it. Ish was still staying with me most of the time, so we did most of the selling together. I had this brilliant idea that I'd save my money from my paycheck and buy a quarter-pound (QP) for $325. The plan was to break the QP down to sell in dimes, make a profit, and have a little extra for us to smoke. That way, we wouldn't have to buy the weed that we smoked recreationally out of our paychecks, since we needed the majority of our checks for living expenses. It was, essentially, free weed. Sounds like the perfect plan, right?

Man, we failed miserably! First of all, our dime bags were way too big. Second, we ended up being distracted from our main jobs because we were trying to sell the weed and keep up with customer demand. Third, we ended up smoking way more weed than we were supposed to. We still had our jobs at this point, so when we'd fall short on "re'ing up" (the term for getting more product, in this case weed), we'd simply compensate for the shortage by adding in our paycheck money. We were horrible hustlers, honestly. When customers would tell us they were short—maybe they'd only have about $8 for a dime—most of the time we'd look out for them and give it to them anyway. We'd also let people buy on credit and promise to give the money back to us when they got paid. Of course, when paytime came around, they weren't anywhere to be found.

Sometimes this would make us late for work, but we didn't care because our boy had our back. Then the unthinkable happened: our boy got transferred. Holy fuck! It wasn't long before a stale manager took over and quickly replaced the whole team. With my track record of tardiness, it wasn't hard to let me go. So I got fired. But I was arrogant! Young and dumb. I didn't care because I got this, right? WRONG. It wasn't long before I learned the valuable lesson about how fast a little bit of money could go, especially now that I had to start buying food again. Then I was back to square one. Within weeks, I was broke. Jobless, moneyless, and back to being hungry again. WTF?

Pops Walks Back Into My Life

It was right around this time that my dad decided to walk back into my life. I was fifteen years old. Our contact had been pretty sporadic since he'd left us without a word when I was seven. The first time we heard from him after he left was when I was about nine years old. He called from California and told my mom that he wanted us kids to come out there and visit him. A part of me didn't want to, but another part wanted to connect with my father again. My mom finally agreed a few years later, when I was eleven years old. She wouldn't send us on a plane, like he wanted. She drove us all the way to California from Richmond. This was the longest road trip I've ever taken and probably the best. We visited so many places along the way.

I saw giant old redwood trees that grew up to hundreds of feet tall and were hundreds of years old. We saw some cactus plants rolling through the desert. I mean, this is just shit I was not used to seeing. This was just amazing and opened my mind to a world outside of Richmond, Virginia. When we got there, my father met us off the highway and took us to San Diego, where he was living. His house was the biggest I'd ever been in, a mansion in my eyes at the time.

California was very different from Virginia. I saw people living the surfboard life, riding on skateboards, and rolling on Rollerblades. I was an East Coast kid and hadn't seen this back home. It was a whole other culture out there. And this was before the internet allowed people to share their lives and cultures instantaneously. Most people where I'm from hadn't been exposed to this. (Hell, for that matter, most people from my neighborhood never made it out of the neighborhood.) The only way you could know what the rest of the world was like was to go!

We stayed at my dad's for two weeks. It was cool to chill with my pops, but I couldn't help but feel a million mixed emotions. Yes, he was my father, but how could I look at him like a dad? I lived in hell back home, and how was he to think that these two weeks were going to compensate for four years of damage? Fuck no. I did enjoy my time out there, but it really didn't do much for our father-son relationship. He bought me my first LL Cool J tape while I was there and my first *Wolverine* comic book (comic books were a major thing out there), for which I was very thankful. Fun fact: This was probably my first introduction to hip-hop tapes, and the comic book led to my love of superhero movies. Other than that, it was a little uncomfortable because I didn't really *know* him. Four years is an eternity to a kid. A lot happened in that time period. Besides, before I could even loosen up, it would be time to go home, so what was the point, right?

My dad lived right on the beach, literally, with one side of the house on the sand and the other facing the street. The house was a tri-level and seemed huge to me. The bedroom where Brandi and I stayed was on the bottom floor. When we walked in, there were two neatly made beds with Reese's Pieces candies on the pillows. We spent about half our time with him those two weeks, and he worked the other half. I have a memory of waking up early one day, walking to the ocean, and seeing him up already, meditating by the ocean as the sun rose. The fly part about it was I remember seeing dolphins jumping in and out of the water in the background. Not bad. Before we knew it, it was time to go home. We took our first plane, by ourselves, with TSA minor guidance back to Virginia. The flight attendants on the plane were so nice that I wasn't even scared. The plane wasn't full, so they let us fly in first class for free. I felt like a king. It was luxury up there.

This Time, Something Was Different

When we got home, reality set back in and it was back to the same shit. My dad would call about once every two weeks for a five-minute conversation. Those talks were usually jive stale as hell, but I was still a little excited to have some connection to a father. It beat having none at all. We didn't talk about father-and-son stuff, though. We had "How you doing in school?" and "Are you making good grades?" conversations, not "This is how you deal with this," or "A man does this" conversations.

Brandi and I went back to California three or four times after that, usually in the summer when we were on school break. Every time we went, it was for the same two weeks. But these times were different from the last. Very different. Sometimes we barely had any food. Sometimes we were in hotels, sometimes in motels. One time we stayed in a motel that was so fucking cheap, I woke up and saw a new mole on my belly! Turned out to be a tick that sucked on my blood for so long, it looked like a huge mole. Thank God these were the days before bedbugs ran rampant! The highlight of our day was going to the free breakfast in the morning and getting as much cantaloupe as we could get for the whole day.

I remember times when my pops would argue with the front desk about paying them when he got off work to scrape up money. Man, we would get kicked out from motel to motel. Sometimes we would luck out and get to spend nights at the apartment of some chick he was sleeping with at the time. They would only be nice for a short time before they were like, "Y'all got to go." With one chick, I don't know what had happened between her and my father but she was so mad at him, she wouldn't let us use her toothpaste in the morning. Who knows what they were beefing about? I was too young to grasp whatever it was, but I understood the bad energy quite well.

Nurse Dad?

So now let's circle back to my life at fifteen. Out of a job. Smoking weed. Dealing weed. And my father called to say that he was in Richmond. My first thought was, *Why?* My next thought was, *Why now?* Why, after all these years, did you finally decide that you should be in Richmond? I couldn't help but think it was for some other reason than me, because if it was about me his ass wouldn't have left in the first place. Or he would've come back here a long time ago.

I'll never forget when I first saw him. He pulled up in front of the house in a beat-up convertible and hopped out of the car wearing scrubs. That's right, muthafuckin' scrubs! The same thing nurses wear. I was confused as hell, like I KNOW you aren't a nurse or a doctor. Bitch, you're a merchant, a salesperson. (In fact, his quality of life in California was a direct result of his sales skills and, more importantly, his money management skills.) The man hopped out of the car in the middle of the neighborhood with EVERYBODY watching and said, "Hey, that's my boy! Come here and give your daddy a hug."

Niggas looked at me like, "Man, who the fuck is this dude?" And at fifteen, needless to say, I was humiliated beyond humiliation. To be honest, this was when I first suspected drug use. This pattern didn't make sense. From just showing up in Richmond to this whole costume and air about him, something didn't click. It felt strange. Plus, I had enough drug addicts in my neighborhood to sense a "druggy" air about someone.

I Saw His Shit Through the Eyes of Pain

How dare you? The nerve of you to feel like you could just walk back into my life like this? LIKE THIS? Really? My love for him didn't grow. It was actually the opposite. I felt resistance. I felt hurt. I felt anger. So I shut down. I was a little older now and I understood the world a little differently. I saw it through the eyes of pain, so I processed it in the same way. In my mind, he fell off in California, maybe hit his lowest point, burned through his connections and friends, and didn't have anywhere to go, so he came back to Richmond. I was just a byproduct of the situation. Of course, he said he came back to be with his kids, but I didn't believe that shit one bit. To me, he was a liar. He just said that shit because it sounded good and he wanted to make me feel special. Or maybe that was the excuse he gave himself when he hit rock bottom and didn't want to accept that it had happened.

The way I saw it, I didn't need him. When I needed him most, he wasn't there. I needed him when I was growing up in a house full of women and wanted a man to relate to, to teach me the way of the world. I needed him when I was getting my ass whipped every day and wanted him to teach me how to fight, teach me how to be a man, teach me how to deal with adversity, and teach me how to survive in the hood. I mean, I was fifteen, Mom dukes left me here in this house, and I survived that. What role could he really play in my life?

> You were the one who was supposed to blueprint,
> My whole life story, y'know,
> Teach me manhood and pave the road out before me, yo,
> I understand you had to handle your biz,
> But in turn, I learned my manhood on my own gambling risk, and this led me
> Into realities of scandals and shit,
> Because of YOU, I ran the streets with a bunch of scrambling kids,
> And I could never really forgive
> What the lack of man in you did.
>
> —Excerpt from hip-hop song by Shiloh Jones

The only time I would call him was when I needed a few bucks (sometimes he had it and sometimes he didn't). What I can say is, when he had it, he would give it to me, regardless of whether he had a habit or not. Might not have been much, but in those days it helped, especially when I was hungry. Other times I would take the money and buy smoke.

Brandi Played Him Closer Than I Did

I think my sister played him closer than I did. She spent more time with him, so she was able to get more from him. This is when she learned how to manipulate men, starting with her father. There wasn't much she asked him for that she couldn't get.

The sad part was that the early manipulation of our father led Brandi to have some fucked-up relationships with men. Drugs got to be a problem, too. She started smoking weed in her late teens and doing other drugs in her twenties. When she was in her thirties, she ended up getting pregnant. She was so accustomed to drug use that she did drugs throughout the pregnancy. She drank, smoked weed, and popped plenty of oxycodone—and I believe her lifestyle led to my nephew having certain developmental disabilities that he has to live with to this day. For this reason and a whole lot of others, my relationship with Brandi is total shit these days. Even though we're not in touch, she tries to use me whenever she can.

My dad and my nephew, Khayri.

My mom would call in favors for her and so has my pops. But I eventually I had to make it clear that I was not going to continue enabling her by bailing her out. And that's where a few of the fibers and strands of our relationship virtually ended.

I see her very, very rarely in passing—usually at some event or by chance. Once, as time passed, I saw her at a funeral after one of our family members died. I hadn't seen her in years. She walked up to me and, when she opened her mouth, all of her teeth were gone but one. The continual use of drugs had weakened and rotted her teeth out of her mouth until they just fell out! This greatly saddened me. How can drugs take someone so beautiful and turn them into this?

This more than put me in shock; it hurt. All my memories of her ran through my mind. When I got back in the car, I literally cried. It broke my heart to see her like that. Even though I was not interested in building a relationship with her, I called my mother and told her that I had decided to pay for a full set of dental work for her mouth so she didn't have to walk around like that! I told my mom that I was appointing her as the handler of the transaction because I couldn't trust giving my sister the money directly. As a matter of fact, I didn't even want her to know it was from me. I spent close to $5,000 on her mouth. Why did I do it? Probably because I knew deep down that if she ever wanted to change her lifestyle, it was going to be ten times harder with no teeth in her mouth. It would have been downhill from there. Nobody wants to hire a toothless person professionally. At least she has a chance, if she so chooses to take advantage of it.

In retrospect, looking at the picture in its entirety, no matter how much of a rockstar my sister was growing up—and such a promising meteorite of motivation, energy, and hard work ethic—these beautiful "natural" qualities about her seem to dissipate once her mind was locked in on hard drugs. It is heart breaking to see her slowly decomposing and rotting from the inside out from drug use.

But what's even more heart breaking is seeing my nephew subjected to being a product of the selfish choices she made. Because of her drug use, my nephew never got to meet, nor will he ever come to know his father. Because of her drug use, he will never know what it is like to have a nurturing mother who truly provides, protects, and teaches him.

Her commitment to drug use has forever robbed him from a sense of normalcy, and has made him face a reality that no kid should have to emotionally endure.

All he wants is his mother . . .

All she wants is to get high.

This is still the effect the so called "war on drugs" has on my community and our families. Truly sad.

Looking back, maybe Brandi's interaction with Pops was part manipulation, part trying to reconnect with her father from the past. Who knows? I mean, what I really learned from growing up without one of my parents is that every child needs both their mother and father in their life for a healthy and balanced childhood. The effects of a broken home run deep for so many black men and women and can be connected to many unhealthy behaviors. It can affect how we treat each other, how we deal with the opposite sex, and how we raise our own kids. It touches our relationships, our confidence, our insecurities, our decision-making ability, our strengths, our weaknesses, our complexes, and our social positions.

In other words, absolutely everything.

8

Age 15: Chimborazo Boulevard, Between P Street and M Street

HERE'S THE THING about smoking and selling weed: it leads to hanging out with people you normally wouldn't spend time with. Here's how it worked with me: my first customers started out as just friends that I'd smoke with. Before long, it was people I worked with. Next, it was people who were down the street on the corners, the hustlers. So, needless to say, the people I was coming into contact with were from different backgrounds and had different influences. My sister started dating this dude named Stash. He was from New York, fresh out of Brooklyn.

When I met him, everything about him was grimy. He was the epitome of street. Still, I rapped with him. He bought weed from me a few times, but I couldn't keep up with the quantity he smoked. I only sold dimes, while he wanted quarters and ounces. Those were out of my league. Whatever. He probably only bought smoke from me because he was fucking my sister.

The corner hustlers bought from me regularly. Them niggas were the ones who haggled with me the most. "Aye, li'l shawty, let me get three for $25."

I thought to myself, *Hey, it's more at once. I can re-up faster. Why not?* Then three of them would chip in close to eight bucks apiece and get a dime for a portion of the usual price. Cheap-ass niggas. Can't knock 'em. They knew the basic rules of the power of buying in quantity. I would sell it to them and they'd be like, "Where you going, li'l shawty? Why you always in a rush? Man, chill out here with us for a second. Damn, cuz, you act like you don't fuck with us?"

So not to be rude, I'd kick it with them for a little. And that turned into chilling with them more and more. All in all, about fifty different niggas hung out on that strip of "the boulevard," which was about five blocks long. To this day, I still don't understand how they all made money. It didn't seem like the smartest business move to me. I would've thought they'd spread out a little bit, develop a territory, hustle a little bit smarter. But hey, that wasn't my business. They sold coke and crack; I sold weed. They would sell coke to each other and sell crack to fiends, and I would sell weed to them. It worked for me.

"One Time!"

One Friday night around 11:30, we were all chilling and about to have a smoke session. Niggas would just smoke and crack on each other, making jokes. Believe it or not, this was fun as hell. I promise you, I met some of the funniest people I've ever known in the hood. The world never got a chance to hear their talent. If the right people had heard them, they could have ended up being the next Kevin Hart.

Anyway, there were about twenty-five of us that night. We were huddled in front of a rinky-dink car lot that nobody bought cars from (it was probably a front) on the corner of Edgewood Avenue and the boulevard. I'll never forget it. A few blunts went in the air, some were still being rolled, when somebody shouted, "ONE TIME!" That was slang for the police. Oh shit! Everybody started to scatter. They didn't run because you didn't run from the police, or you'd look guilty. They just started walking in all directions as if they hadn't just been standing in a big-ass huddle.

What was I doing? Well, I was skillfully crafting my "L" (slang term for blunt) out of my dime bag and had the rest of the bag on a car trunk. After I processed the commotion, I scattered my blunt and its weed guts on the ground and scuffled it around, like a dog does when it's marking its territory. I took the bag I had on the trunk and stashed it in a crevice by the car's wheel well. Then I ducked as the police focused their light onto the lot, and I tried to open a car door. It was locked.

So I moved quickly to a truck right in front of it and tried to open the door and that bitch was unlocked. YES! As I was doing this, one of the fucking boys from the corner ran to the other side, jumped in, and stretched out toward the center of the bench seat. When I tried to do the same, his big ass was in the way. I just squished myself as much as I could onto him. So he was lying inward, and I was lying inward, and our shoulders prevented us from being flush.

Everything was silent. I heard footsteps getting closer. I literally held my breath. Next thing I heard was "GET OUT OF THE CAR!" It was a female's voice. Nigga, I ain't budging. Told myself that she must have been talking to someone else.

"I SAID, 'GET OUT OF THE CAR WITH YOUR HANDS UP!'"

Nope! Still ain't moving. Then I heard, "I SAID, 'GET THE FUCK OUTTA THE CAR NOW OR I WILL SHOOT THIS FUCKING CAR WITH YOU IN IT!'"

Well, time to get the fuck out! I ain't messing with those words. Dude, I'm smart enough to know when to hold 'em and when to fold 'em. I lifted up my hands and kept them there as a lady cop opened the truck door and told me to step out.

"GET ON THE GROUND!" she yelled.

As I got on my knees, one cop held me at gunpoint while the other cuffed me. They did the same to the dude who'd been in the truck with me. I knew that his copycat ass was the reason I got caught. I confirmed it when I asked the cop how she even saw me and she said she could see a couple of the twists from my hair poking out above the window line. (I was starting to grow dreadlocks, and they stuck out of my head like Pinhead from *Hellraiser*.) I knew it! Just a couple of inches down, that one shoulder length, and I would've gotten away with it.

School Saved My Ass Again

The female cop bombarded us with questions. She also tried to contact the lot owner to see if he wanted to press trespassing charges but couldn't reach him. She couldn't get us on anything. She looked at the guy who'd been in the truck with me. "I know y'all were up to something. I can't prove it, and I can't do anything to you 'cause you're over twenty-four years old." Then she looked my way. "But you? You're a different story. First off, you're under eighteen, so I'm taking your ass in for violating curfew."

She left me in cuffs and put me in her squad car. (By the way, do you know how uncomfortable it is to sit in a cop car with handcuffs on, with your hands behind your back? It's not the most pleasing of positions, but I didn't complain. I shut my mouth and took the longest ride ever to that precinct.)

When I got to the precinct, one of the cops asked for my address. When I gave it to her, she realized that my mother worked at Elkhardt Middle School. That's what saved my ass! My mother had given up her hard labor doing wallpapering and painting shortly after she had met Vinnie and gone back to teaching school. Elkhardt was a pretty rough school at the time and required the presence of police officers. That's how this cop knew her. She talked to me differently from that point on, with genuine concern, asking why I was hanging out with those guys.

"Those guys aren't going to be shit in life. Just because you live in the hood doesn't mean you have to 'be' hood." She looked at the other cops and said, "I got this one! His mother is a personal friend of mine." And so they didn't finish the booking. I don't think I was even logged into the system.

Then she called my mom, who was at Vinnie's house, of course. She didn't have a clue as to what was going on. My mother came up to the station and smacked the shit out of me in front of the officers. (Remember, she didn't do embarrassment well, so she was super-pissed.) If the last one was a nail in the coffin, dude, this one was surely the caulking to seal it tight.

After that, she attempted to place me in a facility. As soon as they evaluated me, they released me. They told my mother that I was brilliant and had scored high in tests for competency, academic skills, and emotional stability. So that didn't work. As a matter of fact, it backfired on her. They started questioning her parenting skills, which enraged her even more.

Bill Jones, You Up to Bat!

She tried to take the behavioral route and put me in a group home. "I can't do nothing with him and I don't want him no more!" she said. "He can't stay in my house!" So the group home accepted me. It was the Oasis House on Chamberlayne Avenue. Man, they had locks on the windows and a million rules. They even confiscated the strings out of my tennis shoes. They treated me like a fuckup. I had to figure out a way to get out.

But how? I was a minor, and my mother had signed my rights away, like a slave, to these strangers. She got what she wanted. She won! I was out of her life. She could do whatever the fuck she wanted with Vinnie without having to deal with me. I went to sleep that first night very distraught. Traumatized. I had to figure out a way to get the hell out of there.

I dreamed about that shit all night. I could barely sleep, waking up every hour on the hour. I woke up the next day with a plan. I figured that if a parent had the power to put me in this joint, then a parent had the power to pull me out as well. Okay, fuck you, Mom. Bill Jones, you up to bat! And there it is! That was my way out. See, I knew if I could just speak to him, I could convince him to get me out of that hellhole. All I had to do now was get those fucktards to let me use the phone.

So I went to the "warden" and asked for permission to call my mother to tell her that I loved her and appreciated her putting me there so I could get my act together. He bought it. Bam! Called my pops and told him the story. That negro was there to pick me up in less than an hour. They tried to deny him at first, but that dude wasn't leaving without me. All I could think was, *Nigga, if you ain't good for nothing else, you alright in my book for this one!*

He got me the fuck outta there. Fuck that warden! Fuck you and your group home! Bye, Oasis House! And I left.

My Stay with My Pops

My pops was from Richmond's Church Hill area, so naturally when he came back to Virginia, that's where he returned. As creatures of habit, we usually only develop new patterns when we have to. He stayed in a rundown apartment somewhere on Chimborazo Boulevard, somewhere between P Street and M Street. Yup, you guessed it: this area was drug infested and hooded the fuck out too in the early '90s. Church Hill had it bad, though. The murder rate there was even higher than Northside's, and there were more people on dope—and by dope, I mean heroin. In our world, both then and now, heroin is "dope," "train," or "that boy." Cocaine is "coke" or "that white girl." Crack cocaine is "crack," "rocks," or "hard." Weed is "smoke," "herb," or "reggie."

Anyway, a lot of niggas around there used to sniff dope. Heroin was the type of drug that would either bring the crazy out of you or make you nod off. It was a different class of drug in the sense that you became both mentally and physically addicted to it. The problem with dope is that once you were hooked on it, the chances of coming off that shit were slim to none. See, the withdrawal symptoms were a motherfucker. You could actually die from going cold turkey. Imagine that. Who in the fuck would want to do this? Or why? It all depended on your level of usage, how much you needed, and how long you could go before "getting sick" (that's what they called the withdrawal symptoms). You mix that situation with a person who is already gangster and you have a recipe for someone who would literally kill you for the shit.

In those days, I saw quite a number of people fall victim to heroin. They either lost their lives to it or fucked up their lives because of it. My mom's brother, my uncle, was hooked on it all his life. Fish is what we called him. Fish went from sniffing it to shooting it. He literally died from the shit. Overdosed.

My mom and my uncle, Fish.

Today, heroin has made a huge comeback through prescription pills like codeine and Percocet. We are now facing an opioid crisis. But that's another story. It's really sad to see how it affected the black community back then and how it's affecting it now. Anyway, because there were so many gangstas around Church Hill when I moved in with my pops, stickups were at an all-time high. The blocks were full of people trying to get one hustle or another on. One group sold stolen goods—anything they could get their hands on—from electronics to bikes to high-end athletic shoes. Another group was the niggas who sold drugs directly to their customers. A third group was made up of certified middlemen who got drugs for you so you didn't have to come up against the dealers. You brought your money to them, told them what you wanted, and they'd get it for you. If you gave them $100, they'd get it for $75 and keep the rest as a tax to earn a few extra dollars, or they'd beat the bag and take drugs out of it before they gave it to you. These middlemen were a buffer and, among other things, they connected the professional world (teachers, car salesmen, and lawyers, for example) to the street.

I didn't know what my father had been up to before I moved in with him. Honestly, I didn't care. The first night I stayed with him was a little rocky, but hey, it beat the alternative, so I didn't complain. The second night, though, was an experience.

Thanks Again, Dad!

Since Pops had a one-bedroom apartment, he'd given me the bedroom and he was staying in the living room. On the second night I stayed there, I woke up around 11 p.m. to get a drink of water. I smelled something funny but didn't pay much attention to it. When I passed through the living room, I saw my father on the couch with some random-ass chick, and these niggas were smoking crack. What the fuck?

He screamed at me to go back to my room. I don't think it registered with him that I'd seen what he was doing, but I had. Now I knew what crack smelled like! (Thanks, Dad!) Now I'd confirmed that he was ACTUALLY on drugs. (Thanks again, Dad!) Now I knew both of my parents were on drugs. (Way to go, parents!) Now I felt like drugs ran the whole world 'cause that was all I saw. (Thank you, world!) I had no fucking role models left. I was officially fucked when it came to people to look up to. Somebody wake me up out of this nightmare, please!

I couldn't help but get a little depressed and angry at the situation. See, I didn't expect much from him, but experiencing more disappointment was even worse than expecting nothing, if that makes sense. After that, being there with him was uncomfortable for me. I'd always felt like crack was a bottom-of-the-barrel drug. I didn't understand why people smoked it, especially when it made them lose all self-respect, living like fucking zombies with only one thing on their minds. My dad was obviously a functioning crack user, but was he going to end up being a crack zombie? Who knew? Thought I might as well prepare myself for it mentally, just in case he fell into the "highly likely" group with most crack users.

Meeting Tyrone

The next day, I met Tyrone. He came to my dad's apartment and immediately took to me. I didn't know how he knew my father. I didn't ask. Once again, I didn't care. The best way to describe Tyrone is that he looked like the logo from the AND1 brand. He was about twenty-seven years old, six feet five inches tall, bald-headed, and cool as fuck.

Tyrone would pick me up every day, sometimes in a red convertible, and we'd ride out while he did his "runs." He always made sure I wasn't hungry, so we'd go to whatever fast-food joint I wanted. We'd also go to his chicks' houses (the man had chicks!), and I could hear him banging them out while I was in the living room watching TV. Then we would ride through several spots, check groups of niggas hanging out on the corner, roll up an L, kick it, and then bounce out. He was my friend, and he kept me close to him all the time.

One day we stopped at the Burger King, and he pulled out the largest wad of hundred dollar bills. Man, this dude was rich. Homie had a few cribs and all of them were decked out. He was quickly becoming my role model. He ain't never judge me, he ain't let nobody fuck with me, and he took me with him everywhere. At the time, this was the most love anyone had ever shown me, especially on a big homie level.

It wasn't long before I put two and two together and figured out he was a hustler. But he was a different kind of hustler, one that I wasn't used to. The ones I knew stood on the corner, ten, fifteen, or twenty niggas at a time, and waited for fiends to come their way. Instead, Tyrone sold to hustlers, and they would sell to fiends. He was what you'd call a "nigga who deals weight." One day, he reached into his pants pocket and pulled out the biggest crack rock I've ever seen. "See, that's an ounce right here," he said. "But this ain't shit. Man, I'll chuck a couple of these before you even wake up."

He schooled me on crack and coke, explaining that cocaine was used to make crack and that everything depended on your "cook game" and how fiends reacted to it. "Little nigga, you cool as shit, cuz," he'd say to me. Best advice he ever gave me was not to turn out like him. I didn't listen to that shit, though. He was everything I wanted to be. Fly cars, bad bitches, dumb respect everywhere he went. The way my life had been up to that point, how could I not look up to that nigga?

I remember us pulling up to the strip one day. He said, "Li'l homie, I need you to count this for me." He pulled a stack of bills from his trunk that was so big, it wouldn't fold. It couldn't fold. It stacked. It was all one-dollar bills, about 1,500 of them. "You good, cuz! Count that shit right there," he said, pointing to the street curb. "Ain't nobody gon' fuck with you out here."

I'd always been taught never to flash your money. So imagine what it felt like for me, when stickups were at their highest, to be out in the open and counting out a stupid amount of money with nobody daring to fuck with me. I thought this dude was invincible. Shit, he ran the street. Trip part about it, those were just the ones he'd made that day! He treated his ones like they were pennies. Imagine what he made in bigger bills!

Like My Long-Lost Big Brother Until ...

Tyrone was like my long-lost big brother, until one day when he was supposed to come to the apartment to pick me up. He was running behind. When he finally got there, something was off. His eyes were bloodshot red. His whole demeanor was different. He pushed right past me at the door. He found my dad, sat down on the couch and, after the most uncomfortable silence ever, said these words: "I'm going to ask you one time! Where my shit at?" He stared like a tiger at my pops, dead into his eyes.

"It won't me, Tyrone," my pops responded.

Yo, I had no idea where Tyrone had gone. This wasn't him! He didn't even look at me. He acted like he didn't know who the fuck I was. He pulled out a gun and placed it on the floor in front of him.

"Lie to me again and I'm going to shoot you in the face!" he said to my pops.

"I promise, man, I wouldn't lie to you," my dad said. "It was Donald." (Donald was my cousin, and he hung with my dad. In fact, my dad was with Donald as often as I was with Tyrone.)

"Matter of fact, where the fuck Donald at right now?" asked Tyrone.

"Tyrone, I don't know. I'm looking for him myself," said my dad.

Then Tyrone said, "I know one thing: somebody betta give me my shit or one of ya niggas 'bout to die today!"

This is where I got scared. Was my pops about to get killed right in front of my face? This shit was over my head. I didn't know what the fuck was going on. This moment right there was as *real* as real gets! Tyrone then picked the gun up off the floor, put his finger around the trigger, and pointed it at my dad's face. I didn't know what to do, so I said, "Tyrone, don't, man. That's my pops, bro."

Tyrone looked at me with the coldest look ever and then looked back at my pops. "Yo, I'll be back over here in an hour," he said. "Have my fucking money!" Then he left.

Have Some Respect

I felt a number of things in that moment. Mostly, I was hurt that Tyrone disregarded me like he did. I get it! It was some shit over money and drugs. They fucked up his work. What-the-fuck ever. But I'm your boy. Or so I thought I was. Maybe I was just a front for him, giving the illusion that I was his son while he rode around selling drugs all day. Or maybe I wasn't. Maybe this situation had him so vexed that this was how he reacted over his money. Still, nigga, this is me, and that's my pops. Have some respect. Does money make you disregard everything? Would you do the same thing to me if you'd shoot my pops right in front of me? Of course you would!

And my pops? Why would he put me in that situation? Why would he bring me into this environment? I came to him—I got that—but why would he steal a nigga's "work" while I was there? How deep in this shit was he?

Putting two and two together after Tyrone left, I realized that he was probably stashing some shit at my dad's crib. My pops and my cousin Donald must have been selling it or went into his stash and now it was either gone or the money got fucked up. (As for Donald, I learned later that he moved to D.C. to avoid being killed by Tyrone.)

Really, who cares what the scenario was? I learned a valuable lesson that day. Street shit is straight-up street shit. It follows its own codes and its own rules and, most importantly, it can give two shits about you. Probably because I was young and immature, but I internalized a lot that I made about me that really ain't have nothing to do with me.

Fact: I knew Tyrone was coming back. Fact: The money was either fucked up or the stash was gone. Fact: Some more shit was getting ready to pop off and this wasn't my business, nor did I want to stick around and witness what was about to transpire. I had to get out of there. Here we go again, another situation I had to think my way out of. Fuck my pops! Fuck Tyrone! I didn't want to, but I called my mom and told her what had happened. I told her that I knew she was going to be mad at me, but for my safety, my well-being, I needed to come home.

Back to Mom's

She had no choice. But man, was she pissed! I know she felt like she couldn't get rid of me. She told me she felt I'd emotionally manipulated her into coming back home. And that hurt, but I had to take that shot on the chin. What was I supposed to do? I chose the lesser of two evils. I was going to have to deal with my mom's shit, but at least I was dealing with it in safety.

To my serious fucking surprise, the situation between Tyrone and my dad never really blew up. Instead, it blew over. I never saw Tyrone again until years later in Church Hill. He looked bad. Small. Skinny. Blood ran from his nose, which told me he was using. As far as I know, he didn't use when we were hanging. But hustlers often have a way of feeling invincible and thinking they can start using themselves. Just goes to show how you can be the man one minute and then totally fall the fuck off the next.

9

Age 16: We Ride Together or We Die Together

AFTER THE INCIDENT with Tyrone and my dad, I left Church Hill and went back to Northside. Good, bad, or indifferent, Northside was my comfort zone. I was sixteen years old by this time, and Northside was all I'd really ever known. But now I was dealing with some new variables. One, I had a highly pissed mother who didn't want shit to do with me. Two, I had no money. I was all the way tapped out. Three, Mom dukes was still gone 24/7 over at Vinnie's, so that meant I was still on my own for food. Four, I had to still maintain at school.

Okay, I figured. Here's the hand I'm dealt at the moment. Time to figure something out.

Meeting Stash

Eight houses up the block from me, there was a new crack house that had popped up. You know these places when they enter your neighborhood by the sheer traffic they generate and the individuals who make up that traffic. I passed that house every day going to the store.

One day as I was passing, I heard, "YO, SON!" in a sharp New York accent. I turned around and saw a dark-skinned figure on the porch. As I got closer, I could tell it was Stash, the guy my sister had dated a while back.

"Yo, what's good, son?" he asked. "What's popping?"

"Ain't shit, Stash," I answered. "What's good with you, big homie?"

"Aite-aite, yo, this my new spid-dot (which was just another way to say *spot*—New York dudes back in that day always had a way of making slang out of slang) now," he said. "Come fuck with me, nigga!"

"When you get over here?" I asked.

"Shit, probably 'bout a month," he told me. "Shit booming, son!"

And from there, we kicked it. Kicked it hard! But this nigga smoked all day long! I don't know how he even functioned, but I guess all those years of smoking weed shot his tolerance way up high. I couldn't hang with his level of smoking. Many a time I told him, "Nah, I'm good" when he tried to pass me the L. He thought that was the funniest thing in the world. He started to call me his little brother. He knew I needed money. He knew I was broke.

He told me, "Son, you need money, my nigga. Ima fuck with you and we gon' get some money together!" And that's how it started.

Now the Street Was Becoming Part of Me

Stash only sold crack. He would sell a little to the boulevard niggas as weight but would always keep a substantial amount to break down for hand-to-hand action for the fiends. He told me it was important to keep a balance between selling weight and hand-to-hand. See, selling weight limits your margins when it comes to profit. When Stash would re-up, he could move weight quickly by selling straight to dealers and make a 30 to 40 percent profit margin. But when he broke it down, he would triple his profits. Downside is that it took longer to sell and he had to see more fiends and take more risk. Both approaches had pros and cons and both had inherent risks, so his strategy was to do a combination of the two.

When the work came in, it went fast, especially on the first and fifteenth of the month, because that's when people got their checks, either from the government or from work. I was surprised to see so many levels of crackheads, from ultra-high functioning to super zombied-the-fuck-out. Stash would let me make runs and deliver the shit to certain people. I did and would make money in the in-between. What was so crazy is that I saw my neighborhood from a new perspective. Keep in mind that up to this point, I'd only sold weed. Selling crack was a different world. I saw people in my neighborhood and suddenly knew what their poison was. Shit was weird as hell. Sometimes uncomfortable for me, sometimes uncomfortable for them. After a while, I got used to it. I made hand-to-hand runs, I made weight runs, and anything else to get the job done. This is how I was feeding myself.

Stash and his homebody, B, were damn near twice my age. In a lot of my circles back then, people were much older than I was. That was an indication that I was too young out there, when most kids were at home where they should be. Bottom line. My state of mind started changing. I was already street smart, but now the street was becoming part of me, part of my makeup. I wasn't really making money like that. I was just making enough to satisfy my immediate needs and a few wants. But that was enough for me back then. I really didn't know the full value of what I was doing so I couldn't assign a price to it. Nor did I truly understand the magnitude of risks I was taking. I just looked at my alternatives and knew this was the best one at the time.

Shit, at least I could eat and buy myself a few outfits. Might not have been much, but it was the world to me.

A More Advanced Level of Hustling

Stash and B's level of hustling was more advanced than what I'd seen before. They moved like they were still in Brooklyn, where the streets were rougher than Richmond's. They'd developed three languages to communicate with, so nobody could understand what the fuck they were saying. They had conversations in front of people, on the phone, and you couldn't crack their secret language no matter how hard you tried. They taught it to me after I asked a million times, "What does this mean? What does that mean?"

So then *we* had our own secret language. With them, I learned how to cut crack, bag crack, and stash it by my nuts. I also learned a lot about guns from them. They taught me how to load them, how to shoot them, and how to properly conceal them. They stashed guns all over the place and even gave me two to hold: a chrome .38 Special revolver and a pistol grip shotgun. I held them both at my mom's house, putting one in the drop ceiling and the other in the basement behind the water heater.

Selling crack was an experience that eventually taught me my boundaries. I sold crack to mothers, fathers, husbands, wives, grandmothers, grandfathers, sons, daughters, cousins, whoever. I remember one time selling it to a mom who was so bent on getting high that she used her baby's diaper money to buy crack. Imagine a drug making a mother go against her nurturing instincts, which are built into the human genetic makeup, and deny essentials for her child just to get high.

I realized one day that all the people I sold to had a couple of things in common: most were black and from the community I grew up in. The very thing that was destroying our community, I was supporting. How did I get here? How did I compromise my moral system so badly to do such a thing? I knew better. No matter how long it had been since I'd been to the temple, part of that morality still lived in me.

The Tipping Point

The tipping point for me came one night at the crack house. We had rules there, including that fiends couldn't come by after 11 p.m. That night, the same fiend who would rather buy crack than her daughter's diapers came around at about midnight. I was with Stash and B. We were counting money and smoking when we heard a knock at the door.

"Yo, who dat, son? Yo, dun, go get the door," they told me.

"Man, it's that crackhead bitch I told y'all about that I ain't wanna serve no more," I answered.

"Yo, why dat bitch knocking this late, tho'? She know better!" they said. "Yo, dun, smack her in her face!"

"Smack her in her face?" I asked. "Man, I ain't gon' hit no female, Stash. I don't do that, bruh."

They both started to laugh at this point. "Yo, dis nigga crazy, son. I don't think he knows how this works," said Stash as he jumped in to school me. "Yo, son, that crack shit will have a fiend brain gone. We set rules for a reason. If these muthafuckas come over here whenever they want to, this house gon' get hot! If this shit get hot, then, nigga, the po-po coming. If the po-po come, then our money fucked up. So you telling me you gon' let this one fiend bitch fuck our money up? That's why you gotta smack 'em when they do shit like this 'cause they don't respond to nothing else!"

I had to admit, it made sense. Still, though, nigga, I wasn't smacking a woman. I refused to let that part of my morals be compromised by that little white devil called crack. Fuck that. What if that was my mother? Even though we had all that shit going on between us, I would kill you if you smacked my mother. Fuck outta here! I refused, and somebody else went out there and handled the situation. That's when my hatred toward that white drug, cocaine, began. This shit was the reality I had to accept if I was going to keep traveling in this direction, so I knew I had to change direction. My options were limited at the time. But the universe has a way of changing your course for you.

The Beef

One night I was out, talking to some of the boulevard niggas, just kicking the shit. A guy named Ronnie pulled up. He was one of the boulevard niggas who would be over Northside and Church Hill way. Ronnie was about twenty-seven years old, a little taller than me, and had three gold teeth in the front at the top. After he got out of his car, the conversation turned to putting up on some smoke.

"Well, shit, I'll put up," I said. "I'll be right back."

I walked to the stash house, about half a block away, and hollered at Stash, who was chilling with a couple of girls, to see if he wanted some, too. I let him know we were headed to the store and he asked me to pick him up a six-pack of Guinness Stout and a box of Dutches. When I told him that Ronnie was driving, he said, "Yeah, I fucks with Ronnie. Tell him thanks and give him this."

He handed me some bread and an extra $10 with it, all ones. I left the stash house with the girls and went back to the boulevard.

As we rode in the car, Ronnie started talking to the chicks about Stash. Damn near kicking it to them. And I didn't understand this because Stash gave him love. Why was this dude betraying him like this? Then Ronnie took it further and started going in on Stash.

"Man, that nigga ugly as a bitch!" he said, and the girls started laughing.

I was thinking, *Damn, all these people in here are fake as hell.* I just shut my mouth for the rest of the ride back. He kicked to one of the chicks and got her number before parking back on the boulevard. When I went into the house, I was hot. I waited to see if the chicks were going to talk about what had transpired in the car. They didn't. Sheisty chicks. After a while, I decided to say something. (I mean, shouldn't he know how grimy these broads were? More importantly, shouldn't he know how fake Ronnie was?) Me, I wouldn't trust that nigga anymore.

I pulled Stash to the side and said, "Yo, Stash, let me holla at you right quick 'cause …"

B came up while I was going over what had happened. "What? He said what? Yo, where dat nigga at?"

"He probably still outside on the strip," I told him.

B ran out of there real quick and checked Ronnie, whose response baffled me. He said, "What? I didn't say that! Cuz, I would never disrespect you or Stash. Ya my people. Why that nigga lie on me like that?"

B looked at me and demanded, "Say what he said, son!"

"You did say that shit, nigga," I responded. "Why you lying?"

Ronnie looked at me, said that he didn't appreciate me lying about him, got in his car, and drove off. Then Stash and B asked the chicks what had happened, but they lied, denying it all. And just like that, it was dropped. I didn't understand why, but it was. The next day, I just so happened to run into Ronnie.

When he saw me, he kept staring at me—glaring at me, to be exact. "Nigga, I see that bitch-ass shit you did!" he said to me.

"Nigga, that's some bitch shit you did," I replied. "That man show you love. How you gon' dog that man behind his back to some chicks?"

"Nigga, fuck that nigga!" he responded. "And fuck you, too!"

"Fuck you too, cuz," I said, meaning every syllable of it. "Ain't nobody scared of you. Fuck you!" We shared a few more words and then walked off in separate directions.

This Was a Declaration of War

A couple of days later, I was at home with Brandi when my mom dropped in on one of her random visits. She had Vinnie with her. They were apparently going to stay there for most of the day, so I decided to leave. So I walked up the block, checked Stash, got some work from him, and headed to the boulevard. I got there and found Ronnie with about ten other dudes.

As I walked past them, Ronnie started popping off shit. "Bitch-ass nigga!" he started in on me. "I'll beat yo' ass right here! Say something."

"Say something?" I asked. "Man, get the fuck out of my face!"

"Cuz, you gon' stop looking at me like I'm your age," said Ronnie. "You a little-ass kid to me, nigga." Then he took two fingers and pushed my head at the temple.

Maybe my heart was too big. Maybe I should've avoided this whole thing altogether. No, fuck that, nobody is going to just disrespect me. Those days are over. Sorry. I swung, he swung and, before long, I was aware of the complete advantage he had at twenty-seven over sixteen-year-old me. He clearly outmatched me. Clearly. He had more fights under his belt, more skill, more power, and more strength. He whipped my ass. Hold up, though, your boy never touched the ground. Dude, I pride myself on that one. The fight seemed to last forever, but in reality it was probably only about five minutes long.

By the end of that five minutes, a crowd of about thirty people had grown around us. I think I even heard someone say, "Damn, Ronnie whipping that boy ass!"

He was. I admit that. But what happened next is what took it to another level. I was breathing hard as hell and looking at him, still ready to fight some more, when he backed up and said, "I ain't fighting your bitch-ass no more." He looked at me and added, "You keep fucking with me and I'll kill yo' little ass!"

And just like that, my mind flipped! This was no longer a fight to me. This was now a life-or-death situation! Nobody had ever spoken those words to me, let alone meant it. That wasn't just a threat to me; it was a declaration of war.

"Oh, That Nigga Ain't Going Nowhere!"

I turned around and walked home as fast as I could. When I walked through the door, my mom was in the living room with Brandi and Vinnie. I pushed past them, went down the basement stairs, and walked straight to the water heater. I found the pistol-grip pump shotgun, grabbed some bullets, and started loading them up. Got about five shells in there and cocked back the pump. Mom and Vinnie were at the top of the stairs by now. When they heard the pump cock, my mom screamed and slammed the basement door shut before I could get to the top of the steps. She locked the door from the outside, trapping me in the basement. I banged on the door like a wild man! "Let me the fuck outta here!" I yelled at her.

"No! What the hell is wrong with you, boy? And where the hell you get that gun from?"

"I ain't got time for this shit!" I said. "Let me the fuck out!" I was amped up with so much adrenaline running through my veins, I probably banged on that door, kicking and screaming, for thirty minutes straight.

Word travels on the street fast and, before long, Stash and B came to my house. They yelled to me through a small window in the basement about a foot from the ceiling. "Yo, son, what happened?"

"That nigga said he was going to kill me!" I told them. "I PROMISE you, I will kill him before he kills me!"

They told my mom to keep me locked in the basement. "Oh, that nigga ain't going nowhere!" she replied. "I got this! Y'all can go."

They left me locked in that basement all night. No food. No water. No nothing. In a weird way, I needed that. I had a talk with myself. A talk with the universe. A talk with God. I ran every possible scenario through my mind. They all ended with Ronnie dead. Imagine that. The one time my mother just so happened to come home, she saved me. She saved me from going to jail that day, and she saved Ronnie from getting killed.

Holding My Circle to a Higher Code

I was so enraged, nothing would have stopped me from killing Ronnie in broad daylight. And for what? He threatened my life! I didn't take that well. I mean, I could take an ass whipping. (Shit, dude was almost twice my age. He was almost *supposed* to win. I was outmatched before I started.) But this was the result of a chain reaction *of a chain reaction* of events. If I had just minded my own business when I was in the car with Ronnie that night, if I wasn't trying to be loyal to Stash, if I hadn't needed to go to the store to get smoke, if I never smoked in the first place, if I never involved myself in this street shit ... You know what? Fuck the ifs. That wasn't going to change the situation.

As I remember it, everybody I was dealing with on the street was in his or her mid- to late twenties. Dude, I was sixteen years old. I was still a child. My so-called homies should have stepped in. *They* should have completed the beef. Why the fuck weren't they at my house asking me what happened? Why didn't they go beat the shit out of Ronnie for messing with their little homie? Is this what the streets are all about? I wondered if I was holding the streets and my circle to a higher code than they deserved. Or maybe that was just my code. And if my code was superior to that of my brethren, if it was at a higher standard, then we weren't seeing eye to eye and they didn't have the privilege of being called my brethren.

This Time, There Was No Coming Back

As I continued to put things into perspective, I lost respect for them. Because if the tables were reversed, I wouldn't have thought twice. My moral compass told me that if you took a bullet for me, I'd automatically take one for you. We ride together or we die together. I started to realize what my problem was. I was too loyal, if that makes sense. Emotionally I was confused, mentally I disagreed, but in reality, this is what it was! What was I supposed to do? I could only play the cards I was dealt. This shit of not being able to trust people was starting to get real old!

My mother had a long talk with me the next day. She told me that all the neighbors had filled her in on my street dealings. She told me how "uncontrollable" they said I was. They told her that I was headed to certain death or jail, or maybe both. Plus, she was still really fucked up about the gun I'd kept in her house. (She didn't even know about the handgun that was still in the drop ceiling.) She told me that I'd chosen my path and she had to choose hers. I'd broken several cardinal rules, all within a short time frame, and I was no longer welcome in her home. She assured me that there was no "coming back" this time, no matter how bad it got for me out there in the world. This what it! She'd had enough! She was done. And so my life began as a sixteen-year-old *adult*. Shit just got real! Dammit, I fucked up.

A couple of things I learned from these experiences:

1. I decided never to treat people in a manner that isn't equally reciprocated. From that day on, trust would have to be truly earned from me.
2. I pledged that I'd never sell cocaine again, no matter how bad things got for me. It went against my principles far too much. I refused to be a catalyst for what was destroying our communities like nothing else.
3. I vowed to stay true to my principles and not to worry about the next man. He and I may stand for two totally different things. What I value deeply, he may not value at all. So be true to what you believe in. Your principles are just that, *your* principles. Bottom line.

10

Age 17: "This Is the Richmond Police; Open Up"

WHEN MY MOTHER kicked me out after my fight with Ronnie, I had to figure some things out, including where I'd live. My sister invited me to stay at her place for a while. She lived over on Southside in Somerset Glen apartments. She was eighteen by then, and she'd talked my father into cosigning for the apartment with her. Since I had very few options—well, none at all—I accepted.

Still Learning, Even with All the Bullshit

Amazingly, I'd still maintained good grades in my turbulent-ass life up to this point. Even though my atmosphere was rocky, it didn't mean I didn't like to learn. In fact, I loved to learn. I stayed reading. I stayed writing. Poetry and hip-hop kept my mind intact, kept it alive, preserved it in the midst of all the bullshit.

A year earlier, I'd been accepted into Richmond Community High School, a school for only the most gifted and talented kids in the city. Only forty to fifty kids statewide got accepted each year. At any given time, the entire high school consisted of only about 160 to 185 students, including freshmen, sophomores, juniors, and seniors. Thinking back on it now, I was blessed to have that opportunity. It was there that I met my high school sweetheart. Her name was Sheila. We hated each other at first. She used to always talk shit to me, and you know I was popping shit right back. That was in ninth grade; by tenth grade, we were dating.

I'd travel from Southside every day all the way to the deep West End to go to school at Community. It was treacherous. Sometimes I could ride with my sister. Sometimes I'd have to catch the bus. And sometimes I didn't go at all because I just didn't want to. I had no guidance from my parents or my sister, who was a senior at the time and starting a life outside of school. I spent most of my time dealing with the situation that was in front of me every day—needing food, clothes, a place to live—so school was really taking a back seat.

Southside: A Different Animal

Southside was a completely different animal than Northside. First off, wait, let me give you a little background to paint a better picture for you. Back in those days, Northside and Southside were mortal enemies. I mean, this was a huge beef that stretched back before my time. Northside niggas hated Southside niggas and vice versa. It was the closest thing to Richmond's version of L.A.'s Bloods and Crips. So I want you to understand what a bold move it was for me, a Northside boy, to move into the heart of Southside. While I did catch a little flak, the way I carried myself surprisingly kept me away from a lot of drama. I was still cool with Ish, my best friend at the time, and I started chilling closer with his brother. Yah was his name. We became just as tight as Ish and I were, and the three of us formed a brotherhood.

My sister started dating females around this time and ended up getting a girlfriend. Before long, she moved out, leaving the apartment to Yah and me. And school? With my attendance teetering on the side of flaky as shit, I violated Community's attendance policy in a big way. And I can't fault them because they tried their best to work with me. Let's just say, I probably violated the policy three times more than the tolerable limit before they decided to have "the conversation" with me, informing me that I was being kicked out for attendance issues, not academic ones. They gave me the whole "you're talented, but a policy is a policy" speech and sent me on my way.

The local truant officer got involved and made me go to my local school, which was George Wythe High School. I was in tenth grade at this point and almost seventeen years old. While Community had been a long fucking way from home, George Wythe was literally walking distance from the apartment. So that killed the whole transportation issue. Now it was time to see how this Northside-Southside thing would play out in a school setting.

Nobody Was There to Learn

How can I best describe George Wythe? Have you ever seen the movie *Lean on Me* starring Morgan Freeman? (Yes? Alright, that just about sums it up. If you haven't, watch it and you'll fully understand this comparison.) The school was so bad that they had cameras in each hallway, metal detectors at the front door, and double the amount of cops than at a regular fucked-up inner-city school. I'm not going to lie to you, the school was rough as hell. I don't think one soul came to learn. From what I saw, they either came for a fashion show, to start beef and fight, to sell drugs, or just because they had to. Once again, I was among animals. But fuck it, by this point, I was used to it. I was partially in my element. There were no real grounds to learn shit. And to be honest, I didn't learn one new thing the entire time I went there. Everything I was taught was shit I'd learned years ago.

I aced the tests they gave me without studying, without paying attention in class, and without even coming to school half the time. I would get to school whenever I felt like it and leave whenever I felt like it. (Of course, leaving was harder than coming because I had to duck the po-po, but I quickly developed an efficient system.) Like I've been telling you, just give me a little bit of time and I promise you I will find a way. That was my natural skill set, problem-solving, being put to use. I just needed to know the variables and the obstacles and then I'd take it from there.

Making Friends by Keeping to Myself

I stayed to myself there. Surprisingly, the more I stayed to myself, the more I attracted new friends. They would naturally gravitate toward me. I met some good-ass people from Southside that I'm still cool with to this day. After I'd acquired a certain amount of folks in my circle, I no longer had to worry about the Southside-Northside thing. I was Gucci! One of the guys I met was a dude named G. He was Jamaican. His brothers were big-time weed dealers. They probably supplied half of Richmond's market. (Not a fact, just my guess.)

Those dudes were wealthy. They had numerous cribs and, as a matter of fact, had just left an apartment for G to stay at. They didn't want him hustling, I take it, because he was the youngest, so they spoiled him. Gave him whatever he wanted. Clothes, jewelry, shoes, money. We became close and would just kick it sometimes. We were in one or two classes together, and his apartment was across the street from mine. He would look out for me and give me free weed. Half the time I sold it to keep me ahead of my food game.

I had another friend, Chuck, who went to Community with me. Chuck was from Southside originally so when I ran back into him, he was excited I was at George Wythe. Chuck got kicked out of Community for the same thing I did: not going to school. Man, he took to me so much, he would come and chill over at the apartment with us all the time. None of us knew it then, but Chuck's life was about to take a very different turn.

The Dogg Pound Was Emerging

See, Richmond wasn't known for much gang activity back then, but a gang was emerging. It was called the Dogg Pound and comprised some West End folks and some Southside folks. These dudes were ruthless and would do stupid shit for no reason, the usual gang activity bullshit. One day, Chuck informed us that he was part of the Dogg Pound. And it made sense 'cause that nigga Chuck was crazy as shit! He was always down to do some violent shit for no reason.

He would always tell me, "Yo, Shi, I would kill a nigga for you. Nobody bet' not fuck with you. If you ever have a problem, nigga, just let me know. I got niggas that all I have to do is say the word. You want a nigga beat the fuck up, nigga, I'll stomp 'em out. If you ever want a nigga dealt with, I got you! I keep that ratchet on me!"

Thing is, he was dead serious! He kept two small chrome .25 Autos with him at all times. Man, I seen that nigga pull them two little twin shits out plenty of times. I promise you, he must've practiced in the mirror a million times before he got his game right for the public. He had a dramatic movie-style way of pulling them out when he had beef! I don't think a day went by that this nigga didn't ask me if I had any problems. Good, bad, or indifferent, that's why I kept him around. Plus, he was my friend. So feel where I'm at right now. I went from a group of friends who didn't ride for me like they were supposed to, to a group of friends who would pull a trigger before I would. Total 180 degrees. There was a certain power that I appreciated about my new situation. I knew that at any moment I could summon an army, just like that. One phone call, one word. I never worried about beef, but now I had that "I wish a nigga would" mentality.

And the crazy part is, I wasn't Dogg Pound! Never claimed it for a second. It didn't fit my principles. I'd always held myself to the concept that if you don't stand for something, you'll fall for anything. So no matter what environment you are in, you have to be accountable for yourself and your actions. At the end of the day, it's you that has to live with *your* conscience. I'm not the gang type. And I wasn't going to compromise my morals to become part of one, regardless of the power. To be honest, the Dogg Pound guys were so rowdy when they got together, it made me hate chilling with them. I quickly realized that with these guys, it wasn't that something *might* pop off; it was that something *would* pop off. It was like this contagious energy. When one would have an urge to set it off on somebody, all of them would get this fever and the next thing you know some random nigga is getting stomped the fuck out. And I'm not talking about no regular, get-jumped-and-you-get-up-and-get-yourself-together bullshit. Nnnnnnope! Usually nine times outta ten, their victims ended up in the hospital. This is the honest truth. I couldn't write this shit if I tried.

Dudes Were Straight War-Minded

One time, Chuck asked me if I wanted to go to the pool hall. I asked who was going and he said about six of the guys. (That was a lie. It was more like thirty.) I went and I'll never forget it. We were at the Game Room on Jahnke Road. All we went to do was to play pool. Let me repeat, all we went to do was to play pool. Tell me why it ended up with five guys being beaten half to death with pool sticks? You didn't have to start shit with them; they would start it with you and then let you respond. It was literally a death trap. They would take turns laughing about the shit afterward, bragging about who did what. I mean, these dudes were straight war-minded and fed off of beef.

Another time, we went to the state fair. I didn't want to go, but they promised it wasn't gon' be no shit. See, I knew Henrico police were going to be out there, and you don't mess with Henrico cops. Everybody knew that. To make a long story short, it was twenty-five of us. Now close your eyes and imagine this, my best recollection of what happened. We were walking in a tight huddle at first when one of these muthafuckas was like, "Man, I'm ready to set it off on one of these bitch-ass niggas outchea." He started to walk fast, which made our group form an oblong type of structure, with the ringleader in front. Next thing I know, he hauled off and hit some random dude who was with a few people, including his girl. The guy who got hit fell to the ground. The guy who threw the punch kept walking.

As our swarm kept walking forward, each guy would throw a kick to the face or body of the dude while crossing over him. Even though I was in the back, I saw a very sharp punt to his face made with the force of a football kick after half-time. The guy's neck snapped back and damn near touched his shoulder blades. That shit was truly awful to watch. I mean, why? What did he do to deserve that? And the people he was with sat back and did nothing! Absolutely nothing! But, really, what could they do? They were helpless. Sheep! Any retaliation on their part and their lives would've surely been in jeopardy.

If you're wondering if I added a kick in, don't. Once again, doesn't fit my morals and principles. That dude ain't do shit to me. He didn't do shit to them. I felt extreme sorrow for him. That man came out to have a good time. It was just another day to him when he got up that morning. And who knows how long that one night ended up fucking up his life, both physically and emotionally. I'm too much of an empath for extreme "uncalled for" violence. It has to be some level of justification for me to go there.

I decided that those guys weren't going to trick me into going out with them anymore. Look, I can call on ya when I need ya, but I ain't down for this unnecessary crazy shit. I would tell them that shit was fucked up and that it was eventually going to catch up with them. And it did. But they just overpowered retaliated beef with a stronger fire. They didn't need to be in civilization; they needed to be in Afghanistan somewhere fighting a war or something. I mean, that's where their talents would have been best put to use. That's the type of dudes you send to war. They were soldiers without a cause, doing stuff for the sheer adrenaline rush. Imagine if they had an actual cause!

> I SEE DRUG ADDICTS, DRUG DEALERS, RAPISTS, CRIME BREAKERS,
> I SEE THE HOOD NIGGA, BEAT BREAKERS, RHYME MAKERS,
> I SEE DEATH IN OUR FRESH BORN, BIRTH IN OUR DEAD ONES,
> I SEE DESTRUCTION WHILE URGED TO KEEP OUR HEAD STRONG,
> I SEE NIGGAS ROB NIGGAS, THEN GET ROBBED BY THEIR NIGGAS,
> THEN TURN AND ROB VICTIMS WHO GOT JOBS IN THE SYSTEM,
> IT'S ALL REPETITION, **FLAWED BY THE SYSTEM,**
> AND THE SUBJECT OF THE JUDGES IS MORE CONVICTS IN PRISON.
>
> —EXCERPT FROM HIP-HOP SONG BY SHILOH JONES

Going Through a Serious Anti-establishment Phase

Eventually, George Wythe stopped holding my attention because it didn't challenge me at all. It just felt like I was going to a prison camp every day. So I stopped going altogether. School just wasn't my focus anymore. I started to feel like, what's the point? I didn't have any positive role models in my life to help me chart a course into the business world. As a matter of fact, the business world didn't exist to me. I didn't interface with it in any facet of my life. This was probably when I went through my biggest anti-establishment, nonconformist phase. I felt like everything I was being taught in school was bullshit. It didn't apply to my life in the least. So I started reading on my own. I became a self-learner. I figured that any knowledge that was useful to me, I could get on my own.

Then a strange thing happened that made me even more anti-establishment. I came home late one evening and was walking toward my apartment when I saw a guy lying on the ground in front of my building. He was moaning. A jug of milk was busted on the ground beside him. Milk ran everywhere. He had on a white T-shirt and was face down. At the small of his back, blood soaked the bottom of his shirt and the top of his jeans. Shit! Whatever had taken place had *just* happened.

I yelled, "Somebody call the police!" Neighbors started coming outside, and a crowd gathered as I stood by his side. I recognized his face. He was the Chinese guy who lived downstairs from me. Before long, cops that I didn't even realize lived in the complex came out using walkie-talkies, requesting backup. They didn't have uniforms on and, had it not been for this event, I wouldn't have known they lived so close to me. (If I'd known, I wouldn't have been smoking weed so openly on my balcony and all around the neighborhood.) The police told me to get back, secured the perimeter, and then took him to the hospital. I didn't think much about it after that. I mean, shit like this happens in the hood all the time. I'm used to it.

And Just Like That, I Moved

A few days later, I was at home and heard a knock on the door. The person on the other side gave some bullshit name and I asked, "Who?"

Upon realizing that the door wasn't going to be opened until they fully identified themselves, the person on the outside responded, "This is the Richmond police; open up."

Shit, I didn't have anything to hide except for a little weed in the fridge, probably just enough to roll a blunt with, so I opened the door. The cop tried to come in. I stopped him, saying, "How can I help you, sir?"

"We want to ask you a few questions, young man."

"A few questions like what? Go ahead."

They started to question me, and I quickly realized that I was being interrogated about the situation from a few nights ago. "We have reason to believe that somebody in this apartment may have had something to do with it," said the cop. "Where were you on the night of … ?"

My heart started beating faster. Wait a minute. I know they are not accusing me! This is bullshit!

"Why?" I asked. "Are you accusing me of shooting that guy? I was right there, trying to get help for him! How the hell you gon' accuse me? What, you think I shot him and stayed and waited for the police to come? What sense does that make?"

"If you aren't guilty, you have nothing to worry about," the cop said. "Now, I'll need the names of all your friends who frequent this apartment!"

"First of all, I know my rights," I said. "You're not supposed to question me without the presence of a parent. I'm a minor. Should I call my father right now?"

"That won't be necessary," said the cop. "We'll be in touch."

"Excuse me, officer, can you please identify yourself?" I asked. "Do you have a card as well?"

He looked pissed at the way I'd responded. He gave me his card. "Where is your father?" he asked.

"He's at work at the moment, but I'll be sure to give him your card and inform him of the purpose of your visit," I said. "Thank you! You guys have a great evening."

He turned around and was about to leave when he said, "Oh yeah, and just to let you know, buddy, your neighbor who was shot? That bullet was an inch away from his spine, so *whoever* it is I'm looking for is facing attempted murder. Any withholding of information is a charge of accessory. Just an FYI. You have a good evening, yourself. We'll be in touch."

After I shut the door, I started to formulate a theory. Could Chuck and these niggas have started off robbing the Chinese dude and then ended up shooting him, too? Why the fuck would they do that shit in front of my house? Man, I ain't trying to get caught up in this shit! Okay, think, Shiloh. Fuck it, let me call my pops. I called him and told him what had happened. He immediately came over and asked for the card I'd gotten from the police officer. He called the cop and chewed him out, saying that I wasn't involved in anything and if they had anything else to say to me, they needed to call him first.

Then my pops turned around, looked at me, and said, "You need to move the fuck outta here now! Do not associate yourself with any of these people. This is the best thing you can do at this point."

And just like that, I moved. Bye-bye, Southside!

11

Age 17: There Was a Weird Energy about the Place

SO BACK TO Church Hill I went. And this go round, I had a little more respect for my dad. After all, when he got the cops off my back, he saved my ass for the second major time. That's two for Bill Jones. And I was grateful for it. I was only seventeen and still an arrogant kid, so I probably didn't show him much gratitude. But now he was showing me, if I really, *really* needed him, he would come through.

I was so stubborn back then. I did so much on my own. I thought I had the answers, even when I didn't. As time progressed, I realized that arrogance comes at a cost, and the lessons were expensive as shit. Many times, I metaphorically wrote checks I couldn't cash and then was stuck figuring out a way to cash them *because I had to*. Like now, I was over on a new side of town again. I hadn't finished the tenth grade because I'd been kicked out of one school and dropped out of the next. I had to figure out this brand new side of town, which meant penetrating the community and developing new friends while figuring out a way to eat on a daily basis. (Shiloh, what the fuck …) This "keep starting over" shit was starting to get real wack!

Let's Start with Problem Number One

Let's start with problem number one. As much as I wanted to be anti-government and anti-establishment, I realized that I was making myself another statistic by not graduating high school. I was falling rapidly behind because of my ideals. This was the worst thing I could do to myself! C'mon, Shiloh, you're way too smart for that. I knew that not graduating would make me feel like a huge failure, even though I was already pretty much at rock bottom. I started to make some decisions that were vital, pivotal.

It was summertime, so I decided to give it my best shot. But where would I start? I found out my new zone school was Armstrong High School. It was a little bit of a hike but within walking distance of my temporary living arrangement with my pops's girlfriend at 35th and P Street. I borrowed some decent clothes from my father, went to the school, and met with the principal. We sat down and talked for about thirty minutes. I didn't know what angle to come at him from so I decided, hell, the truth works. (When in doubt, the truth *always* works!) I told him the whole story. He listened and, surprisingly, had a soft spot for me. He saw the fire in my eyes and understood that I was 100 percent motivated to graduate and get on with my life.

He said, "Let me check your transcript, young man." After about five minutes, he told me that I was in luck. Since I'd taken so many honors and advanced classes in middle school, combined with my time at Community (where all classes were advanced and college prep), I only needed three classes to earn my high school diploma. He set my classes up so that they were back-to-back, which allowed me to get out of school by 11 a.m. every day. This, he told me, would give me the rest of my day to figure out how to survive.

"Now don't disappoint me!" he said. "You have a good head on your shoulders. With a little bit of focus, you'll find your way. It may be a struggle, but life is not easy, son. It's not about the hand you've been dealt; it's about how you play it. If you ever need me or want to talk, my office is always open to you. You hear me, son?"

"Yes, sir, and thank you for your time today! I really appreciate it!"

"Anytime. But do me a favor?"

"Yes, sir?"

"By any means necessary, I want to see you walk across that stage and get your diploma. You hear me?"

"Yes, sir! I won't let you down. I promise!"

And there it was, two things that sealed the deal for me. The first was "by any means necessary." Ever since I'd first attended the temple, those words were so powerful to me. They were the powerful words of Malcolm X, which have always moved me on a deeper level and activated my inner warrior. The second was the fact that I said, "I promise." In my code, your word is your bond. I don't take that lightly. If I make a "promise" to you "by any means necessary," I will deliver. It all boils down to sheer willpower and determination. The principal didn't know it, but I knew when I walked out of his office that I'd already graduated. I'd already walked across that stage. I just had to fill the time between then and now with classes.

Next Up: A Place to Stay and a Job

Okay, so school was one thing checked off my list. Next thing, my living situation. I knew the first night I stayed with my pops's girlfriend that I was going to be kicked out soon. She was not having it. That's not his home; that's her shit. And she fucked with him, not me!

It wasn't long before she started to openly express this. So I decided that I'd get in front of the bullet. I convinced my dad to rent me an apartment down the street from her place. It was on the top floor of a duplex at 35th and M Street. Place? Check!

Next came food. At the time, my dad was selling meat. He was the guy who'd knock on your door, tell you he had a great deal for you, build value in the product, and then offer you a "one-time deal" you couldn't refuse. The way he worked was that he got the meat wholesale from a guy at distributor rates and then was a middleman for the customer. The customer came out winning, getting the product 30 to 40 percent cheaper than from the grocery store. The only downside to the situation was that the customer had to buy in bulk. But the more they bought, the more the price came down and the more unbelievable the deal.

My dad's goal was to move units. The more units, the more profit. I knew I could help him do that, so I convinced him to let me work with him on weekdays and Saturday mornings. In exchange, my rent would get paid and I could make some pocket change for food and clothes. Now my day-to-day living expenses were also taken care of. Check!

Starting to Grow My Social Circle

Now I had to figure out the social piece of my new situation. You know what? I was going to carry it like I normally do and stay to myself. Whatever friends I made in the process, I made in the process. Don't stress it. Part of my father's family was from Church Hill. He had grown up there and knew a lot of people around there. I stayed a block away from Bill Robinson's childhood playground. And guess who lived directly across the street from the playground? My grandfather!

My grandfather was highly revered in the community. I mean, no exaggeration, I don't know many people who could fill his shoes, no matter how hard they tried. He was a model citizen. Not only was he the first black firefighter in Virginia but he was also a chairman on the advisory board of the Greater Richmond Transit Company (GRTC) for twenty-five years. He was also president of the community crime watch association, helped establish the neighborhood's Boys & Girls Club, and repaired lawn mowers for everybody in the area as a part-time hobby and business.

He was truly a respected pillar in the community. How much value did this have for me at the time? None. Zero. He really didn't like me that much back then. Or at least I thought he didn't. When he'd see me, he'd go straight in on me with, "Boy, why are your pants hanging down like that? You need to be more productive with your time. Don't make no sense! What's wrong with you kids nowadays?"

I promise you, I got the same conversation every time I saw him, just regurgitated in different ways. He never really said anything positive to me, only telling me that I looked like a thug. Thinking back on it, this probably was his way of showing me love. He just needed better wording for his intervention speeches if he was going to be successful at reaching me. He would've made a terrible counselor! LOL.

Pissed at My Parents for Their Life Choices

I had a couple of cousins around Church Hill that I started chilling with, along with some of my old friends from past neighborhoods, like Yah and Ish. Plus, I would meet a few new cats a week. My circle started to grow, and before long I had a decent amount of connections to navigate pretty much any situation. I was able to work with my dad for a few good months before things started to get shifty between us because he was still doing drugs.

Church Hill was a pretty bad influence on him. It got really bad between us one day when I was supposed to get paid. I knew we'd closed deals that day. When my pops dropped me off, he told me that he'd be right back with the money. I kept calling and calling his phone, but no answer. I didn't have any money, and I was hungry as hell from not eating for the majority of the day. He ignored every one of my calls until I was so pissed off, I had to go for a walk to calm down. While I was walking, I saw this dude, my pops, near 32nd Street, leaving a drug spot.

He continued to ignore my calls after that, we ended up having a big falling out, and I decided to stop working with him. My hotheaded temper put me in a lot of situations where I would fly off the handle too quickly, and then my pride would paralyze me from moving forward and squashing the beef. Should I have made things right with my pops? Yes. Was it in my best interest to squash it? Yes. But I didn't. I just held onto my anger toward both of my parents. I was pissed about their involvement in drugs and how it affected their personalities, life choices, and treatment of me.

Transforming Into an Artist

I was still doing my thing with my music. I continued to murder cyphers every chance I got. And the times when I wasn't as great as I could have been only sent me back to the lab to reinvent myself for the next cypher.

I took every opportunity to write, in school, on the bus—everywhere! When a thought came to my mind, I was anal about getting it out before it was lost forever. I think that anal quality is what breeds the most talented MCs because great ideas don't come when you plan to sit down and write a rhyme. No, the mind doesn't work that way. Some of my best thoughts came when I was having a random conversation with someone or when I was focused on something else. You have to capture those thoughts in the moment. In the long run, this is what gives your "writtens" that extra edge.

At this point for me, hip-hop was purely for the neighborhood culture and for myself. Verses, freestyles, and cyphers were all I cared about. It wasn't until I linked with a few others like me and we formed a group that I started to take on other hip-hop skills like making songs, performing, and recording in the studio. I went from being a rapper to transforming into an artist. I started making concept songs rather than just spitting out rhymes. It's like being a boxer who just punches at stuff and then transforms into a professional fighter. There were more rules and structure to what I was doing now.

My first group was named Tribe of Judah. We formed the group because we were all like-minded. We had the same spiritual outlook on life and all studied different ways of thinking, ways of living, and ways of breaking down life in our free time. We weren't religious at all, but we considered ourselves spiritual. Studying the science of religions and how these world religions controlled people intrigued us. This was a point in my life when I was introduced to scrolls and the teachings of Dr. Malachi Z. York. He had very interesting scientific perspectives that led to reasoning for modern-day thinking, as well as a bunch of ideologies behind government and elite conspiracies. What's crazy is two of his sons were in my actual rap group. A lot of us were street dudes, but we were intellectually gifted. And that's what gelled us together. This was our common ground, putting us on the same frequency. Plus, we were all dope-ass rappers!

We started making songs, which were really just independent verses over beats and with a hook that unified our braggadocious rhymes and viewpoints. Sometimes we would rap about what we studied and regurgitate it into a song. We were a group, yes, but we were really more like a clique of independent rappers who could hold their own in any cypher. It worked. And it sparked my next period of evolution in music, but not without some memorable interruptions.

My First Real Girlfriend

I started to chill around my neighborhood more. I was still dating Sheila and, because she lived nearby, we were hanging out a lot. Her mom and stepfather couldn't stand me and thought I was a big distraction for her, so she'd have to sneak over to my house. She was my first real girlfriend, and I had an exceptional love for her. There was just something about her. It was the way she looked at me, without judgment. It was the way she accepted me for who I was. It was like she adored me, perfectly, the way I was. She would tell me this all the time. I could do no wrong in her eyes.

We were having sex damn near every day. Eventually, we just stopped using condoms. Not surprisingly, one day she informed me that she was pregnant. We both knew we were in no position to have a baby. That was absurd. Bring a baby into this? Are you crazy? Neither one of us was stable. It just made no sense. Somehow we were able to come up with the money for an abortion. After it happened, we promised each other that we would stop having sex. Dude, that lasted about two weeks before we were back at it like bunny rabbits. You can't hold two young people with all that chemistry back. The sun, the moon, the stars, and a million armies couldn't stop us from seeing each other, loving each other, sexing each other. I mean, shit. Honestly, we couldn't stop ourselves.

Church Hill at the Time and Its Weird Energy

There were so many factors at play at this point in my life, all determining my destiny. Relationship factors. Family factors. Societal factors. Economic factors. Something else was affecting me in the bad times and even in the best of times: my environment. Church Hill was different from Southside and definitely different from Northside. There was a weird energy about the place. I always felt a black cloud over it. I couldn't help but think it was connected to the history of the area. At least it felt that way to me.

Richmond was the major target of Union campaigns during the Civil War. It was also the destination for Confederate soldiers horribly wounded on the front lines of these campaigns. Chimborazo Hospital in Church Hill treated thousands of these sick and wounded soldiers. In nearby Oakwood Cemetery, many of their souls were resting. (How peacefully is anybody's guess.)

As if all that darkness wasn't enough, Richmond's slave trade was centered about a mile away from Church Hill—and it was fucking huge. It was a major industry in Richmond in the years before the Civil War, second only to the trade in New Orleans. There were slave markets. Auction houses. Jails. Traders. Receipt books for buying and selling human beings.

My brothers and sisters generations back endured more than I can imagine, and my heart aches for their unending sorrows. The chains that bound them back then still bind the black community today. I felt that energy magnified in Church Hill when I was a teenager.

Getting to Know the Neighborhood

So at this point, I knew my fair share of people in Church Hill and I was pretty community-bound. Some of them I went to school with, some I knew from seeing them around all the time, a few knew my cousins, stuff like that. Down the street, in the last house on the corner, was Sherrod. We'd walk to school together in the morning. Sherrod was a comedian, always had something funny to say. You ever met those people who are so cool-headed that you could never catch them mad? That was him. Nothing could take him off of his square.

Every morning, he'd tell me, "Spit a new rhyme for me, Shiloh," as he was one of the folks who was genuinely impressed by my ability to rap. In fact, he was one of my motivations for crafting new raps at night, memorizing them by morning, and then acting like I just randomly came up with the shit. I amazed him every time.

Throughout this time, I was still rhyming and ended up forming a new group with Ish, Yah, and a guy named HT after the guys in Tribe of Judah split off because of regular life bullshit we all had going on. Still, good feelings all around. All those guys are still cool to this day. Most stopped rapping and have families that they care for. The new group was called Metaphysic. But our rap group names changed often back then in an effort to find ourselves and our ever-evolving style. HT did most of our beats, and we ended up taking recording to a new level. We started to work more on concepts, song structure, sixteen-bar verses, and hooks.

Ish and Yah were dealing with some personal things, so I was with HT, who considered himself a producer, all the time. I shifted gears and started focusing more on solo projects. HT would only jump on tracks to rap every now and then, so the majority of the songs we created featured me by myself. I believe this is when I grew the most in my music. We challenged ourselves to do three songs a day for five or six days of the week. I was hustling during this time, so I was able to put a lot of time into recording.

There was also a girl named Kiki I used to pass who was about twelve years old. She had it rough and would always be out in the streets, smoking cigarettes and hanging out with people who were always into shit. I used to school the little homie. (Get that? Me trying to school someone else on how to get their life together.) I took to her and didn't want her to go through what I'd gone through. I always had a passion for not wanting people to go through what I had to. I would look out for her whenever I had extra cash on me and even when I didn't have much. I would buy her food but never cigarettes. Kiki hung out a lot with a neighbor of mine. His name was JuJu. He was about two years older than me and lived with his grandfather. JuJu's grandpops was old and had health issues, which pretty much gave JuJu a free pass to do whatever he wanted.

I didn't really fuck with JuJu that much; he just wasn't my type of person. Nothing was wrong with him. Certain people just don't mix. Plus, it was a little too noisy around his place. He always had a bunch of people on the porch and in and out of his house. Across the street from me was a dude named Dale, cool as hell. Dale was about seven years older than me and was always on the move. I used to appreciate kicking it with him, as he used to come over and check on me all the time. "Yooooo, Shi, what you doing, big dawg?" he'd say. Dale was a hustler who stayed low and kept to himself, always on the move but super-cool as shit.

One day, I came home and found Kiki on my front porch. She was crying.

"Yo, what's wrong, Kiki? Why you crying, boo?"

She went into a long story about how her dad had kicked her out again and she had no place to go. She felt like he'd let her back into the house after he cooled down, so I knew that she really just needed to vent. So I let her. We walked down to Chimborazo Market and ordered two chicken-nugget-and-fries combos from Mr. Chou, the crazy Chinese store owner that the whole hood knew not to rob. He had guns everywhere. We got our food with a couple of strawberry can sodas and walked back to my porch to eat. As we ate and talked, she did a sidebar, asking me for a cigarette. "Nah, baby, you know I can't do that. Look, why we gotta go through this every time? You think one day you just gonna catch me slipping and give you one?"

"Hey, you don't know if you don't ask. It's okay, I'll get one from JuJu."

"Oh word, he be giving you cigs?"

"Yeah, but he starting to get creepy to me. I think Ima stop hanging out over there."

"Why?" I asked.

"You know that nigga be trying to fuck all of us."

"Fuck who?" I said. "You?"

"Yeah, I mean we did it like once or twice, but I ..."

"Hold up. What you say, Ki? You had *sex* with him?"

She confirmed, and I was furious. JuJu was a nineteen-year-old man. Kiki was a twelve-year-old girl. WTF! Plus, she was my little homie. I looked at her like a little sister. I didn't fault her because she didn't know any better. But him ... I sat on the porch and talked with her for an hour about what it means to have a person take advantage of you. How her body was a temple and how sex is something she should save until she is a little older and more mature. Man, it hurt me to my soul that somebody was taking advantage of this innocent little girl.

The next day, when I saw JuJu, my mind kept telling me, "Mind your business, Shiloh. Mind your business." As I walked across the street to pass his house, he was on the porch, smoking a cig.

"What's up, Shiloh? How you doing today, cuz?"

"Just the dude I wanted to see," I responded. ("Stay out of it" kept running through my head as I stopped and looked at him.) "JuJu, come here for a second, I want to holla at you right quick."

He walked toward me. "What's up?"

"I want to ask you something in private, bro, so walk with me for a sec." We went through his yard and up the alley. Eventually, I said, "Soooo, I was talking to Kiki yesterday and I want you to be honest with me about something." By now, we'd walked to the asphalt of Bill Robinson's playground.

"Yeah, go 'head, Shi. What's up?"

"Yo, are you sleeping with her?"

"What you mean sleeping with her?"

"Nigga, are you having sex with her?" (I responded back swiftly, bluntly, with an extra air of sharp enunciation.)

I looked right into his eyes before he quickly looked away. "What, she tried to say I fucked her?"

BAAAAAAAAAAWWWWWW! Before he got his last syllable out, I threw a right hook at his face that connected between his nose and his mouth. He could molest a young girl but he damn sure couldn't take a punch! That punch knocked him off of his feet, with his shoulder blades hitting the ground first. I stood over him and yelled, "Get the fuck up! Get the fuck up, bitch!" He looked up at me, grabbed his mouth, and rolled over. Then, in the quickest recovery move I've ever seen, he got up and ran at full speed back to his grandfather's house. I didn't bother to chase him. He knew I saw him for what he was. A coward. A bitch. A child-molesting cowardly bitch!

I looked up, still standing in the same spot, and who did I see? My grandfather on his front porch looking dead at me! I couldn't write this shit if I tried. He just shook his head in disappointment.

Breaking Ground with My Pops

But hold up. While my grandfather thought he'd confirmed his suspicions that I was nothing but a thug, he didn't understand that I was totally justified in doing this. This time I was actually doing the world a favor. I was standing up for what I believed in. Should I go and explain to him my reasoning behind what I'd done? Would he even agree with me if I did? Better yet, would he even believe me? You know what, fuck it! He'd judged me already anyway. Who cared what he thought? I knew the reason why I reacted like I did and that's all that matters. Sometimes in life when you act on shit and you have resolve behind it, it don't even matter who don't agree with you.

I walked back down the street to my house. JuJu already had a mob of people on his porch yelling at me, calling me all sorts of names and throwing threats. I simply looked over there and said, "Fuck dat nigga! Ya know where to find me. I'm right here every day." And that was the last of that.

My grandfather called my pops, who came over to my apartment. "Shiloh, what the fuck just happened?" he asked me.

"First of all, don't yell at me," I said. "We ain't got that type of relationship! Second, he deserved it." I went on to tell him the story. Pops was cool about it and admitted, "I hear you. Yeah, fuck him. You did right! But you gotta watch yourself out here. These mufuckas crazy out here! Watch your back. And don't trust nobody round here."

And just like that, he earned another cool point from me. Was my dad agreeing with my moral compass, the code I'd developed for myself? Was he starting to understand me for real? I felt more comfortable with him talking to me like this than with him trying to be a father to me. In fact, that was the first time we really broke ground with each other.

12

Age 18: "I'm Pregnant, and I'm Keeping It"

IT FINALLY FELT like things were coming together. Took damn long enough, too. But once I had my principal's support combined with my own motivation, it felt like graduation came around in no time. I attended school every day, killed every class, aced every exam. Rain, hail, sleet, or snow, I made it to school. And then the day I'd visualized back in the summer, talking to that principal, was finally a reality.

Of course Armstrong's graduation was hooded out, ghetto as hell. But who cares? I had done what I had set out to do, and accomplished it with flying colors. Man, I felt great that day. In the words of Kanye West, *You couldn't tell me nothing!* My mother came to watch me cross the stage. Vinnie was there, along with my sister, my father, and some other family members. I felt supported. It was truly a happy day for me. In spite of all the bullshit I'd been through, had to put up with, had to maneuver around, I still made it. Big middle finger to the adversaries! I was eighteen years old. I was officially an adult now.

"I'm Having the Baby"

I partied all that evening. The whole neighborhood partied together; there were a lot of people in that graduating class. Somebody threw a big shindig at their house, like *House Party*, the old classic Kid 'n Play movie. They had food, weed, and liquor. It was everywhere! Man, I got so smashed, I remember waking up on the front lawn of my crib at 4 a.m. with no idea how I'd gotten there. Apparently, somebody was nice enough to carry me all the way up the street and place me on the small patch of grass in my front yard. Also, apparently, I thought it was my bed. All I remember was getting to the party, *maaaybe* about an hour or two into it, and then sheer nothingness. Somebody don't know how to hold their liquor!

I had the worst hangover ever when I came to that morning. (It was more like afternoon, to be exact.) Regular routine. I got up, brushed my teeth, hopped in the shower, and put clothes on, all to come downstairs to a white piece of paper on my front door. *What's this?* I thought. I unfolded the paper to find the first eviction notice I'd ever seen. It was a pay-or-quit notice. (Bill Jones, you didn't pay the rent?)

I'll deal with it later, I thought. I was on the way to meet Sheila, who wanted to talk to me. I met her halfway, at our usual rendezvous point. She hit me with something from out of the fucking blue. "Look, I don't know how to tell you this, but I'm pregnant. And I'm keeping it this time."

"I don't think we're in any position to support a baby right now, Sheila."

"Yeah, well, I mentally can't go through another abortion," she said. "I physically can't either. I thought about this long and hard, and no matter how I look at it, my conclusion is the same. I'm having the baby."

Somebody pinch me! I wished I were dreaming. Fuck me! What was happening? Did I just get an eviction notice and an "I'm having a baby" notice within minutes of each other? Are you serious? I felt a wave of stress come over me, like somebody was aiming a hair dryer at my face at full speed. What's the plan, Shi? What's the strategy?

CHECKMATE! I'M DONE

For the first time ever, I was stumped. I didn't have any answers. I was stuck. I was cornered. Checkmate! I was done. I was tired of fighting. Tired of these unexpected turns. Tired of this roller coaster. So what did I do? I ran. I ran away from the problems. I shut down. I lost my fight. I froze.

When eviction time came, I had to figure out where I was going. I called my sister and asked if I could stay with her for a while. She was reluctant, but she agreed. She had her boyfriend, a guy from New York, living with her at the time. (She'd started messing with dudes again and laying off the chicks.) He always had a lot of people around him so, needless to say, the house stayed packed. I slept wherever I could. On the couch. On the floor. Wherever there was a space a body my size could fit.

Sheila would call me damn near every day, several times a day. I avoided each and every one of her calls. I couldn't face reality and, even when I tried to, the stress would overwhelm me until I just shut down again. I hated that I couldn't face it. I mean, I loved her. She was truly the love of my life. And here I was, the person who was supposed to protect her from anything, hurting her the most. The trippy part was, I knew I was causing extreme mental and emotional damage to her. But, like I said, I froze.

Maybe in the back of my mind, I thought that if I didn't talk to her, the problem would go away. I mean, I wanted to have kids one day; I just wanted to plan for it. We went from talking fifteen times a day to not speaking at all. And I couldn't fault her because she tried everything she could to get in touch with me. What was I doing? This was the same girl who'd bought me food when I didn't have shit to eat. You don't shit on people like that. I mean, nobody had been in my corner more than she'd been. Needless to say, this was a terrible demon that haunted the fuck out of me. Before long, I heard that she was going to college, Virginia State University. I passed up the chance to see her before she enrolled and started campus life.

Working Another Shit Job

Meanwhile, I worked whatever jobs I could find. Most were through the Labor Ready temp service. Like everybody else, I'd literally get there at 5 a.m. and wait for a job to become available for that day. I was battling for a spot against crackheads, alcoholics, and people twice my age who were down on their luck. Most of the jobs were complete bottom-of-the-barrel bullshit. Mostly construction temp labor, doing demo work, or carrying cement broken up by jackhammers, loading it into wheelbarrows, and then rolling it to dump trucks to be hauled off. (Oh, did I mention this was in 105-degree weather?)

We were paid minimum wage ($5.45 an hour at the time) for eight hours' work minus the ride there and back and minus the materials you had to rent for the work, including gloves, a safety helmet, and safety glasses. For all the math geniuses out there, that's $43.60 a day, gross. After taxes and rental fees, I walked away with about $24 a day. Indentured servitude wages, right? I was thinking the same thing myself. That was just enough to take care of my most basic needs, like food and shit.

Before long, my sister wanted money for me to stay there. How was I supposed to do that? I truly felt like a hamster on a wheel. Running hard as hell but not going anywhere at all. I didn't have the energy to come up with a plan. Every day was just about focusing on making that $24. And then there were the days when you would go all the way there, early as hell, and wait until 9:30 a.m. or so and no jobs would come through for that day. Or your number wouldn't get called. Those were the worst because now yesterday had to support the lack of work for today.

Picking Up a Better Gig

Walking back to the house after one of those days, I decided to get dinner from Chanello's Pizza at 3rd and Grace Streets, two blocks from the temp joint. I saw a "Help Wanted" sign in the window and went up to a guy with glasses, a manager who was working the whole place by himself. I inquired about the sign and he said that he needed help right away. So just like that, I picked up a regular gig. The two of us got close and I worked my way up to assistant manager-in-training. They didn't pay me shit, but it was better than $24 a day. Thank you, I'll take it!

I took every shift I could, whenever he needed me. I did whatever: answered phones, made pizzas, made nearby deliveries. He slowly put more and more responsibility on me. I then enrolled in college for electronics technology. It was a community college, but at least it was college. I had only two classes, twice a week, on Tuesday and Thursday evenings. That was all that I could fit into my schedule. My father helped me with the enrollment process, which I was thankful for. And I'm not going to tell you that it wasn't a struggle trying to make it to class and balance my life because it was. I would study between my shifts at work, which was complicated whenever I had to pull doubles. I would bum rides, pay people to take me to campus, take cabs, whatever I could. Things started to feel as if they were turning around slowly but surely. Then one day ...

The Grill of a Cadillac, Just Inches from My Face

I was outside the pizza joint, taking a fifteen-minute break and talking with a coworker. Two of my every-other-day customers—girls who worked across the street at the *Richmond Times-Dispatch*—walked up and joined the conversation. Somebody inside Chanello's called for one of us to come back to work. Since I was on my break, I stayed outside and carried on my conversation with the girls. We were inches away from the corner of 3rd and Grace Streets in the middle of downtown Richmond. It was around lunchtime and traffic was crazy. My back was turned to the street. The girls were facing the street.

The next thing I knew, I saw a flash of light. Then I was looking up at the sky. Then I was thrown to the ground. I was in shock, so time kinda passed me a little, but this is as accurate as I can get. I looked around and saw that my shoes had flown off my feet. One was ten feet in front of me; the other was five feet in the opposite direction. I couldn't process what had happened. All I could hear was ringing in my ears. A few moments later, sound started to settle back in and I heard chaos coming from every direction. I turned around toward the noise and saw a black old-school Caddy up on the sidewalk, touching the Chanello's building. The grill of the Caddy was just inches from my face. A second car—a green Hyundai Sonata—had also spun up onto the sidewalk.

All of a sudden, I saw the girls. Their legs had been crushed. The Caddy hitting them head-on between the knee and the thigh had bent their legs away from their bodies in a way I'll never forget. It was a horrible sight. They were screaming in pain. Pedestrians who ran over to help were screaming in panic.

Then I realized what had happened. The Caddy had run the red light at the intersection, hit the Hyundai, and sent both vehicles crashing into pedestrians on the sidewalk. I just happened to be one of those pedestrians. I tried to get up, but my right leg felt broken. I wiggled my foot and it moved. I was almost fully conscious and aware by this point. I deduced that if my toes could wiggle and my foot could move, then my leg couldn't be broken. After a three-minute struggle with myself and with gravity, I got up. Before, I'd felt shock. Now, I felt pissed. I started to limp over to the black Caddy, which I surmised had caused the accident. My coworker saw me heading fast toward this guy, ran up to me, and said, "Nigga, if you don't lay down and act dead, then I don't know what the fuck is wrong with you, 'cause you 'bout to be paid."

He Told Me I Was Lucky—Very Lucky

Because I was in shock, I couldn't hear him. More than that, I didn't want to hear him. I wanted to confront the dude in the Caddy, an old white man who wasn't injured but stayed in his car like he didn't give a shit about what he'd just done. I got in instant-retaliation mode in response to his reckless-ass driving that could've fucking killed me, by the way! But before I could do anything about it, the pain hit out of nowhere. Excruciating pain! It stretched from the upper part of my knee to my hip on my right side. I was rushed to the hospital in an ambulance.

I was there for hours. My doctor said that I had a serious contusion in the right leg. He told me that I was lucky. Very lucky. He said that, because of the nature and point of the impact, I'd been knocked upward onto the Caddy and slammed back down to the ground from the force. If I'd been standing beside the girls rather than facing them, I might've lost my ability to walk. He prescribed me strong painkillers. I told him I didn't have any insurance, so he gave me some sample meds from the hospital pharmacy for free. Then he sent me on my way to pick up a cheap, generic version of the meds he'd just given me. He told me that he was restricting me completely from work and gave me a doctor's note saying so.

When I left, he said, "You're not going to be able to do much walking on that leg for a while. In fact, you're gonna be in some serious pain for the next few weeks."

Man, about two days later, my whole body was in pain. My lower back, especially, was killing me. I accumulated some extra hospital bills from additional visits to see if they could help my back. I was assigned a physical therapist and told to go to him three times a week. Meanwhile, even though I couldn't have worked if I'd tried, the people around me advised me not to work because all of this was going to "build my case." The higher my bills, the better it would look in court when it was time to pay me.

Speaking of getting paid, I heard through the grapevine that the girls got over $100,000 each from the settlement. I can't be sure because I never saw them again.

13

Age 18: That Soul Connection Was in Her Eyes

AFTER THE ACCIDENT, my life fell apart. Not working meant no money. No money meant no transportation to school and, sooner or later, no food. Life got so bad that I had to stop going to physical therapy, too, even though I really needed it. According to Maslow's hierarchy of needs theory, our attention focuses on our most immediate level of need. And once again I was back to survival mode, the most primary plane of need.

Mad at the World

I ended up losing my job at Chanello's (my manager *had* to fill my spot) and dropping out of college, all because of a lack of money. Then, after all this, my sister had the nerve to inform me that her boyfriend felt that I wasn't contributing enough to the household and, besides, she had too many people staying at the house, so I had to leave. And I thought the last point was my lowest point? This was truly rock bottom! I couldn't get no more rock bottom than this rock bottom right here. The same day my sister gave me notice was the same day she kicked me out. I couldn't believe it. She let a million muthafuckas stay in her crib, but she allowed someone to tell her I couldn't stay there? And none of them paid rent.

You talk about being angry? I was angry at everything and everybody. Mad at the world. Mad at my mom. Mad at my pops. Mad at my sister. More importantly, mad at myself. I had exhausted all of my resources.

I had nowhere else to turn. I'd pushed my one true love away. I had no money in my pocket. I was hungry. I kept thinking to myself that I was an eighteen-year-old failure. At around midnight, I started walking. I walked so long and thought so hard, I was physically and mentally exhausted. I found the nearest bus stop and sat there until I dozed off. And that's where I slept that night, in the middle of downtown Richmond, outdoors, under the shit overhang of a city bus stop.

Somehow the camera got me in one of my stressed moments.

SURVIVING LIFE BY BEING MY OWN SAFETY NET

This is the point when I had to be clear with myself. I knew that I could *never* depend on anyone else again. I knew that if I was going to survive this thing called life, I was going to have to be my own safety net, my own backbone, and my own support system. My trust for human beings went out the window. They say when you are at your lowest point, you can't go anywhere but up from there. I knew that, somehow, I was going to have to harness this fire, this anger, this pain, and convert it into fuel to drive me forward. I just didn't know how yet.

SUCCESS IS A MINDSTATE   129

The next month or two was dark. Really dark. Maybe too dark to even go into detail about here. But I will share one of my darker moments to give you an example of how things were going. My homie, Yah, was still close to me. He was in a similar situation but had a way of meeting people who'd extend the courtesy of letting him spend the night with them. Sure, it only lasted a few nights, but it got him through. Me, I'd find places to crash here and there, always careful not to overstay my welcome. When it was time to move on, I'd go back to spending my nights outdoors, resting wherever I could until it got light again. The worst hours were between 2 a.m. and 6 a.m., when a whooole different crowd came out into the streets.

Not My First Robbery but Definitely My Last

Around this time, I remembered that I still had that handgun from my days with B and Stash hidden at my mother's crib in the basement. Somehow or another, I made an excuse to get over there with her one day and got it. Now, before you judge me, I want you to remember that I was at my lowest point. Some days I literally didn't eat if I couldn't find a way to manipulate my way into food. So Yah and I decided that if we got any hungrier, we would result to robbing. My primal animal instincts were being activated. We didn't want to hurt anyone; we just needed money. One time we went to rob somebody and ended up with a crazy story to tell. It wasn't the first time we'd committed a robbery, but it was most definitely the last.

We walked around for hours looking for the "right" person to rob. We really wanted to rob a drug dealer, not an innocent working person. (Even in the face of darkness, we still had somewhat of a code we followed.) The extra benefits of robbing a drug dealer were that they were more likely to have more cash on them and less likely to call the police. It was a calculated risk.

That night in particular, when we were all pumped up to do it, we didn't see one damn dude who fit our drug dealer profile—until we got to a gas station on Broad and Grace Streets near Virginia Commonwealth University (VCU), where we spotted our perfect victims. Two white boys.

They had a tricked-out whip, flashy rims, and chains on. One of them was on the pay phone arguing with his girlfriend. The other was just sitting on the hood of their car smoking a cigarette. Yah and I had an unspoken body language style of communication between us, so we knew what to do. We approached him and said, "Yo, you got a light, homie?"

"Yeah, sure, cuz," the dude replied. He handed us a light. We sparked up a generic-ass conversation with him for about ten minutes. Told a few jokes, got him laughing. Yeah, now we got him comfortable. I looked at Yah and he looked at me. We both knew that we were too out in the open. We couldn't pull the shit off here. VCU police were driving by every five minutes or so. We had to think fast, get the dude away from here.

"Yo, where y'all going next when your man get off the phone?" I asked the white boy.

"I don't know, man. We'll probably go back to Southside. I gotta get back over there soon as this nigga get off of the phone." (Yes, white boys in the hood call themselves niggas, too.)

Okay, that's not going to work. Think fast, Shiloh. "Yo, you think you can drop us off up the street, man? It's too far to walk. We can give you a couple of dollars." Our guy went to ask his homeboy, who was arguing on the phone and just waved his hand like, "Whatever." And so it was on.

"C'mon, I'll take you guys," he said. "How far is it?"

"Just up Broad by the Sixth Street Marketplace," I said.

Got in the Car with One Gun, Got Out with Two

When we got in the car, I jumped in the back seat, Yah in the front. I had the burner on me. I was thinking we needed to get just a couple of blocks down the street and then it was time. We pulled out of the parking lot and this white dude, in an effort to impress us, turned the music waaaay up. (Sidebar: He did have a booming set in that car, competition level. I could barely breathe when the bass kicked in.) We didn't even get a block down the street before blue lights were flashing behind us. What the fuck! The cops were pulling us? He quickly turned the music down, looked over at Yah, and said, "Oh shit, I got a gun in the car. It's in the glove box."

"Whaat? You got a *gun* in the car?" Yah said in awe, as if we were innocent. And me, I got a gun on my waist. Oh no. This was going from bad to worse, and quickly.

I said, "Yah, man, put the gun under your seat. Everybody act normal."

Yah took the white boy's gun out of the glove compartment and slid it under the seat. He was careful not to look like he was hiding something, as the cops were shining their spotlight on us from behind, looking for suspicious movement. With the dude's gun under his seat, I took mine and placed it under my seat as he brought the car to a stop. The cops got out of their car and one walked up to the passenger's side of the vehicle with a flashlight shining into it. The other went to the driver's side and requested a license and registration. "Do you know why I pulled you over just now?" the cop asked.

"No, sir. Oh, did I have my music up too loud?" the dude asked. His hood slang had totally disappeared. He sounded like an official white boy who'd just stepped out of Harvard Business School. By this time, another cop car had pulled up and two more officers jumped out. They started asking us questions like Where were we going? and What we were doing out so late? My heart raced.

But when in doubt, pull out your best de-escalating tactics. I thought fast. I knew if I didn't say anything and sat there like I was guilty, they were going to assume suspicion. In a bold move, I rolled down the window and started to converse with the cops. I told them I was fresh out of school, had just graduated, and that I was interested in becoming a police officer. "What steps do I need to take?" I asked them.

This short-circuited the cops, stalling them while one ran the white boy's license. When it came back clean, the officer walked back to us and noticed that we were all conversing. He let the white boy off with a warning. "Look, turn your music down from now on. I could've given you a noise pollution ticket! You guys have a great night and drive safe."

Just like that, he let us go. I flipped out on the white boy like, "Why would you not tell us there was a gun in the car? Dude, just drop us off on the next block!" I acted like I was pissed as I slid the ratchet back on my waistline. I reached under the seat and grabbed his ratchet, too. We weren't robbing nobody tonight, that's for sure! But we would be walking away with this new burner. Long story short, we got in the car with one gun and got out with two.

Feeling Like There Was a Bigger Purpose for Me

I saw this as a sign! Dude, my life could have taken a dramatic turn for the worse. There were two scenarios: One, Yah and I could've robbed the dude and gotten shot while walking away because we didn't know he had a gun in the car—that is, if we didn't search the glove box looking for valuables, which was a great possibility. Two, the cops could've searched that vehicle and we could have all gotten felony convictions and gone to prison for a minimum of five years under the "no illegal gun" law. And remember, I got my gun from B and Stash, so who knows what was done with it before they gave it to me to hold. I felt like I got out of that by the skin of my teeth. This was life changing for me. I started to believe that being caught up in all this bullshit was not the universe's plan for me. I felt like I wasn't going through all of this for nothing, that there was a bigger purpose out there for me. I just had to find it.

I went to sleep that night with my thoughts racing. I felt shitty. I'd allowed my desperation to cloud my judgment to the point that I had compromised my morals. I mean, c'mon, this ain't me. Had I really reduced myself to the level of robbing another human being? No matter how bad it got for me, that went against the code that I'd developed for myself over the years. The fuck was I doing?

Then I thought about my life. My mom. My pops. I thought about Sheila. It had been about nine months now. Was she still pregnant? Then I thought about the baby. Then about my pops. Then about the baby again. Wait a minute. I knew I was being a bitch, running from the problem, but think, Shiloh. What was the greater evil? Bringing a life into this world when I wasn't ready? Or doing the same thing to my baby that my pops had done to me? Once again, that whole "not becoming another government statistic" nightmare started playing in my head. And I was finding myself rapidly getting on that path in multiple ways with the lifestyle I was living and the choices I was making: illegal activity and repeating the cycle of another child born with an absent father.

It was time to open up my closet and face my demons. I knew I was right! Fuck the fact that Sheila was pregnant and I wasn't ready, I had no right to put a child through the same shit I went through. Neither did I want this child to experience the same pain that I did. I made a vow to God that night. I was no longer going to let this haunt me. I would do whatever it took not to make this problem—this hell—generational. I made a pact to stand by this child no matter what the odds were, what the obstacles were, what mountains I had to climb, what sacrifices I had to make, even if I was going to kill myself trying. This child was going to have a father! Correction: She or he would have a real daddy—and a great one! By any means necessary! This was another moment when I knew I needed to stand for something greater than myself.

It Only Takes a Second to Change

Procrastination and stagnation can seem to go on for an eternity, but it only takes a second to change. One second. And that second is when you truly shift your mind to stop accepting your old way of doing things, formulate new ways of thinking, and adopt them into your life. Fueled by this new motivation, I rushed to get in touch with Sheila. It didn't take much effort because she always left a paper trail for me to follow. Soon as I spoke to her, I asked her when the baby was due. She responded that it could be at any moment. I told her that I really needed to talk with her. We made a plan to meet that coming weekend when she came into town.

When she arrived, I explained how much I'd missed her. I apologized to the best of my ability for the way I'd treated her, the way I'd abandoned her, and especially for the way that I'd shut her off emotionally. Then I gave her this speech: "Look, Sheila, I know I've shown you that I'm not the most trustworthy person you know, but please allow me to fix this. I admit, I was scared. And instead of facing the situation, instead of facing you, I avoided us. Because 'us' reminded me of what I couldn't face. I've thought about this long and hard, and I want to be there for the baby. I want to be there for you. I want to have a family together. You didn't get a chance to meet your father. I didn't have mine with me at the most crucial times in my magic years. We can't do that to this baby. My soul can't live with that. The only way to break what has been done to us is to do the opposite for this baby of ours. I know you just started college, but I will do whatever I need to support this baby and get you all the way through school. My word! Let's move in together and do this right. What you think?"

I saw the wheels in her mind turning. I knew she was thinking, *Is this nigga crazy? Move in together? He just threw me away like trash. I'm fresh in college. He doesn't even have a job. How can he support the baby and me while I go to school? Can I even trust that what he's saying is real?* And I knew her mind was giving her every reason to say no. Her heart wanted to say yes. This was a heavy moment for her. I saw it in her eyes. I knew how much hurt she'd dealt with and the confusion she had at that moment. But she still had remnants of genuine love for me in her heart for that can't be falsified. It was authentic. And all I could do at that moment was connect to the part of her that loved me unconditionally, no matter how distant it was. She took a while to respond and said, "Can I think about it?"

"Nope! You can't think about it!" Lady? You've been trying to get back with me since I coldly distanced myself from you. Now I give in and you want to think about it? Fuck you mean you have to think about it? But I knew I was wrong, so I took one for the team and I quickly adjusted my inner perspective.

I just laughed and said, "I'm only joking. Take your time."

I obviously didn't mean it at all because I started to put pressure on her right away. I called her every day. I gave her the best part of my personality every chance I got. I gave her "new chick" energy, spending countless hours on the phone catching up with her. Mind you, it cost me a quarter every time I called her (quarters that I had to scavenge) because I had to use a pay phone to talk to her. I made sure she couldn't resist all this "Casanova" juice I was spraying in her face.

A week later, she gave in. "Okay, let's do this," she said. "I trust you!" She then went on to explain, "I have to finish my semester at school, so I'll have to stay on campus until May, when school is out. I've arranged for the baby to stay with my sister until I come home. And then that gives us enough time to find a place for the three of us."

An Amazing and Spiritual Moment

Two weeks later, Sheila had the baby, Ree, at the Medical College of Virginia (MCV) hospital. It was January 22, 1998. I was there to see my baby born. It was a girl—a healthy girl. It was a trip. She came out blue. (I didn't know babies come out blue; that baffled me.) It was such a beautiful sight to see life giving life. It's an amazing and spiritual moment. I was the first to hold my daughter, and then I cut the umbilical cord. (It's funny how easy it is to cut the umbilical cord when they are babies but how hard it is to cut it when they're grown.)

Ree, my first daughter.

When I looked into that child's eyes, I connected with her soul. This being was a product of her parents' love. Truly incredible. Her full name is a derivative of "Charis," which means "grace" in Greek. It fits her. What also fits her is the Urban Dictionary definition for her name: "A beautiful, intelligent, crazy, yet creative individual. Although sometimes she may have trouble expressing her feelings, those around her love her anyway. Give her a challenge and she will rise to the occasion. There is *nothing* this girl can't do once her mind is set on it!"

If you had been in the hospital when she was born, you would have seen a grown man cry. I made these promises to her on the day she came into this world:

1. I promise I will never abandon you.
2. I promise that you will never struggle like I did.
3. I promise to never leave you hungry.
4. I promise to provide you with everything you need to prosper.
5. I promise that, no matter what your mother and I go through, I will always be there for you.

You know, all the promises that I wish were made to me.

And so it was. With those words spoken, the integrity of the actions *must* follow. Time to man up!

14

Age 19: Elated, Scared, Empowered, Refueled, and Reborn

WOW! I AM a father. I am officially a father. *Oh shit, I am a father!* I was elated, scared, empowered, refueled, and reborn, all at the same time. That's a lot of emotions for one little guy from Northside to have all at once. But I was excited about change. And this time, I was going to do things right. A fresh start.

Everything Was Coming Together

During the four months that it took Sheila to finish her second semester in school, I had to get my shit together. With everything that had been going on, I'd forgotten all about the lingering case I had around the accident in front of Chanello's Pizza. I contacted the insurance company in an all-out move to settle. The insurance agent knew he had me by the balls for a bunch of reasons: I was young and represented myself; I hadn't built up enough doctor's and physical therapy visits because of my living situation; and, frankly, because I seemed desperate. He played hardball with me and settled me out at $2,700. Fuck it, I'll take it. I made three moves:

1. I bought myself a car for about $1,200. It was a piece of crap, but it was a car.

2. With the car, I was able to get a job.
3. With the car and the job, combined with the fact that we had a baby and Sheila was in school, I was able to get us into a government-subsidized apartment through a program for low-income families. It was on 32nd Street in Church Hill. Our rent was about $250 a month starting off, with the expectation that it would increase every couple of months.

This was good. Everything was coming together. By the time Sheila was out of college for the summer, I had the place situated. Then my baby came home. The first night was one to remember. I think I might've woken up a million times just to make sure she was alright and still breathing. I thought I was going to break her somehow. But honestly, that first night with her home, I think I made the most mind-shifting change I've ever made, one that chain-reacted and made me the person I am today. Of course, I would have to evolve in stages before I could turn these mind states into fully matured attributes. But the seeds were planted when Ree was born. The fire of not wanting to struggle, the promises I made to her, and the huge responsibilities on the road ahead were catalysts for turning those seeds into trees.

Hard Work Trimming Trees to Make Ends Meet

I had a job working for Asplundh, trimming trees. It was very hard physical labor, as I had to be out in all types of inclement weather, from extreme cold to blazing heat. I would climb trees in an attempt to prune the branches. I would *fall* out of trees in an attempt to prune the branches. Then, after the pruning, we would gather all the trimmings and branches and feed them into a chipper, which would spit wood particles back at your face with the force of a BB gun. I hated doing physical labor jobs, but they were all I seemed to land in those days. I always felt that my sharp mind would be more of a benefit to a company. But apparently I was the only one who believed that.

Our new family stayed on 32nd Street for about three months before the apartment complex gave us some news: we had to move to Cool Lane Apartments, a very small complex in the middle of the Fairfield

Court public housing project. It was literally the same as living in the projects, except for the fact that we paid rent for the apartment. To this day, I don't know why they made us move, but they did. Before long, our rent went up, just like they said it was going to. It went to $325, then $350, then $375, and then $425. As the rent went up, our cost of living was also going up. Asplundh was no longer cutting it for me for a few reasons, including the fact that it just wasn't paying enough. I would work all week and barely have enough to fuel the car with gas for the next. Besides that, working there didn't leave me time to do anything else because I was physically exhausted at the end of the day.

A New Opportunity

I figured this much: if I only had a finite amount of physical energy to exert in a day, I might as well get jobs that were less physically stressful. In turn, that would allow me to effectively put more work in. If I could put more work in, then I could make more money, whether that meant overtime or part-time jobs. So that's what I did. I searched my ass off and, with a little bit of creative digging, I got a job at a semiconductor plant. I also started working part-time in a clothing store my aunt owned on Brookland Park Boulevard in Northside. (It gave me extra income and gave her a chance to have a life.) She paid me what she could. It was cash, so that worked for me. I was willing to work every chance I got, and I did. I think this was the point in my life when I learned about true work ethics, developed resilience, and started on my way to becoming the workaholic I am today.

Northside hadn't changed much since I'd lived there a few years earlier, so it was still rampant with crime. I was on a twelve-hour-a-day schedule at the semiconductor plant, working three days a week. The other days, I would work for my aunt. As much as we tried to sell a variety of clothes, the neighborhood thugs were mostly interested in white tees and jeans. We kept a few pairs of Timberlands on deck just in case somebody wanted them. The problem with shoes, though, is that you have to maintain a lot of inventory, and inventory means money is tied up, which means that less cash is available in other areas the business may need for day-to-day operations, especially for a small business. Cash flow is incredibly important for a very small mom-and-pop-business style of operation.

Enter Supreme and His Strip Club

One day, while I was at the shop, one of my mans from back in the day came in and hollered at me. His name was Supreme. "Yo, widdup, Shi?" he said to me. "What's good?"

"Ain't nuttin'. What's Gucci with you, Supreme?" I asked.

"Shit, my nigga, back in town. You know me, always on a paper mission!"

"True that. What you got popping now, tho'?"

"Yo, I got the spot next door," he answered.

"Spot next door?" I was oblivious to what the hell he was talking about. The neighborhood was full of barbershops, beauty shops, and clothing stores. But I'd never noticed the building next door. In fact, it looked abandoned. I hadn't known anything to be there ever since I'd lived in or moved from Northside.

"Yeah, my G. I got an after-hours strip spot."

"After-hours strip spot?" I asked. (This was starting to make more sense. My aunt's shop closed at 8 p.m. A strip club wouldn't open until about 11 p.m., so it wasn't a surprise that I hadn't really noticed it.)

"Yeah. Alright, so what I do is, you know how I be on the road all the time, right? Man, I plugged in with these strippers from out of state and we break bread for them to come and strip. I've been doing that joint for about two months or so now. Matter of fact, I need some folks I can trust to do some security for me. Ain't too many real niggas I fuck with. These dudes be too shaky. Man, I could really use you, bro."

"What you mean? To do security? I don't know about that one, bro."

"Look, Shi, I'll pay you $100 cash a night and all you gotta do is be there for four or five hours max, homie."

"Let me think about it, Supreme," I told him.

"Yo, here go my number," he said. "For real, holla at me, Shi."

I went home and talked to Sheila about this opportunity. On one hand, I needed the money; on the other, I knew it was a little sketchy. Of course, since Sheila was usually worried about me, she said, "Even though we need the money, I don't think you should do it."

"Look," I said. "Let me just do it for a couple of weeks. We can catch up on some bills and get out of the hole."

She had a way of supporting me, even when she didn't want to. "I'm going to roll with you on this one, but I am telling you, I don't agree! Just be safe, babe."

I had a thing I would always say to her: "I don't care if the world falls apart, I will always make it home. Don't worry." A promise I vowed to keep. And with that move, I called Supreme and told him that I was on board.

He wanted me to start immediately. It was a Friday. I was off from the semiconductor job that day, which meant I would go to work at the clothing store from noon to 8 p.m. and then hang around until about 11 p.m. to work at Supreme's spot. Three hours to kill in the process. No problem. It was just going to be a long day.

I did the first shift, no problem. Got me something to eat and chilled for a second. Now it was time for Supreme and his strip party joint. Fast-forward a little. Everything about that joint was illegal. I'm going to skip most of the details on this one and get to the meat and potatoes. That night, a fight broke out inside the club. As we were kicking the people involved out, another fight broke out on the outside.

The second fight led to a huge, uncontrollable brawl—a shoot-out—that spilled out into the street. It was total chaos. Some guy ended up getting shot. He was wearing a white T-shirt and it was soaked with blood. He ran back into the club to get away from the shooters before falling into shock and passing out. Supreme, knowing his place was illegal, knew that he had no choice but to drag the guy out of the club and back to the street, fearing that the police would somehow charge him for running an unlicensed strip club. My first night working, and somehow I was in the middle of all this action. I was literally breaking up fights when bullets started whizzing through the air. Needless to say, that was Supreme's last night running his business in that particular spot along Brookland Park Boulevard.

I didn't even want to tell Sheila, but since we told each other everything, I did. I couldn't even get the whole thing out before I was bombarded with withdrawn body language and a million I-told-you-sos. That's another thing about Sheila: she supported me, even when she didn't agree, but she was right there to deliver the famous "I told you so" faithfully afterward. You better believe it!

"Let Me Stop You Right There, Homeboy"

A week later, I was at the shop, business as usual. A guy came in, looking stupid suspicious. I had several customers who I was tending to. Keep in mind that I was in the shop alone, as I usually was when I worked. He kept asking me dumb-ass questions and seemed to be stalling for time and waiting for everyone else to leave. In my head, I was like, "Nigga, I know this trick." My inner street Spidey sense went off.

As I noticed this, and especially while there were customers in the store, I said, "Excuse me for one second, I really have to use the bathroom. Be right back." I went in the back and grabbed the pistol that my aunt kept for protection by the camera system's DVR. I quickly put it on my waist. I wet my hands, grabbed a paper towel, and came back to the front of the store, drying off as if I'd just finished using the bathroom for real. I immediately picked back up with helping customers.

As they dwindled down to just one, and after more questions from the suspicious guy, I prepared myself. If it's about to go down, then it's about to go down. Bottom line. I started to ask him stupid questions, turning the tables on him. The air began to get thick and uncomfortable for both of us. He knew I sensed something. I could tell. Then he went into his spiel: "Yo, man, Ima be honest with you. I hate to do this, but I got a habit and I need money, and look ..."

This is it! No time to think. Fight or flight. You promised Sheila that you would make it home, no matter what happened. Fuck your life, Shiloh, you got other people depending on you. And that was the only thing that mattered to me in that moment. As he started to say the word "look," I pulled out the pistol and pointed it at his face. "Let me stop you right there, homeboy," I said as I looked him dead in his eye. "Put both of your hands up where I can see them." He complied. "I don't know what the fuck you came in here to do, but let me tell you something. You walked into the wrong shop today, bruh!" He just looked at me and I looked at him for what seemed like an eternity. I broke the silence with "Man, you look the same age as me. Sup wit' you?"

He shook his head and looked down at the floor.

"Talk to me, nigga!" I said. "The FUCK is up with you?"

"Man, I'm trying to get it together," he said. "It just seems like I'm falling deeper and deeper into this shit. Ain't nothing going right with me, man. Then I got this habit. I be getting sick. I want help, I just don't know how to get it."

"Let me explain something to you, homie," I said. "I could have reacted out of fear and shot you in the face and it would have been self-defense. This was a life-and-death moment for you. The next time, you might not be so lucky. Now you need to choose what path you're going to take. You say your hole is getting deeper and deeper. Your choices as to how you deal with that hole are going to either get you killed or change your life." He started crying as I spoke that real shit to him. "Think of this as the universe giving you a second chance. Now get the fuck out of this store. Get yourself together, bro."

I swear to God, this was one of the most intense moments in my life. But I meant every word I'd said. Even though he was going to strong-arm rob me, I felt the pain in that guy. The hell he was trapped in. No, that didn't mean I was going to be soft toward him or that I wasn't going to protect myself. But I *know* I touched him. I *know* he heard me. And even if he had been running on "criminal autopilot" for the past few years, I know that moment pierced through to his conscience and, if only for a second, he thought about the bigger picture, his life, and change.

"I really appreciate this talk, man," he said. "I promise, this ain't falling on deaf ears. Man, thank you. You like an angel, shawty. For real." Those are the words he spoke as he left the store, giving me a nod of his head.

Everything was caught on the store's cameras, and my aunt viewed it when she came back that day. We never reported the incident because of the way it was handled. However, she sadly reported to me two weeks afterward that he had gotten locked up after making Richmond's Most Wanted list. Oh well.

The Universe Was Driving the Point Home

What made me do that? What made me care enough to even give him that speech? Hold up, this was twice within a week that I had been in some serious, life-threatening shit. At the rate I was going, I could potentially do great harm to my family. This was not what I meant by "sacrificing." Sure, I made a promise to my family that I would do whatever it takes, but this was starting to not make sense. I came to a realization about something: I couldn't be so willing to put my life on the line for other people and their causes. That alone would end up indirectly making me neglect my own cause, which was, ultimately, taking care of my family's essential needs. Even though I knew what really mattered, I couldn't help but feel like a hamster on a wheel.

Sometimes the universe has a way of driving the point home. The tipping point came one day when Sheila and I were driving to our apartment on Cool Lane. When we got to Mechanicsville, I told her to stop at the gas station so that we could fuel up. As I was pumping gas, I gazed off into the distance. I saw a car pass me and the guy's face looked familiar. Really familiar. As my memory started to kick in and my facial recognition software analyzed my mental databank, I realized, "Oh shit, that's Ronnie." He was the guy I had beef with a couple of years earlier when my mom had to lock me in the basement of her house. Was I sure? No. But I *had* to be sure. The guy's car slowed down and turned into a parking lot. After pumping the gas, I pulled into the same parking lot. "What you doing, babe?" Sheila asked, intuitively sensing that something was wrong.

"Nothing," I said. I drove by his car and saw that he was getting out to make a call on a pay phone. I slowed down and saw his face. He saw mine, too. I thought fast and said to Sheila, "Look, I gotta drop you off right quick."

"Why?" she asked. "What the fuck is going on? Talk to me!"

I kept tight-lipped, didn't say anything, and drove her to our apartment. "Get out, I'll be right back."

"No," she said. "You are gonna tell me what the hell is going on!"

"I SAID, 'GET THE HELL OUTTA THE CAR!'"

She looked at me, concerned, and got out of the car. I ran in the house and got my gun. Then I immediately pulled off, heading to the parking lot. He was still there. Good! With the gun in the front passenger seat, I pulled up and looked at him in his face. He saw me. It's about to go the fuck down. "What up, nigga?" I said. "You thought you won't gon' see me again?" He took the phone from his ear. "Yo, put the phone down, nigga," I said, speaking more assertively. "We got business to handle."

And the craziest thing happened next. He hung up the phone, looked at me, and said, "Yo, that shit ain't have to go down like it did back then, bro. I was young and stupid. I'll be the first to admit that it didn't need to happen like that. Look, man, that shit behind me. That shit squashed. Man, I got more important stuff to worry about. Seriously, that shit dead."

What the fuck was he saying to me? My heart was pounding. I was ready for war at that moment. And nigga pick *this* moment to say this. He short-circuited me. Confused me. This ain't the same dude who said he was going to kill me with so much conviction. *I'm here like a man*, I thought. *Just me and you, no spectators, no instigators, just us.* Before I realized it, I was back in that situation like it had happened just yesterday. When I paused to figure out how I was going to respond to all of this, I had a flash of awareness.

Shiloh, what are you doing? What if he had responded differently? You would've killed him. Without a thought. Right in the open, on a main street, right by the projects. In the passion of the moment, you wouldn't have thought twice. Nigga, you just yelled at your girl, dropped her off, and once again put yourself in a situation that could have taken you away from your family. What if he'd been ready like I was and closer to his heat than I'd been to mine?

The thought didn't even cross my mind until later that night. I couldn't believe my anger took me to this place. I was ready to handle this years-old beef in broad daylight when I probably had more to lose than he did. *What was I doing?* I looked at him and, without speaking a single word in response, got into my car, pulled off, and went home.

I was embarrassed to face Sheila when I got there. I was still pumped up on adrenaline, but I knew I was wrong. I felt like an idiot. Was I really becoming the thug my grandfather said I was? When did this happen? I never wanted Sheila to think I had uncontrollable rage in me. Nor did I want her to think that I made stupid decisions without thinking them through. If she did, I knew she'd lose trust in me. Lose faith in me. Women are about security, and I had just threatened her feeling of security in so many ways.

Not only did I need to check what I was willing to make sacrifices for in life but I really needed to check my anger as well. Life has an interesting way of humbling you, propelling you toward evolution. I knew I had some growing to do and some real prioritizing.

A Bad Start in the Corporate World

We ended up saving enough money to move out of that apartment on Cool Lane and into a duplex on Oakwood Avenue in Richmond. Sheila ended up getting pregnant again, so new responsibilities were getting added on. The more Ree grew, the more expensive she was getting. Sheila's school and commuting every day were getting more expensive, too. Food for the household was being consumed at a faster rate than ever. Bills started stacking up. I had very little time to write and record music. All I did was work. My semiconductor job started to become uncertain when I was assigned to a supervisor who just couldn't stand my guts. He took the opportunity to harass me every chance he got.

One day, I'd had enough. The company supposedly had an open-door policy, so I decided to go over his head and report him to his manager. (I figured the open-door policy was bullshit but gave it a shot anyway. He was eventually going to find an excuse to fire me anyway, so what did I have to lose?) Well, after reporting him, that whole thing backfired and then I was targeted. I ended up getting fired just two weeks later.

I hated the corporate world for that. I'd had a million jobs by this time and it always baffled me how managers had so many control issues and how they would take this control and use it negatively, abusing their power to satisfy their egos. So often, especially with larger corporations, the powers that be are so disconnected from their lower-tier workers that they usually aren't aware of the abuse that happens on a daily basis. I've come to learn, however, that this disconnection is a result of the sheer incompetence of the organization. It is the organization's moral, ethical, and operational responsibility to ensure that everyone from the bottom up is being treated fairly, and not to just see things from the top down. You know, I couldn't see what the road ahead had for me at the time, but I did know this: if I was ever in a position of power, I would not abuse it. Yes, I was motivated by the wrongs that had happened to me, but this was a principle that attached itself to me and would stick. And it proved to be very valuable in the future.

Once again, I found myself in that same place of needing to change. I took whatever jobs I could get to make ends meet. Most of them didn't last long. Frankly, I started to lose the motivation to work, or at least to work these bullshit odds-and-ends jobs.

15

Age 20: Only Thing I'm Left with Is You, Weed

I ain't trying to tell you how fucked up my life was, but how beautiful my life turned out! There's a difference!
— Shiloh Jones

My daughter, Ree, at the height of some major moves and shifts I was about to make in my life.

SO THERE I was, with a wife, two daughters, and bills that never stopped coming at me. Fucking relentless. I thought about every possible solution I could. Short of get-rich-quick schemes, which I didn't believe in anyway, I was stumped. I didn't have any answers to build a foundation for a strong-enough strategy. Then it came to me. I might have to hustle again, sell drugs. No! That's too much risk. But hold on! Wait, I've been willing to lay my life on the line for other people's causes. Why not a cause of my own? I listed my pros and cons:

Pro: If done right, I could make the free time I need to do music while also creating resources to fund my music.

Con: If done wrong, I could get locked up.

Pro: If done right, I could generate enough income to take care of my family and hopefully save some money for a rainy day.

Con: If done wrong, I could get locked up.

Get In and Then Get the Fuck Out

I thought about this constantly for about a week straight. Look, I was already sacrificing. My goal needed to be get in and then get the fuck out. I was going to go the hustle route. Failing my family was not an option. Desperate times call for desperate measures.

Once I'd made up my mind, there were a few things that I needed to be honest with myself about. First, I was terrible at hustling when I'd tried it before. Why was that? They say hindsight is 20/20, so I examined all the reasons and came up with countermeasures to avoid making the same mistakes in the future. Second, I had to be very careful. I knew I couldn't afford to make any mistakes. Plus, I had this big thing about never becoming a statistic. Third, I could never lose sight of my purpose. I knew I had to make a pact with myself to not get caught up in the street life. If I did, I just knew I would get stuck.

Nope to Ecstasy, Acid, Crystal Meth, Dope, Coke, and Crack

Okay, so the ground rules were out of the way. Now I had to determine what I needed to hustle. Well, my options were coke, crack, dope, weed, or—well, those were it. We didn't have much of a market for anything else in the inner city. The counties had other drugs like ecstasy, acid, and crystal meth, but we just weren't exposed to them like people outside of the city were. It would have been too much of a market transition for me to offer drugs beyond the basics and, frankly, too complicated.

Alright, first off, we can take coke and crack off the list. I'd promised myself a long time ago I would never sell either one of those items again. I refused to deteriorate my own community like a cancer. Next up? Dope? No! The customer base is too risky, too violent. Plus, that's just as bad as selling coke or crack—or worse. Only thing I'm left with is you, weed. Let's take this journey.

The cons associated with selling weed are based on the fact that it's the least profitable drug to sell. Other drugs can be cut, stepped on, and stretched to produce more profit. You can't cut weed. (At the same time, that's what I respected about it.) Weed is weed. The only advantage I could create was getting it for a cheaper market price (below market value) so that I could make a decent profit on the sale (higher margin). However, this often meant buying wholesale. And as with any business, the larger the quantity you're looking to purchase, the more bargaining power you have. (That's the power of buying in bulk.) Okay, Shiloh, sounds like you need to sell weight. But how can you do this, sir? You don't have the main ingredient necessary to buy in bulk. *That's money, genius.* Not too big of a deal. I just had to formulate a plan.

Plan Number One

Save up enough to sell weight. I had a check on the way for about $430. So I went and hollered at a guy I knew who sold smoke. I asked how much he would charge me for a quarter-pound of weed. His answer was $325. Okay, let's do the math. A quarter-pound comprises 4 ounces, with each ounce weighing 28 grams. The going weight of a dime in those days was anywhere from 2 to 3 grams. I figured if I could come in the middle of about 2.5 grams per dime, I was mid-market, which was acceptable. That meant I had to make sure this smoke I was getting was good. Not good but great! I got a sample from him, smoked it, and confirmed that it fit the plan.

Now let's continue doing the math. If I took one ounce and bagged up 2.5 grams, it would yield me 11.2 bags. Multiply that by four (because there are 4 ounces in a quarter-pound) and that's a little over forty-four bags. Forty-four bags at $10 apiece and that's a grand total of $440. Now take $440 and minus out the original purchase price of $325, and that equals a net profit of $115. Add that to $105, which was what would remain of my check since I was only going to pay $325 out of $430 for the weed. Now take that $105 plus the $115 profit plus the return of the original stock, which was $325. Total, I would have a gross of $545. Sounded solid!

I bought the quarter-pound and advertised to everyone in my circle who (1) I trusted and (2) I knew smoked. My plan was to reach my first short-term goal. Nothing else mattered to me. Knowing that every dollar counted, I took no shorts. If a buyer only had $9 for a dime rather than $10, I would pass on the sale. I wasn't even willing to lose one dollar. No three-for-$25s, either. I couldn't do it. I had a strict plan, and the only way I was going to reach it was to account for every dollar. No shorts! And no spending money!

Before the week was over, I'd sold everything. I did it! I'd reached the goal that I'd set for myself. I had the $545. Now, what next? Time for me to start exercising buying power. I called my connect. I figured if he sold me a QP for $325, then common sense would say that he'd want $650 for a half-pound. I convinced him to let me get it for the $545 I had to spend based on the following negotiation points: (1) I promised I was going to come back to him to buy future stuff; (2) based on how fast I'd sold the QP, it would mean bigger profits for him if he allowed me to grow; and (3) if he did this for me this one time, I would be able to purchase a whole pound next time, based on my previous calculations. He went for it! Okay, let's get busy.

Plan Number Two

Back to the math board. A half-pound was 8 ounces. Applying the same mathematical formula as before, the half-pound would yield roughly $110 per ounce. That would bring $880, which was not enough to buy a whole pound. My connect wanted $1,200 for a pound. Okay, that meant I had to make some adjustments. What if I sold two-gram dimes? I mean, it was acceptable by street standards, and some of my customers would be repeat customers.

Let's do the math. So, 28 grams in an ounce divided by 2-gram dimes would yield a potential profit of $140 per ounce. At 8 ounces, that would bring a grand total of $1,120. That was only $80 short. Now this worked. Math checked out. I had to do like I'd done last time and not spend any money. Don't take any shorts.

Problem this time around was that I hadn't paid any bills and I was quickly running out of money for the household expenses. It was all or nothing! Okay, fuck it. I was gonna take a risk and let the bills pile up while I made this move. Once I bought the pound, I could take the profit money from the pound flip and pay bills with it.

It was a bold plan, but I stuck to it. It worked. I sold the entire half-pound within a week and a couple of days. I had grossed $1,120. Now it was time to re-up. I knew of a friend who sold weed and he wanted a pound as well. I went to my connect and again used the concept of buying power. He wanted $1,200 for a pound. I first asked him about one pound and had him verbally repeat the price for clarification. This was just a setup on my part, though. Once he said "$1,200," I followed up with, "So if I buy two of them right now, you'll do it for $1,100 apiece?" This was me putting the principle of buying in bulk into action. He conceded to my negotiations. (Sidebar: Your boy doing good for just two and a half weeks of work and a starting point of $325, right?)

Ready for the Math Board Again?

I took that pound and ... ready for the math board again? Sixteen ounces. I figured I would do my customers right ethically. Since I pretty much shorted everybody before with the two-gram dimes, I would go back to 2.5-gram dimes. I wanted to balance out the bold move I'd pulled last time. Just because I got away with it didn't mean I should keep doing it (a lesson and jewel in itself, by the way). So, 2.5 grams out of 16 ounces would yield 179 dimes. That's a total gross revenue of $1,790. I figured that my boy who went in with me last time would do the same this time. That meant my repurchasing inventory fee would be another estimated $1,100, which ultimately gave me a net profit of $690. That was a good amount to throw on our house bills until the next flip.

I repeated this process and eventually came out of the hole where our bills were concerned. I did roughly three flips in the next month, totaling a net profit of $2,070. Business picked up the following month and I did five flips. That was a net profit of $3,500.

Now I was able to profit *and* save while still paying all the bills. I still worked at my aunt's shop every once in a while, so that was extra money that also added straight to the "house" cause and never touched my pocket.

I was quickly developing a new problem, though: traffic to and from our house. Now, while it was good to sell dimes for the greatest profit potential, this was increasing my "hot" factor. If I got too hot, I'd attract attention. If I attracted the wrong attention, I'd jeopardize everything. Time once again to change up my strategy a little. I had to reorganize. I had to remind myself of my original goal, which was to sell weight. See, I knew selling weight had its pros and cons:

Pro: Selling weight meant less traffic around my house.

Con: Selling weight meant less profit per unit.

IN ORDER TO SELL WEIGHT, A FEW THINGS HAD TO HAPPEN

One, I needed great pricing. I had to get the product at lower-than-market rates in order to make a profit. The lower wholesale price at one end and the going market value at the other would equal my profit.

Two, I needed a better connect. While my connect was a great guy who worked with me as much as he could, he was only at a certain level. He could only offer pricing at his value placement in the market. I needed a distributor who dealt with higher quantity and could make better deals per unit. A distributor's mind state is about moving units. The more units, the more profit. And then they can move on to their next batch. (This is a business principle I learned from hustling, by the way.)

Three, I needed more buying power if I wanted to increase my inventory enough to sell weight. Plus, I knew that if I wanted to deal with bigger distributors, they would have to see the value in doing business with me. How was I going to accomplish this? I knew it would be a process, but I've always been a firm believer that what you focus on, you bring to fruition. Where focus flows, energy goes.

Making My Transactions More Efficient

Meanwhile, I decided to stop selling dimes and to start selling quarter-ounces. That would cut down on the number of people I had to see per batch, making my transactions more efficient and bringing less attention to my business.

So, four quarter-ounces come in a full ounce. If I sold each quarter for $25 (the market rate at the time), that would bring me to an even $100 per ounce. With 32 ounces—I'd started buying my own 2 pounds every time I re-upped just to take control of my own buying power—that was a total of $3,200 gross per flip. That was also $1,000 net profit. This time, though, instead of making 358 total sales, I only had to make 128. The frequency of actual transactions was reduced. Not bad. And all I truly lost was a potential profit of $190 per pound, or $380 per batch. Less profit but less attention. Sacrifice a percentage of profits for efficiency. The plan was to shave some of my clientele down as I made the bigger transitions. Plus, some of the dime buyers were truly aggravating. They'd call me at all times of the day and night. It was just too much headache and too much motion.

In the midst of my hustling days, with Ree, one of the main motivations behind extreme decisions I chose to make.

Next, I started selling quarter-ounces, half-ounces, and full ounces. I figured that as long as it yielded the $100-per-ounce quota, I was Gucci! I gave no break for bigger weight. I made sure that I kept those even numbers for profitability purposes. At this point, I couldn't sell quarter-pounds, half-pounds, or full pounds, because it didn't make sense. And if it don't make dollars, it don't make cents (sense)! It would have killed too much profit.

16

Ages 20 to 22: Let's Hear It for New York

MY SECOND-BORN came into the world on June 29, 2000. Her name is a derivative of the Greek word *gaia*, which means "of the earth." Another absolutely beautiful moment. Another life-changing experience. Another conversation with myself had. And a new set of promises. It's funny. Just when you think you have the most beautiful thing that God can create on earth, He creates another that's just as beautiful.

When Kai was born, reality was still setting in that I was officially a father. Shiloh, Sheila, and Ree—the three of us—definitely felt like a unit. But when Kai came, it felt like a family. Two kids, two parents. Having Kai gave me that much more reason to work hard, that much more reason to dream, and that much more reason not to fail. And I know that I may be a little biased because I am their father, but those two girls are among the prettiest I've ever seen in my life.

The most powerful experiences I've ever had were when I met my children, the two diamonds that came from me. But naturally, I couldn't help but think that reality was sitting in. Now I literally had three people depending on me. The big irony was that I was drawn to the street in order to provide for them and eventually found myself needing to leave the street in order to ensure my provisions were secure. I didn't know then, but the same reason that got me in pushed me out. I found myself with three extremely huge reasons why failure was not an option, three reasons why I couldn't fall short—not even for one month.

If I fell short, I would be neglecting my family. This was not a failure that I was willing to accept. I wouldn't have been able to live with myself. I had *one* responsibility, *one* purpose. By any means necessary.

It seemed the bills would race the paychecks to the house—and the bills were always two steps ahead.

> I GET A CHICK THAT I'M FUCKING, THAT TURNS TO MY LOVER,
> TO BABY MOTHER, TO SIGNIFICANT OTHER,
> GOT USED TO EACH OTHER, FUCKING WITH NO RUBBERS,
> OUT COMES A SEED, NEXT COMES ANOTHER,
> FAMILY IN NEED, NOW IT'S FOUR OF US THAT'S STRUGGLING,
> I WORK HARDER, STILL SOMEHOW WE KEEP SUFFERIN',
> EVER SINCE A MUTHAFUCKIN' CHILD I BEEN SUFFERIN',
> TO MINES I CAN'T DO SHIT, BUT SMILE LIKE IT'S NOTHING,
> RAGE IN MY HEART, TOO MUCH VIOLENCE AMONGST US,
> TO WE PUSH HATE IN MUSIC, CAUSE IT'S TALENT AMONGST US.
>
> —EXCERPT FROM HIP-HOP SONG BY SHILOH JONES

Music was my dream, but I just didn't have time to invest in it as I was building up my other business to pay the bills. But it never left my mind. I mean, shit, I had the talent. I knew that I could make it and we wouldn't have to worry about money if I did. My goal was to pursue my dream of making music and to take care of my family in the process. I knew this would be hard, but I could do it if I stayed focused. I couldn't spend all my time working odd jobs here and there because I'd get stuck. I would end up caught in the rat race and, next thing I knew, it'd be thirty years later and my life would've passed me by. I didn't feel like this was what life was supposed to be about. Or, at least, I wasn't accepting that as *my* reality.

By this time, my sister, Brandi, was living in New York and would call often to check on me. She ended up meeting a guy named Keith

Shocklee. He was one of the founders of the Bomb Squad, the main producers for Public Enemy back in the day (with Chuck D and Flavor Flav). This was years after Public Enemy stopped putting out music. Keith had become a label owner for his own production company. He was actively working with artists and trying to find talent to help his company get off the ground.

See, the way things worked back then was the only way people really made it in the industry was by getting signed by a major label. And you either did this by meeting A&R people (talent scouts) from the record company or by plugging in with those who have connects with a label, like a manager or producer. They would develop you into an artist, create an album, and then shop you to a major label. If the label liked you, it would either buy you from the label that introduced you or sign the label altogether. If it signed the initial label, it was that label's responsibility, under the control of the major, to fully produce, market, and break you as an artist to the world.

My sister kept talking about me to Keith: "Yo, he is one of the nicest rappers I know." Finally, Keith got curious and wanted to hear some of my work. I sent some recordings to him. Immediately, he called me and said that he wanted to work with me and headline me as the first artist off his new label. I was excited—nervous but excited. *This is it!* I thought. See, back then, it seemed every artist on the East Coast literally had to be broken out of New York. That city was the Mecca back then. The entertainment hub. So I talked with Sheila and built a plan to move to New York for a while. She agreed and supported my dream, as she always did. We knew that she had to stay in Virginia while I chased the dream up north. And with that, I packed my bags and moved with HT (my friend and producer at the time) to New York.

Working to Get to the Next Level

I knew that achieving this dream was important to me and to my family. Growing up in those times, there were only two ways people really made it out of the hood: sports and entertainment. I knew if I made it in the music world, I'd be able to take care of my family and achieve financial freedom while pursuing something I loved to do. I think that's everybody's dream in life, really: to do something they love and make money while doing it. I moved to Long Island, near the Hempstead area. It was a great experience, especially working with a professional like Keith. We worked almost every day in the studio. Then every other weekend, HT and I drove back to Virginia to see our families. It was rough being away from home constantly; I knew that my being away put a lot more pressure on Sheila because she was taking care of the girls by herself. But we had to make sacrifices if we were going to move to the next level in hitting our goals.

> THINK I AIN'T BEEN THROUGH MY FAIR
> SHARE OF SHIT, HOW YOU FIGURE?
> I CAME FROM A BACKGROUND THAT'S FUCKED UP, MY NIGGA,
> BUT I PUT THEM DECK OF CARDS ON THE SHELF,
> CUZ I AIN'T TRYING TO DISH THE SAME CARDS I'VE BEEN DEALT,
> CHAINS ON MY BRAINS, I SEEN PAIN TO RAISE MY DAUGHTERS,
> IN THE SAME ORDER AS WHAT I'VE BEEN BOUGHT UP,
> SO CATCH ME ON THE CORNER CUZ MONEY I NEED MORE OF,
> AND I PRAY THIS MUSIC POP OFF BEFORE YOUR BOY CAUGHT UP.
>
> —EXCERPT FROM HIP-HOP SONG BY SHILOH JONES

MY TIME IN NEW YORK

Here's another thing about being in New York: living there rather than just visiting, I got to see it from an entirely different angle. We lived on Long Island, so if we wanted to attend a "happening" event, we had to travel into the city.

Being around Keith, I hung out with a lot of celebrities, some relevant and some not so much. He was real close with DJ radio personalities Dr. Dre and Ed Lover. At the time, I think they either had a radio show or were trying to kick one off. We got to kick it with Chuck D at his crib, and he gave us some really good industry advice. We saw a lot of behind-the-scenes entertainment-industry shit, too. We also got to compete in a rap battle where I took third place and HT took first. HT was nice at off-the-dome freestyle battling, I have to truly admit. Doing this in the heart of the place where hip-hop was born was a true honor. It gave me a new level of confidence and added to my overall music skill set.

Here Comes the Drama

We were almost halfway through the album when I started to sense some drama that would end up affecting the operation. What happened was that Brandi got jealous that Keith was working so hard on my project and not giving enough time to her project. Keith only had so much time to devote to any project because he was married with kids. The more work he and I put in with the limited time he had, the more emotional she got.

Then it became obvious that Brandi and Keith were fucking. Oh boy! But that didn't bother me because they were grown folks and that was their business. But the way my sister was acting crazy, it wasn't hard for the wife to put two and two together and things got ugly. Next thing you know, everything was shut down! The whole project! It got too personal. Keith couldn't balance the world he'd created between the two women he had, and now it was affecting business. Needless to say, the Shiloh project was shelved, and HT and I had to take the long drive home to Richmond. Keith told us this pause would be just for a while until he sorted the situation out. But for now, this shit was too close to home.

No Stopping My Grind

Of course, that was a little disheartening, but did that stop my grind? Stop my dream? Hells no! I chalked it up as *everything happens for a reason*, got right back in the lab, and started working. Damn skippy! But now, I came to the board with much more experience.

I took everything I'd learned in New York—recording techniques, song structure, bridges, layout—and continued to develop myself. What doesn't kill you makes you stronger! I continued to work solo with HT, knowing that one day I'd have another opportunity. And when it came, I'd be even more ready than when I went to New York the first time.

Meeting Foots

It was around this time that I met Foots, a younger dude from the neighborhood when I lived in Church Hill. He'd always pass me when I was on the front porch of my house and ask for a cigarette. I'd never give him one because he didn't look old enough to smoke, but that didn't stop him from asking. He was persistent. One day I asked him, "Yo, what's up with you, man? Why you always walking down the street like you got nowhere to go and asking for cigarettes?"

We talked a long time that day and just kicked it. He told me that he didn't really know his pops and that his mom was always looking to get high on crack and that she often kicked him out of the house. That explained why he was always scrawny, dusty-looking, and ungroomed. It also explained why he walked the streets every day like he had nowhere to go. We kicked it more and more and eventually I grew a soft spot for him. I started to look out for him. Give him a little dough sometimes and clothes here and there. One day he came to me crying and said he'd had a big falling out with his mother. She'd kicked him out and he didn't have nowhere to go. I ended up letting him stay with me and taking care of him, almost like he was a little brother or a son.

Foots had dropped out of school, so I made him go back, bought him school clothes, and introduced him to a stable life. He lived with me, Sheila, and the girls for a couple of years. Through those years, my influence over him grew. Because he looked up to me, he started getting into music as heavily as I was. I was pretty hard on him because I had a high level of expectation for him since we came from similar backgrounds. But to be fair, I had a high expectation of myself, so if I love a person and they close to me, I naturally start to impose the same standard on them as I do on myself. My own projection of self-love.

Plus, there were a few things about him that we needed to fix. One, he used to get bitched a lot in the neighborhood. Before I started fucking with him, niggas used to bully him constantly. After taking him under my wing and defending him a few times, the bullying stopped 'cause niggas knew I had his back. Plus, I taught him how to stand up for himself. Two, he was lazy as hell. I had to break him of that. You are not going to live with me rent-free and think laziness is an option. And three, he had a lot of greasy ways about him. Thieving was a problem for him and was sometimes the reason for his ass getting whipped in the neighborhood. In many ways, I taught him how to be a man through being a positive role model and acting as a big brother to him. This was my give-back project, and I did it from the heart.

I carried myself decent and he lived under the blanket of respect that I had developed for myself. Naturally, his confidence grew and he reached a level of notoriety he'd never had before. When he turned eighteen, he started helping me with my hustling business. When I had work to be delivered, he would take it. He knew who I messed with and I taught him how to move like me so that he was as safe as he could be. In return, I gave him money, smoke, and clothes, let him drive my cars, and let him participate in anything I did to reward myself.

Forming a Group, Bo-Gard

Here is a little picture paraphernalia from that time.

Eventually Foots developed his hip-hop skills to the point where he was dope. So the two of us formed a group with a dude named Rah. We called it Bo-Gard, which was symbolic of our intent to strong-arm the industry. I upgraded my studio equipment to higher-end items so we could produce a better-quality sound. We'd have producers come into the studio and lay down tracks or we'd have them send tracks digitally as WAV files. Then I'd engineer the recordings and mix the songs to the best of my ability before sending them off to an official engineer for mastering.

In addition to pictures, we had sticker paraphernalia posted everywhere.

My goal: to produce the best-quality music I could within the confines of my home before sending it to somebody else to master it, resulting in a product that sounded like we recorded it in a $50,000 studio. We did good. (We did great, actually.) We released a project called "It's Not Music, It's a Movement." (What we produced was actually in the form of a CD but, because it was unofficial and unpublished, it was known as a "mixtape" in the music industry.) Since we were directly in touch with relevant artists in the hip-hop industry, we got them to give us drops. I made 10,000 copies of the mixtape and released it in the street. We pushed it everywhere in Richmond. We sold it for whatever a buyer had on them at the moment. We got anywhere from as little as $1 for it to as much as $50 from people who were really in love with the music.

One of the mixtapes we dropped.

CATERING TO AN AUDIENCE

Since we knew we were releasing the mixtape in the street, we focused the direction of it to the street audience. I'm going to say this and I am going to stick with it 100 percent: I am a well-rounded artist. And I usually don't like to concentrate too much in any one direction because I don't want the listener to put me in a box. That's my personal pet peeve. While I loved the product, I didn't want people to think that all I had to offer was street shit. But I did it anyway to achieve our goals: to release the project, give listeners some well-rounded shit, and get the streets on our backs while we marketed ourselves and looked for a record deal. That was our strategy.

This approach ended working against me. The more I spit street shit, the more people wanted to hear it. I had people come up to me regularly and say, "Shi, nigga, I love when you kick that real shit. Man, your other shit hard, but that street shit, niggaaaaaa." They'd say that when, in actuality, they hadn't heard much of my other shit. My other shit was in the lab. It was just the street shit that I was flooding the neighborhood with. There were so many other sides to me I wanted to express to show who I was. I wanted to give the world all of me, not some of me! This is the paradox of any true artist. And the fucked-up dilemma I was starting to have was that while I was kicking street shit, *I was doing street shit*. (Meaning that I was hustling. I was reeeally out there in them streets!) That was the crazy part. That's kind of why I didn't want to show just that one part of my music. It was like telling on myself. Yes, it was honest! But fuck, it was incriminating.

The Business Part of the Music Business

I knew that Bo-Gard had something special. So I had to put all of my music experience to work if I wanted us to have a chance at blowing. All we had to do was let the world hear our music. The labels were sure to sign us. There was only one problem: we had to get out of Richmond.

See, the Richmond music scene operated under a "crab in the bucket" mentality at that time, meaning that artists liked to pull each other down rather than lift each other up. And I don't know if you've done your homework on the music industry and Richmond, but nobody has ever successfully blown from here. You could make a case for Trey Songz. He was from Petersburg, but he was an R&B singer. No rappers, though. The closest thing we had was Mad Skillz, and he never officially *made it* made it.

Richmond Ain't No Atlanta

Richmond had talent. The problem was, we didn't support each other musically. I've always said I wish we were more like Atlanta. The artists there support each other so heavily that the market alone can financially sustain an artist, even if they don't blow nationally. But Richmond's limitations didn't stop us from trying to create a buzz. And we had to do it in an industry that was starting to advance rapidly. The www. era had arrived and was changing the way artists broke themselves. With the internet at their disposal, they could get enough buzz from their local community to attract the attention of the major labels. It was a powerful tool. Even though we didn't have that type of market in Richmond, we figured we would still defy the odds.

> WHEN YOU FEEL GOOD ABOUT YOURSELF, YOU PERFORM BETTER. AND WHEN YOU PERFORM BETTER, YOU FEEL GOOD ABOUT YOURSELF. BOTH ARE ESSENTIAL. NEITHER CAN ENDURE ONE WITHOUT THE OTHER.
>
> —BRIAN TRACY, AUTHOR AND MOTIVATIONAL SPEAKER

Taking Matters Into My Own Hands

If we were going to beat the odds, I had to strategize properly. One problem was, I had more business experience than the other guys in my crew. The other was that they didn't have any money and it would take a lot of cash to accomplish what we were trying to do. If we were going to get somewhere, I had to play both of those roles and I knew it. So I did. I supported us financially and led the group in the business side of the industry. And taking matters into my own hands meant that I would have to employ all the business skills I'd learned up to that point, from hustling to watching the industry from up close in New York.

It was me who conceptualized and financed the idea for 10,000 mixtapes. I paid for the mastering, the duplication of the posters, stickers, T-shirts, and other paraphernalia. I even bought promo items such as matchbooks! Tell me I wasn't a genius. What other artist had lighters and matches with their logo on them? My goal was direct marketing, guerrilla marketing, and subliminal marketing. All angles. I paid for DJs to play our shit at clubs. We created a few singles that I paid radio personalities to play on the radio. We did shows whenever we could. Hit cyphers every chance we got. Promoted everywhere we went.

Going Beyond Richmond

Even though we managed to create a nice buzz for Bo-Gard, I realized that Richmond wasn't going to do it for us. I decided that we should take our music out on the road. We started traveling to nearby cities to move our music product and give out promotional items. The road trips were starting to get expensive, but I knew we had to continue to get the music out, which meant going further and further to get where the action was. One place where the action was? Las Vegas during the NBA All-Star Game. We couldn't afford for everybody to go, so I went alone.

I took about 1,000 mixtapes with me, hopped on the plane, and got busy. Fuck an All-Star Game, I'm here to move units! I was dedicated. I was focused. I was moving like a man possessed. I went to every exclusive party out there and pushed my music on anybody who seemed to fit the "I like hip-hop" profile. I got several contacts—which was great—and hit it off with a dude named P, who worked for Koch Records. He was in Vegas with some of the label's artists who were performing during the All-Star weekend event. He told me he would listen to our music and then call me when he got back to New York.

He didn't lie either. About a week later, he called me and we rapped. He said he loved what he'd heard and wanted to work with me. From there, we kept in weekly contact. P told me that Koch Records was losing money because of the internet and other changes rapidly taking place in the industry. He said that the label was downsizing and he didn't think it was a good idea to take my project over to Koch. He explained that he had a lot of industry connects from being in that world for so long in an artist development role. He personally believed in the project and wanted to take it to a major label rather than an independent like Koch. "But there's one thing, Shiloh," he told me.

My man, P, from Koch Records at the time.

NIGGAS CATCHING A FEW FEELINGS

"Yo, we gotta bring you out first," P said. "Then when we make your project pop, you can start a label and bring your crew in. I feel like you're the most polished on your crew and this is going to be the best shot we have of breaking y'all in the industry. Think Method Man to Wu-Tang. It's going to be dope!"

When I told my crew about the plan, they said that they were down for it. It wasn't until a little later that I found out that niggas had caught a few feelings over this. I think they thought I went in there pushing myself and not them. What they didn't understand was this: if I was just pushing myself, I would have told them. I would have been honest. I mean, I did most of the back-end shit anyway. Plus, I had my own dough. What was stopping me? There I was with my "trying to be loyal" shit and niggas still caught feelings like somebody was doing them wrong. But I didn't hear it back from them. The sad part is that it was coming back from other people. Like, really? If you felt like you'd been underhanded, why didn't you say that shit from the beginning? I was doing it all with the right intentions. Taking one for the team. To me, it didn't matter who stepped out there first so long as we all benefited in the long run.

I was with it. I mean, whatever it took, right? As long as we all got in, I didn't give a fuck! Plus, I figured P knew what he was talking about because he'd been in the industry for so long. He knew how that world ticked more than I did, so my best bet was to follow his guidance. If that didn't work, I could judge, but until I followed his blueprint, could I accurately critique it? So I sent him some songs and started banging out new ones. I put all my oomph into developing the most polished product that P could use to shop to the labels.

After a few months, he had a package he was confident to shop, one we thought was surefire. He started requesting meetings and finally landed one with Ampora Sapp, who was a head A&R for Sony. On the day of the meeting, he hit me up and said, "This is it, nigga! Keep your fingers crossed." Then he went into that meeting for what seemed like hours.

When the meeting was over, P called and gave me the rundown. He detailed how he let Ampora hear all the music. She liked it! She thought it was dope! Okay, great, we're doing good so far. Then he told me about their conversation. It went more or less like this:

"Yo, P, your artist is dope. I would personally ride around and listen to his music. But there are a few things I have to take into consideration these days given the state of the industry. More than ever, our necks are on the line with the artists we sign. With everything going digital, the money ain't there like it used to be, so there's no room for mistakes. If I make a bad move, I'm done. Right now, I have projects for four known artists on my desk and I'm trying to make decisions about them, starting with Kelly Rowland's solo project." (Ampora was talking about Kelly's solo project after stepping away from Destiny's Child for the first time.) She continued, "I'm also looking at somebody from E-40's camp and a Bun B collab. Is Shiloh getting any sound scans or BDSs, something I can work with?"

"Well, right now, that's why we're here," said P. "We've developed him as an artist, we've got a solid album together, and we want to get some funding for the right marketing campaign. Po, we don't even need a big budget. You already know I can make it work. Let's figure something out and we can hit the road and get busy."

"P, you know how the industry is changing," said Ampora. "The easiest way for you to get the money you want for his project is to make Shiloh and his team hot in his locale first. Build some buzz and then bring me back something more than good music if you want me to hit the go button. Some sound scans, something. Otherwise, the best I can offer you guys is a $50,000 contract with him being put on the shelf for however long until I crank these other artists and projects out, and that could be up to four years. But you know what that comes with, right? He wouldn't be able to touch another label in the process *and* I can't make no guarantees."

Kelly Rowland's Project Came First, No Surprise

P was disappointed. So was I. At first, I was like, "P, fuck it, let's take the $50,000 and just work."

P advised against it, said it didn't make sense. It was a bottom-of-the-barrel contract. "Think about it, Shiloh," he said. "Four years is a long time. We can do a lot on our own in four years. Let's just start working on building buzz and do it that way. After that, they're going to have to pay us what we're worth."

Sidebar: No surprise. Ampora went with Kelly Rowland's project first. I understood that. Shit, Kelly was already known and had dumb recognition from her time with Destiny's Child. It seemed like the label's logical best shot.

About eight months later, Kelly's "Like This" came out and underperformed, which goes to show how hard it is to predict success in this industry. "Like This" took flight in its first week, selling a little over 86,000 copies. It went downhill from there. Sony and Columbia expected the album to do much, *much* better than that. And they pushed it like shit. So remember how music execs stick their necks on the line for the projects they cosign? Well, sadly, Ampora lost her job at Sony after Kelly's album was released, and the rest was history. (An industry rumor circulated for a while that Mr. Knowles, the executive producer of Kelly's album, had secretly sabotaged Kelly's success. But I don't put any stock in that 'cause

I don't know them muthafuckas. If the rumor did have any truth to it, though, it goes to show you how cold and fucked up the industry can be.)

Bullshit from My Crew

Anyway, back to my story. What happened with Sony knocked the wind out of me. It wasn't like I'd never heard "no" before or never had to re-strategize, for that matter. But this was during the height of my hustling business on the streets, and I was experiencing an extreme level of stress from that. So I started to think, *Fuck re-strategizing, I need to start thinking about my life choices now. Is music something I need to invest so much time, energy, and money in?* With a family, I couldn't afford to play the starving-artist role. And now P was telling me we had to start doing our own campaign and ramp it up?

That meant the amount of money I'd have to put into this thing called music—my dream—would increase. Where would it come from? That would mean I'd have to hustle harder to make more dispensable income to drop in it while taking care of family, bills, and living expenses. No financial equation was making sense to me at that point. The police were cracking down, so I couldn't risk hustling more. The whole time I'd been sacrificing everything for my family and my dream, and now life was throwing me an ultimatum: either choose family or the dream, or risk it all. I sat and thought about it hard before realizing that I didn't have any options. I needed to choose family and sacrifice my dream.

That's exactly when I started to hear about the bullshit my crew was saying, coming back to me from other people. And it was not so much Rah as it was Foots. That shit was so corny. After hearing it a few times, I didn't even confront them. I fell back. I ended up kicking Foots out. He was an adult. It was time. And, because I knew that I was going to have to slow down hustling, I would no longer have the expendable income to support him. Besides, he started to get way too ahead of himself.

Beware! The same thing that attracts a person to you will be the very same thing they will envy when they are close to you!

— Shiloh Jones

17

Age 22: It All Started with a Cough

REE WAS A fat baby, greedy as hell. Kai came out slim. At about three years old, Ree finally started slimming down and shedding all that chubby babyness, while Kai never had it to shed in the first place. Then one day, Kai got a cold with a very bad cough.

Kai, my second daughter.

We gave it a few days, didn't panic, but her cough got worse. She would cough continuously for a minute straight. At this point, we felt this warranted a doctor's visit, so we took her to her pediatrician. He examined her and ruled that she had whooping cough. I don't even remember if he gave us meds or not, but he definitely gave us some directives, like making sure she got rest. He said it would go away. Over the next three months, her cough would leave and come back sporadically. We took her back to the pediatrician over the course of the next three months as he "practiced" and experimented with different strategies for getting rid of this cough that wouldn't go away.

At some point in her first year, Kai began to lose weight she didn't have to spare. She went from slim to skinny. Something wasn't right. (This wasn't supposed to be happening. I mean, babies are supposed to be chubby, right?) We lost confidence in that doctor and decided to take her to the hospital. You can imagine how worried we were. We just couldn't figure out what was going on with her. The more she ate, the more she lost weight. And she still had that crazy cough.

When we got to MCV, they put her on an IV, saying that she was dehydrated. The doctors came in, probing us, asking us a million questions. (Some were very offensive, by the way.) I started to feel like they were accusing us of neglectful parenting. They informed us that they would have to hospitalize her for a few days to run tests and monitor her to ensure that she was getting proper hydration and nutrition. Sheila stayed at the hospital the entire time and never left Kai's side. I was back and forth to the hospital, working, taking care of Ree, and bringing food and other things from the outside world when Sheila needed me to.

After So Many Tests

One day, the doctors came into Kai's room and said that we needed to talk. They escorted us to another room, the "I need you to sit down for this" private conference room. This is when things started to move fast for me. One of them said this:

"Hey guys, so you've been at the hospital for about two weeks. I know it's been rough and that we haven't been able to produce much in the way of answers up to this point. We've run a lot of tests on Kai based on what we suspected could be wrong with her, from blood tests to scans. Then we thought, *Let's run a sweat test on her*. The test measures the concentration of salt in a person's sweat. It showed that Kai's sweat has five times more salt than most people's. Then we thought, *This explains her coughing*. Your child, unfortunately, has what is called cystic fibrosis."

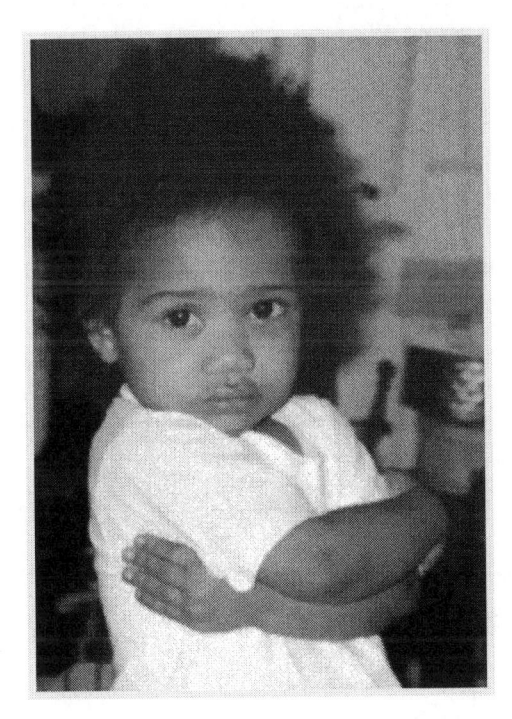

Kai, around the time when we received her diagnosis.

My heart dropped. Cystic fibrosis! What? But wait, what in the hell is cystic fibrosis? The doctor then educated us. Cystic fibrosis (CF) is a life-threatening, inherited genetic disease. I'm going to get scientific for a minute. We all have dominant genes and recessive genes embedded in our DNA. Some of these genes carry mutations. In order for a child to get CF, both parents have to carry a specific mutated gene. Even then, there's a slim-to-none chance that the recessive gene will result in a child having CF. I'll give you a better idea of how rare it is: only about 100,000 people worldwide have CF. But one in every twenty-five people actually carries the faulty gene. Most likely, you have the recessive CF gene in you. CF can't be caught. It can only be inherited in the rare occurrence that the faulty genes from two parents become active in the child during pregnancy.

So what does CF do to the bodies of the rare people who are born with it? Good question, I'm glad you asked. First, it affects the lungs by clogging them with very sticky mucus, which usually results in chronic infections and constant inflammation of the lungs. (This explains Kai's uncontrollable cough. It's like having mucus in your chest that you can't cough up.) Also, it affects the digestive system because, for some reason, CF prohibits the pancreas from creating enzymes. (Okay, nerd time: the way your body processes food is with enzymes that break the food down so it can be used as fuel. The enzymes are biological catalysts that speed up the rate of chemical reactions taking place in the body's cells. This process is essential for proper digestion and metabolism. Remember that Kai's pancreas wasn't producing enzymes like it should have. This explained why, no matter how much food Kai ate, she got skinnier and skinnier. Her body couldn't process the food she was eating. She was just eating it and shitting it out.)

The sweat test was important because CF patients lose water five times faster than other people, making their sweat five times saltier. Also, this is super-rare in white folks and extremely rare in blacks. The chances of a black person getting CF are 0.00000000001. Yes, our genetic makeup leaves us more prone to sickle cell anemia than white people, but CF is very rare in us.

Now back to the doctor and the conversation. The conference room was completely silent as the next words came from his lips: "There is no cure for this. And it's fatal. Now, depending on treatment and the individual, life expectancies can vary. We've even seen some reach the age of nineteen, twenty, and twenty-one."

When I heard this, I said, "You're wrong. Test her again! I want a second opinion."

They tried to talk to us, saying, "I know this is hard to accept ... " but I damn near snapped. I walked out of the room. I couldn't believe it. What had just happened? Was this because of me? Was God paying me back for all the fucked-up shit I'd done in my life? Was this a test? I couldn't understand why God was doing this to me. Not my baby! I cried. Man, I cried for fucking weeks straight! If you think I was angry when I was younger, well, I was truly on fire now. I went through a very dark period internally, emotionally. I continued to blame myself. How could I not? I was probably the only fucked-up thing in my family's world. They were innocent and pure.

The doctors kept Kai in the hospital for a month or two after diagnosing her and then released her to come home. This was around the time that gave me enough reasons to justify my decision to start hustling again—and go hard at hustling. Sheila was stressed out. I was stressed out. Now, all of a sudden, there's a special needs kid in the mix?

They sent her home with a million medicines, a million directives, and ten million "Do this and don't do that" instructions. It was really rough on the family. I swear to you, in certain ways, I'm very thankful that I was in a position to hustle. It was the *only* thing that kept us afloat and gave us the flexibility to deal with Kai's treatments and constant hospital stays and the very unpredictable nature of this disease. I mean, she had to go for regular checkups every week or two at the Nelson Clinic at MCV Hospital all through elementary school, and we never knew when we took her in if they were going to admit her or not. And when they did admit her, she was in there for a month minimum. The school system even had to work out a way for her to receive schoolwork while she was in the hospital so she wouldn't fall behind.

I rejected the sympathy of people who said to me, "I know what you're going through right now."

No, you don't! How could you possibly know what I'm feeling? Do you have a daughter going through the same shit Kai is going through? Do you really know what it's like to stand there while doctors perform procedures on her while she cries, looking up at me for help?! Do you know what it's like forcing her to eat three times more food than normal, just so she can maintain her weight because the doctors are saying she can't afford to lose any more? Have you ever had the constant, nagging thought that your child may die before you do? And you may have to watch that shit?

Can't nobody love-love me like you do,
Sweetheart, this statement couldn't be more true, boo,
Through the fabric of life, you fine texture,
Look, to make a diamond, you need pressure,
So don't sweat it, all this pain is for a reason,
It just hurt to know that daddy can't ease it,
I love you, baby, with all my heart believe it,
God, get her lungs like they supposed to be breathing,
If you can't, why the fuck you put her here?
She shouldn't have to suffer and I
could've saved the tears,
But while you here, we gon' make the best of life,
Even if I have to hustle, you gon' be alright.

—Excerpt from hip-hop song by Shiloh Jones written for Kai

18

Age 22: Money in Motion: Approaching Hustling as a Business

SO, HERE I WAS after all that, back to hustling. But I was approaching it differently this time. Let me stop for a minute and say this: I don't want to give you the impression that hustling is easy because it's not! And I would never suggest it to anyone. There are too many dangerous factors involved and too many risks. Never take your life for granted or your freedom, for that matter. At any time, I could've gotten locked up, robbed, or shot in a stickup. And that's just for starters. So please don't read this and follow what I did. I'm sharing the story of my hustling days simply to give you my experiences and life story.

I am one of the very, *very* few lucky individuals who made it out of the game. Most don't. And for that reason alone, I highly suggest that you *never* play this game. As a matter of fact, there is no circumstance that would ever make me go back to the game again in this life! In the immortal words of Jay-Z, "No, Hov' did that, so hopefully you won't have to go through that!" By all means, choose a different route. Please do not take these words lightly.

Closest Thing I've Ever Come to a Hands-On MBA

I approached hustling as a business. I was forced to learn many core business principles if I wanted to survive in that life, successfully take care of my family, and not get caught. Hustling was the closest thing I've ever come to receiving a "hands-on" MBA, as I acquired skills that the best colleges teach. My education also included what you can only learn from field experience.

I learned exceptional customer service skills and became a superior judge of character. I came to understand the principles of accounts receivable and accounts payable, management skills, leadership skills, risk assessment, strategy implementation, contingency planning, forecasting, cash flow, product demand, supply chain, customer acquisition risks, customer relationship management, and financial management. These are just some of the skills that I used to transition into the corporate world, skills that eventually made me a great businessman. The only difference was that this wasn't a test.

You weren't going to get fired if you lost, change schools if you failed, get loans if you made the wrong move. My consequences were more severe if I didn't play this game right, if I slipped. Imagine a tightrope walker learning how to walk a slender rope a thousand feet in the air with no safety net! That's the best metaphor I can give.

Transitioning to a High-Quantity Customer Base

Anyway, back to the story. I rocked out for a while as a "semi-weight" specialist while continuing to transition to my core, high-quantity customer base. Before long, I felt growth stagnated. One of my close friends at the time, Mark, introduced me to a Jamaican who was extended family to him because he'd married Mark's cousin. For purposes of identity protection, I'll call him Trevor. When I met Trevor, he'd just come home from prison after being locked up for eight years for distributing weight. He still had connects but was scared to touch anything because he knew that he was still being closely monitored. (This happens to most folks who get out of prison for moving large quantities of anything. The thought is that it's hard for an old tiger to grow new stripes.)

Trevor knew I sold weed and knew what level I was at. He would talk to me and drop little jewels here and there about how to do this smarter and what not to do. (These pieces of advice came from lessons that he'd learned the hard way. Of course I would listen. I was past the days of being arrogant, because I'd started to understand how expensive arrogance could be.)

Trevor had a dilemma. See, he couldn't put his hands on anything. (The key word is "he" couldn't.) I knew he needed to make money. He'd just come home and was going to start running out of it soon.

A Little Light in the Situation for Me

There was a little light in this situation for me. A little silver lining. There was an opportunity for me and Trevor, I just had to pitch it to him so that he saw the value in it, too. If I could play this situation right, I could swing this to my advantage. I knew that he could get his hands on the amount of weight that I needed to take myself to the next level. What was in it for him?

He could make some money without having to take the risks. I would take all the risks. We'd all benefit! Win-win situation.

> The shortest and best way to make a fortune is to let people see clearly that is in their interest to promote yours.
>
> —Jean de La Bruyère, philosopher and moralist

I got comfortable enough with Trevor that I was able to give him my pitch. I knew he wouldn't jump on it immediately, because that's what smart hustlers do. They take their time. They don't rush shit. They move slow. After a while, he came back at me and asked, "Are you really ready to make some real money?" BOOM! I got him. I acted nonchalant and told him that I was ready when he was. He informed me that he'd put an order in with his old people and that the shipment was supposed to arrive in a few weeks.

Time to Rock and Roll!

Several weeks later, it came in. Time to rock and roll! My strategy was to again restructure and transition to a new customer base. At the same time, I would refine my old base with customers who were willing to grow by buying more quantity, this time stepping up. I figured that the lowest quantity I would sell was a pound. Question was, how cheap was I going to be able to get the shit? Trevor first tried to tell me $1,100. I explained to him that this was too high and immediately went into my negotiations. I didn't know his price, but I did know he was going to try to profit off me as much as possible. That's the name of the game. I haggled my way down to $900. BAM! Now I was in business.

The $900 price was below market value enough so that I stood to (1) offer great wholesale pricing, (2) unload the pounds quick enough to satisfy Trevor, and (3) make a profit I was comfortable with. The market rate for a pound at the time was $1,200. But to successfully acquire new business, I'd have to recruit hustlers who already had a relationship with a supplier. That meant *beating* their supplier's price. People are creatures of habit, so why would they deal with me if they already had a positive working relationship? I had to offer *better value*. Bottom line: it's always about the bottom line. Business 101. I decided I was going to set my price at $1,100 for one pound. Two or more, the price would be $1,050. This should be good enough for *discount incentive*. I chalked this discount up to the cost of customer acquisition.

When we broke the package down, it came out to be 20 pounds of weed. At $1,100 apiece, 20 pounds would yield a net profit of $4,000. If I sold them for the bulk discount incentive, the least I would bring in would be $3,000. Not bad for making twenty or less gross sales. Pro: Way less traffic. Con: Bigger risk. Math checks out. Let's rock!

Business 102: Meeting Supply-and-Demand Requirements

So I did just what I decided. I went to everyone who sold weight to me and said, "Look, my people got some work in, the shit good. I probably could get you a good number on the shit because I fucks with you, plus you always look out for me. I want to repay the favor." They bit.

I went to others who I knew sold weed and changed the pitch up a little: "Yo, my folks Gucci, I don't know what number you're getting now but they are willing to beat out the number." They bit, too.

Before a week and a half was out, I'd dumped the entire 20 pounds that I'd gotten from Trevor. He was shocked at how fast I had moved it. I came back with straight money. "How fast can you get the next shipment?" I asked him.

"I'm going to put in an order, little bro," he said. "Calm down."

The supply chain *must* meet supply-and-demand requirements. This was a problem. If I allowed this to happen every time I moved the work, it would counteract my efforts. Hustlers don't wait for you to come through if they have several connects. Simply put, if you don't have it, oh well, they'll get it from somebody else. One monkey can't stop no show. Plus, they had to keep up with the supply-and-demand requirements in their own world. They had customers to please, money to make, and business to maintain, even if that meant paying extra for the next batch.

I explained this concept to Trevor and went into detail about how we'd have to have a reliable, consistent supply to make money. Trevor was new to the game this time around. He couldn't control the inconsistency of these 20-pound batches, so we had to carry on like this for the moment. So when I didn't have the shit, I just didn't answer my phone. When it came in, I made calls. I really wasn't comfortable just making my $3,000 to $4,000 when it dropped, but hey, it was better than nothing. Plus, those breaks gave me peace of mind. Those were the times I focused on making music.

ON THE ROAD TO NORTH CAROLINA

When one of the batches came in, Trevor told me that he wanted to take it to North Carolina. He had an old customer by the name of Buck who'd gotten back in touch with him and he wanted to take the work down there. First off, I wasn't going to take this trip by myself, so I wanted him to get the thought out of his head pronto. "These are *your* people," I told him.

For all I knew, he could've been trying to set me up. That's one thing about the streets. You simply can't trust anyone, no matter how much you know them. Eventually, every street nigga becomes paranoid, even of the people closest to them. It's just something that comes with the territory. He understood.

I wanted to be smart about this. I won't try to get caught the fuck up. Sorry. So I came up with a plan. I paid a dude I knew, Cory, to drive with the work while I rode behind him. Trevor would ride with me. Trevor and I spoke of the deal in detail, settling on what was in it for him and what was in it for me. He explained that since Buck wanted to buy the entire 20 pounds of weed straight up, he could only charge him $700 a pound.

Trevor claimed that since his connect was "looking out for him" (yeah, right), his price had been $600 for each, so we'd split the $2,000. I felt like it wasn't entirely worth it, but Trevor kicked me a story about how his connect said that if we kept moving the 20 pounds, he'd make them cheaper as we went along. He explained that a person like Buck would be valuable as the prices dropped. While it didn't seem like much at the time, it was going to pay off in the future, he told me. Cory agreed to make the run for a QP's worth of work. This was cool since after we broke down the 20-pound block, there was always just about that much left over. Cory was doing the drive with us virtually for free because it didn't really bother our total product.

All in all, I decided to take one more for the team. We made the trip. When we got down to Greensboro, we had to put the work in my car. According to Trevor, the extra person (Cory) meant that "too many" people were involved and we didn't want to scare Buck. Plus, it would've just looked too sloppy. As we were on the way to Buck's crib, an undercover cop in an unmarked vehicle came racing up behind us at full speed. Oh shit! All I could think was, *This is it! I'm going to jail! That's 20 pounds' worth of work? They 'bout to give me a kingpin charge. WTF!*

I rode for a second, heart beating fast as shit. What do I do? And what Trevor didn't know was that there was a gun in the car. (I told you, trust no one!) Now I had a gun and weed in the car.

I tried to calculate how much jail time I was going to get. I'm never seeing my kids again—ever! When I get out, they won't even know me. I don't have money for this type of bail. I'm fucked! I looked in the rear-view mirror and saw the policeman aggressively telling me to move over. I thought about slamming my foot on the accelerator and going on a high-speed chase, but I didn't do it. Fuck it, let me just pull over and deal with the consequences. I steered into the next lane, slowed down, and pulled onto the shoulder of the road. The cop zoomed past me into traffic ahead. He was pursuing a call unrelated to me! What the hell?! My heart felt like it was going to jump outta my chest. Oh my gosh! To date, hands down, one of the scariest moments in my life. Shit almost got real!

Double-Dipping Like a Muthafucka

When we got to Buck's house, Trevor went in by himself and hollered at him. They talked for a while and then came outside. Trevor nodded at me and I grabbed the work, which was in a plain trash bag, out of the trunk. We kicked it with Buck for a minute. He was a good guy. A true hustler. Laid-back fellow. The minute Trevor left us alone to make a phone call, Buck started talking to me in a dissatisfied manner. "Man, Trevor told me this shit was supposed to be $700. But then he got down here and changed up the game and said it was $900. He know I don't play that shit. I don't know what he trying to do, but you gotta watch that nigga, cuz."

And right there I knew what Buck was thinking. He was thinking that I was the connect. He thought Trevor was trying to middleman *my* price to him. But what I was thinking was, *Damn, Trevor, you just played me, bro!* This nigga making an extra $4,000 *over* the $1,000 we agreed on. Double-dipping like a muthafucka.

So what did I do? C'mon, I ain't no dummy. I played it smart! I acted like I *was the connect*. I let Buck assume whatever he wanted and let him lead the conversation.

"Yo, Shiloh, bro, I get this about every two weeks. And I pay straight cash! Dawg, you ain't gotta middleman through him. Let's holla at each other straight up. Ima thorough nigga, man. Fuck with me!"

"Are you willing to drive up to Virginia?" I asked, knowing there was no way in a cold day in summer I was gonna make this scary-ass drive again. Fuck that!

"Yeah, man, if you deal with me directly, bet!" he said. "But I need that $700 number. At worst $750."

"Done! Say no more!" I told him. I made the deal without even having a solid plan. But one thing about your boy: give me a little bit of time, Ima figure it out! That's one thing I can guarantee.

Trevor came back and we carried on small talk. An interesting turn of events had happened in just a few minutes: Trevor thinking he got over on me, me stealing his connect, and Buck being an unsatisfied customer. Business 103: Treat your customers right or your competition will be eagerly waiting to do it for you!

Needing a New Connect

I got back to Virginia and realized I had some work to do. I needed to find a new connect. I couldn't trust Trevor anymore. You show me a little bit of larceny and that's enough for me to know that you're a sheisty individual. I'd dealt with enough larceny-ass niggas. I never told Trevor that I knew what he'd done. What was the point? It's better for a person to think you don't see their true colors when you really do than for you to alert them. "Let his slip show" was the street term for that way of thinking.

I put energy out into the universe about needing a better connect. As always, the universe sent something my way. I ran into my old friend, G, from George Wythe High School. While we were catching up, he informed me that he was in the game. He had taken over where his Jamaican brothers had left off since some were locked up and some had moved and so forth. He was the one holding it down for Richmond. (Boom! Here's my chance.) I quickly freestyled my pitch.

Knowing what I could move on my own in combination with the plug I'd just hijacked from Trevor—Buck and his 20-all-at-once demand—I said, "Yo, I can definitely move about 50! Can you handle that?" Going from moving 20 pounds of weed to 50 was a bold move, but I was ready to show and prove.

G was a little hesitant. He said he could probably do 30. "Just one thing," I added. "Ima need you to throw them joints to me." (That was the street term for fronting work, getting now/paying later. Credit.) He was cool with it. So now the blueprint was starting to make sense. Then we got to the inevitable topic of price. I asked him how much he was charging "per one."

"How much are you getting them for now?" he asked, referring to pounds. I knew that this moment would define everything that was to come. Whatever price I gave him, he would have to come close to my current pricing. But it had to be believable. Without hesitation, I responded, "Shit, I'm at $600 a joint now." It rolled right off my tongue. Then I followed up with the closer: "You think you can do $550?"

"Nah, I probably can't do $550, but I can match your current $600, though," he said. "I can do that for you." And just like that, my positioning changed. Not only was I getting better pricing—stupid pricing—but I was getting the product thrown at me as well (in other words, fronted to me on consignment). This not only gave me the immediate leverage I needed but also kept me cash-flow positive. Now it's on and popping! I'm formulating a formula.

What Did I Get Myself Into?

A few days later, G met me with the work. He surprised me and gave me the entire 50 pounds, not the 30 he'd offered. It was kinda weird seeing all that work at once. It came in a big, compressed block. It was wrapped tight with Saran Wrap, then a layer of car grease, and then more Saran Wrap. I cleared off one layer of wrap, washed off the car grease, and then took a knife and sliced through the final layer. The weed was so compressed, I couldn't break it with my hands. I had to take a metal object (later, this would be a butcher knife or a screwdriver) and pry it apart before I could break it into pieces.

My scale at the time only weighed a maximum of 2.2 pounds, so I had to literally bag each pound up a pound at a time. I used gallon Ziploc bags. The freezer bags were better because they had more weight to them, which ultimately gave me about a half-pound of weed left over after I'd finish bagging up all the work. I could smoke the extra if I wanted, break it down to my closest family and friends, give it away, or sell it for $750. Man, it took me about two hours to bag all that shit up. My fucking back was hurting from bending over constantly to scoop more weed chunks into Ziploc bags.

When I was done, I remember feeling paranoid. I mean, this was a lot of work! I sat back, looked at it, and thought, *What did I get myself into?* (It's a thought, by the way, that every entrepreneur has when they finally get what they ask for.) But I refocused. I knew what I'd gotten myself into. And that's the next level. It was time to get busy. I knew I had to off this shit as quickly as possible.

My Goal: Undercut the Market

I called Buck and told him I had him straight. He asked me about the price point. "What's the number?" I told him the price was exactly where he wanted it, being careful not to talk in too much detail on the phone. He knew I meant $700 apiece for pounds. It was cool. That was twenty straight up. A quick $14,000 sale of which $2,000 was net profit. I hit up everyone else I'd sold to before. I used a "buy in bulk" strategy. I told them that the number was $900 for one (already beating their price) but I could do three for $800 apiece or a five-pack for $725.

This strategy was similar to the way convenience store products are priced, offering one item like a Big Bite Pizza for $1.59 but two for just $2. It's like a deal you can't refuse. My goal was to get them to buy more. If they bought more, I could get this shit off me in a shorter amount of time. I wanted to discourage people from just buying one from me.

I wanted to undercut the entire market. I knew if I did, I could sell the product faster, satisfy my supplier quicker, and profit by moving units. I was officially a distributor now. My goal was to move quantity. Let's do the math again. Selling 20 pounds at $700 gave me a net profit of $2,000. Now I had 30 pounds left from the 50. If I encouraged everyone who bought from me to make at least five-pack sales, I would make a net profit of at least $125 per pound. Multiply $125 per pound times 30 pounds and that's a net profit of $3,750. Add that to the net $2,000 and you had a grand total net of $5,750 in profit. With any smaller amounts I sold, my customers were getting taxed at a higher rate, but fuck it, that just meant my profit margin was greater.

$6,500 Profit in Two Weeks

I cleared the 50-pound batch in two weeks max. I think I totaled over $6,500 in profit. Lots of people couldn't get the five-pack, but that was okay. I put the word out to them and, trust me, they would get it either the next time or the time after. This I knew. They just had to get their money up. Remember, all business boils down to the bottom line. I took G his money. (If you were doing the math properly, you'll know that it was $30,000 cash.)

I'd never seen that kind of money before in my life. But now I had, and I did it all by myself. I remember when I took the bread to him, I took all the big bills for myself and gave him the small bills. He had a fit! "Yo' always give me the largest bills," he said. "Remember, bro, I have to go get more work with this, so I have to carry the most money to my peoples. If everybody gives me small bills, I would have dumb trash bags. I can't be rolling up with trash bags. C'mon, bro, that shit hot as hell."

"True, true, true," I said. "You right. I got you pimpin'. I ain't think about that." Made sense. That was my amateur mistake. From that point on, I kept the small bills and delivered him the large ones.

After the first flip, I knew I had to be smarter. Stealthier. I mean, with greater power comes greater responsibility. I knew I had to be smarter than the next nigga, than the average hustler. Smarter than the police. Smarter than the snitches.

A New Quality of Life

        I ain't depending on this government,
Let dem joints move out,
        I got a hundred coming in,
    Covered in coffee beans, packed in a luggage bin,
I don't buy smoke,
        I just put away a couple 'dem,
        Fuck them!
        Foots get the scale, bring the smoke in,
    So compressed you need screwdrivers to break 'em open,
        No shit!
        Grind time, peddle for bread,
        Paranoid, stay focused, keep a level head.

—Excerpt from hip-hop song by Shiloh Jones

G kept the work steady. With two flips on average, I was making $10,000 to $15,000 a month. My quality of life started changing. The quality of my family's life started changing. No more were they going to want for anything. If Sheila wanted something, I bought it. If the kids needed something, I bought it. I got tired of paying for studio recording time, so I purchased and built myself a studio for the house.

    I was smart with my flips, though. The more money I saved, the faster I could pay off my supplier before all the actual product was moved. I would pay him about halfway through. Half was his money, the other half was my saved money. So the second half of the work I was moving was actually me recouping my saved money. The more I did this, the more I had in the kitty, so to speak. So I moved to a different strategy. I would start throwing work to dealers I trusted. I did this *only* because I knew I had enough money in reserve to pay for it if something happened. I mean, this was the streets. Anything could happen. Some things are beyond our control. This gave me considerable leverage. To the layman's eye, it appeared that my money was always in motion. In reality, it was constantly growing.

19

AGE 24: BEWARE THE WOUNDED EGO

I THOUGHT I was done with Foots when I took him off the streets, but there was a lesson lurking in that move. See, the problem was, I didn't recognize the classic homeboy bullshit happening right under my nose. It's a mistake I'll never make again. A huge lesson for me. At the time, he was extremely grateful and took every chance to say so. I can confidently say that I did more for him than anybody had ever done or ever will, for that matter.

While he was with me, he got to experience money, power, and respect. The very things that attracted him to me. The things he admired in me. But those things can drive a person down the wrong path. After a while, he started getting the homeboy perspective that so many black brothers have when they're next to powerful people. They start to expect the lookouts, the money, and they think you're supposed to keep feeding it to them.

When people spoke to us, they generally looked at me. They always gave me more respect than him, 'cause of course they looked at me as the big dog. They automatically assumed I was the one who called all the shots. They naturally assumed I was the brains. Yes, I was. But I was always very humble about it. I never walked around poking my chest out like I was the man. I wanted everybody to look at the people around me as if they were the man as well. I was the type of brother, I would let a nigga rock my chain, drive my whips, whatever, because I wanted them to shine. I shine, we all shine. I didn't want to be the only fly chick among a group of ugly girls, a king among peasants, a gorilla among chimps. There's no props in that.

That was the mentality I had. But just because I had that outlook didn't mean that others—people in the street, dudes we knew, other rappers and chicks—felt the same way. I didn't care, but Foots did. That shit started to eat away at him and bruise his ego. I fault myself for not seeing it sooner, but there was nothing I could do to change it. To keep something like that from bothering you, you have to be a confident dude, a strong dude, and now yourself. But this is where the ego part of the mind fucks you. And this is where the money, the power, and the respect corrupt you. The more you feel it, the more you want it. The more you see, the more you desire. And the more you see others getting it, the more you envy them (even if it's the nigga right beside you who's helping you get it). It blinds you. Thwarts your purpose. Changes your being.

If it were up to him, Foots would be under my wing to this day. He had no motivation to get on his own. I wanted him to learn how to fish, how to adapt the principles he'd learned from me into his own life, and become his own man. But he didn't have the same inner "why" as I had. And when I saw this happen to him, it was too late.

No matter how much you do for niggas, they feel like you owe them the world. Pure arrogance.

I Had to Cut Him Off

When I kicked Foots out, to him it symbolized the end of his world. How was he going to survive? Was this going to affect his power, money, respect? For several weeks, he came asking to borrow money and I gave it to him. I stopped when he started asking for amounts I wasn't confident he could pay back. At that point, it's no longer borrowing; it's charity work, with him taking advantage of me and me enabling him. "You a grown-ass man, Foots. You need to start making ends meet. Ain't no way you been around me that long and didn't learn one ounce of hustle. Man the fuck up!"

Plus, the bullshit that was coming back to me in the last few months over the music didn't motivate me to help him or even be around him. It got to the point where I had to cut him the fuck off! He wasn't my child. I had my own kids. He'd built such a dependence on me, he didn't know how to cut the umbilical cord. I had to cut it for him. He went pillow talking with a few chicks, telling them I was treating him fucked up, whining to them, and they would run back and tell me.

After a while, I didn't hear from him anymore. He stopped coming over. He stopped calling. *Good!*

But a couple of months later, I got a phone call from my daughters. By that time, I'd entered the legitimate job market. The call came a week before their summer program started, so they were staying by themselves during the day while Sheila and I were at work. About thirty minutes after I got to work, Ree called. She was whispering, "Daddy, somebody's in the house."

"What do you mean, 'Somebody's in the house'?"

"I just saw somebody and they saw me, so I ran to my room."

"Ree, get your sister, close the door to your room, hang up the phone immediately, and call 911. Then call me right back. I am on my way to you!"

I raced home at a thousand miles an hour! My mother lived a few blocks over from where we did. I kept a gun at her place that she could use for protection if needed. I called her and said, "Bring the gun outside and walk down to the street. I can't talk now, just hurry!"

"Why, Shiloh?" she asked. "What's going on?"

"JUST WALK OUTSIDE WITH THE GUN NOW!"

I pulled onto her block, going the wrong way down a one-way street. While I grabbed the gun from her, she continued to probe me about what was happening. "Somebody broke in my house. Just call the police! Send them to my house now!" I floored the gas and headed home. When I got there, I walked in with the gun out. I had Ree—who was hiding in her bedroom closet with her sister—on the phone. "I don't know what to do, Daddy!" she told me. "I'm scared!"

"I'm here, baby," I told her. "Just stay in your closet with the door shut."

I searched the entire place. Nobody. Then I went to my kids. They were scared and crying. I comforted them and let them know that they were safe now that Daddy was home. They didn't have a reason to be worried anymore. The police took about twenty-five minutes to arrive. While we were waiting, I questioned Ree about what she'd seen.

She explained everything that had happened and then concluded, "I think it was Foots. It looked just like him. He tried to put a scarf around his mouth, but I know what his head and his body look like. He even had on clothes that I remember him wearing. Plus, I saw the mole by his ear." Yup! That's him. Foots had a distinctive mole on one side of his face, by his ear. Bubblish and protruding. The kind you want to take a needle to just to see what happens. FUCK ME!

You. Don't. Fuck. With. My. Family.

I'm not proud to admit the thoughts that entered my head next. Fuck the police. Foots had bigger problems on his hands. You fuck with my family and all bets are off. There are no rules now! This is war!

Here's what happened. After I kicked Foots out, times got hard for him. He got desperate and people in desperate situations don't think logically. He had nowhere to turn, figured that he needed a quick lick, and targeted me.

The big thing he had working for him was information from living with me for years. He knew I kept money in the house; he just didn't know where. (I changed up my hiding spots monthly and randomly.) He knew who Sheila was. He knew from acquaintances we had in common that I'd started working a regular job. And he knew that the kids attended a summer program from 8 a.m. to 5 p.m. every day, every summer.

What he didn't know on the day he targeted my house was that my girls would be at home. So he parked down the block early that morning and saw that Sheila's car was gone. Then he watched and waited until I headed out. A couple of minutes later, he went to the only fucked-up door of our house—the back door to the basement—because he knew the trick to open it. He also knew my dog, a 95-pound pit bull who wouldn't let anybody he wasn't familiar with get past him. Trust me! There was no doubt in my mind that it was Foots.

Once he got in, he started searching and made his way upstairs toward my bedroom. My daughters heard noises as he approached and looked out into the hallway. That's when Foots and Ree locked eyes, and he took off running.

"Yo, It's Me, Foots"

His plan didn't go the way he'd wanted it to. He didn't find any money. In fact, he didn't find shit. He thought he'd hidden his identity with that scarf he put over his face, but I knew for sure that it was him who'd broken into my crib. Great! This was an advantageous position for me to be in. I spent the next few days searching hard for him but not telling people why. And then I got a phone call.

"Yo!" said somebody on the other end of the line.

"Who this?"

"It's me, Foots."

"Yo, Foots, where you at, homie? I need to rap with you. It's kind of important."

"Nah, nigga, you ain't gon' be able to find me."

"Fuck you mean I ain't gon' be able to find you? Where you at, bro?"

"Look, man, your mom told me you was looking for me and shit. She told me how you think I broke into your crib. Nigga, I ain't break into your shit."

"Okay, I hear you. Let's get up face-to-face and rap about it. Where you at, big dawg?"

"Nigga, I'm way out in the country. I don't even stay in the city no more. I told you, man, you ain't gon' be able to find me ..."

"Let me stop you right there, homeboy," I interrupted. "Oh, I'm going to find you! You would have to leave this muthafucking state for me *not* to find you! And your money ain't long enough to keep this hide-and-seek game up forever!"

And then the conversation went left. I cracked him and his true feelings came spilling out. He told me how selfish I was, how fucked up it was that I had cut him off, and a few other things. But the worst part was, he said that he had heard all of this by way of my mother. I was extremely pissed. I couldn't believe my mother betrayed me by calling him and telling him that I was looking for his ass! The fuck are you doing, Mom? This ain't the time for me and your beef! For your revenge. It was my fault, though. I kicked it into motion when I called her to get my gun that day.

"Look, man, fuck dat," I said. "Ain't gon' be but a matter of time. I'll see you when I see you!" I hung up the phone.

We started a race against the clock, with Foots trying to make something happen to me before I got to him. He texted me that if I pursued him further, he'd call "the boys in blue" and tell them he knew where drug activity was taking place. Those were the exact words of his text. That text was the first but not the last. In fact, he texted me this same message for a week straight. No exaggeration, he did it about a hundred times. Then he did like my mom and told everyone he could that I was looking for him. Even though I was more than heated, I knew I couldn't do anything to him because of the fuckery that originated with my mom's bullshit. That's okay, I got patience.

Now to Deal with My Mom

As I tried to protect and preserve my family, that included trying to reconnect with my mother. Shortly after I started really hustling on another level, things were getting rough between my mother and Vinnie, her girlfriend at the time. They ended up separating. While this was going on, I was attempting to repair my relationship with my mom. (I mean, you only get one mother, right?) Things got bad between Vinnie and my mom, often ending in everything from extremely bad arguments to physical fights.

Once or twice, I had to step in and help Vinnie understand something: even though my mom and I had issues when I was growing up, she was still my mother and I would be damned if Vinnie was going to keep putting her hands on her, whether my mother started the argument or not. Vinnie was bigger than my mom, so getting physical with her was something I couldn't accept. The first time, I gave Vinnie a verbal warning; the second time, I gave her a threat. I meant it, and I'm pretty sure she knew I did! See, beyond what I could physically do, I had something on my side that outweighed what she had, and that was money. Make no mistake about it, money goes a long way in the street world and is never to be taken lightly.

After a while, they officially separated and my mom was by herself. She had finally paid her house off, so her monthly expenses consisted of utility bills, cable, and gas for her car. She retired. (Well, she actually ended up being hit by a school bus one day at work, which resulted in a workers' comp claim that eventually rolled into retirement.) She was on a fixed income, but she was comfortable. Her monthly income from workers' comp and retirement totaled around $2,300 a month. With her minor monthly expenses, she was really set.

The Thing about Money

Money didn't change who I was, but money did change the people around me. My experiences kept me grounded with who I was internally. Sure, I was able to buy things that I was denied as a child and young adult, but it didn't make me a different person. But it was interesting to see how money altered people's interactions with me and changed their opinion of me and their level of respect for me. This always aggravated me because it was a superficial response to my character. And, because I was still dealing with a lot of anger, my thinking was, *If you didn't fuck with me then, don't fuck with me now.* So while I associated with a lot of people, I rejected a lot of new relationships. Old, damaged relationships I would re-enter with extreme caution.

It was no different with my mother. She was on the side of damaged, so I handled her with care. Didn't mean I didn't love her. I just had my guard up constantly. She knew that I hustled. I was always honest with her about that. As I started to make money, our relationship started to get weird. The more money I made, the more she wanted from me. My viewpoint on giving her money and doing things for her? I wanted to do things for her when *I* wanted to, not because I was forced to. I wanted to be able to take her to really nice restaurants, throw her a couple hundred here and there, buy her a few nice things. But her viewpoint was different.

She felt as if I should shower her with gifts and spoil her. I mean, she openly expressed this to me. "I took care of you when you were younger, so it's your time to take care of me," she'd say every chance she got. And it was never enough! The more I gave, the more she wanted. This ain't the reason I'm hustling; I'm hustling to provide a better life for my daughters, not for me to shower muthafuckas around me with gifts.

Confronting the Demons from Our Past

Why does she feel like I owe her? I'd wonder. *She didn't spoil me. Why the hell does she think it's my job to spoil her? And I'll be damned if I was gonna be locked up potentially without shit to show for it because I spent all this extra money showering people with gifts just because I had it.* Hells no! I felt that my mother didn't have the right to come to me like that. Most of the time, I wouldn't even bring up the way I really felt because we were trying to patch our relationship up. I felt this would've been counterproductive to our progress, so I didn't speak up. But as it got worse, I had no choice.

When we were eventually forced to confront the demons from our past, our relationship got even rockier. My mom had a distorted perception of the past. She had truly built up an alter ego, super-parent view of herself and felt that she'd done the best she could for me as a mother. Of course, I felt differently. And I no longer wanted to play along with her delusional view. Doing that just perpetuated and justified her behavior, solidifying her idea that I was supposed to spoil her with 50 percent of what I made out in the streets. So how did we move on from this conundrum?

The answer is, we didn't. I continued to act from my own viewpoint and she continued to nag me from her distorted reality. I was only going to give when I wanted to, not because she forced me. Eventually, this led to her going to every one of our family members and involving them in the problem—from her viewpoint, of course. People thought I was being fucked up and would come to me and try to defend her way of thinking.

This didn't usually end well for them. How the hell do they have the nerve to tell me what the fuck I should do with my money? And why would my mom think this strategy would work on me? She didn't have the right to involve other people in an issue between the two of us. I felt like she was being disloyal. I felt betrayed. If you're gonna do that, Mom, then tell them all the fucked-up shit you did, right? Be fair about it. Tell them how we got to this space.

The Tipping Point

She didn't stop there. When going to family members didn't work, she took her case to random people in the community. She went to the same barbershop as I did, and would speak awful shit about me to the people there, changing their perceptions of me. She'd even talk about me to people I didn't even fuck with. As a result of this campaign to defame me, I started to distance myself from her. More and more, I stopped taking her phone calls. And when we did talk, we would argue. It was just too negative to be around her at the time.

The tipping point came with the situation with Foots, the kid I had taken under my wing when I was in my early twenties. When he broke into my house, my mother sent word to him that I knew he'd done it. That bothered me. Until she told him, he didn't know that I knew he'd done the break-in. I'd told her specifically not to say nothing to anyone 'cause I had a strategy for dealing with him. I felt she did it out of a need for revenge, and no other reason.

This created a bit of a situation for me. Not only did it deprive me of time to deal with the situation at hand, but it also put the wrong message out in the streets. How was Shiloh going to allow someone to break into his home? What was he going to do? Now anything that was done put me on blast. And if anything had happened to Foots, fingers would have pointed to me, regardless of who did it. Thanks a lot, Mom! Way to fucking go! I'm dealing with some serious bullshit and you take this opportunity to be vindictive? That's wack as hell.

I cut her off.

As if things weren't bad enough, she created a new situation. She had people coming up to me from all walks of life, questioning me about the Foots situation. I felt so double-crossed—one person stabbed me in the back, while the other betrayed the fuck out of me—that I decided to accept the fact that I would go through life on this planet without any communication whatsoever with my mother. She had no positive intention for me. She meant me no good. And at the rate we were going, what would her unpredictable nature do next? I wasn't going to give myself the opportunity to find out. So I cut her off. I blocked her phone from making calls to mine. If she was going to keep defaming me, it was going to happen. Fuck it! It wasn't nothing I could do. I accepted the fact that nothing was going to change.

We ended up having to get Ree counseling after what happened. She started having nightmares and was scared of being by herself. And just as her counseling sessions ended, I got a random phone call from Sheila one day. She and Ree were shopping.

"Baby, where are you?" said Sheila.

"Why? What's up?"

"That nigga, Foots, is right here in the store where we are."

"Word. What store you at?"

"I'm at the Family Dollar on Laburnum Avenue."

"Say no more, I'll be there in a second," I told her. I immediately stopped what I was doing and got my *Starsky & Hutch* on, racing to the Family Dollar.

By the time I pulled into the parking lot, Sheila was arguing with Foots, and she was doing most of the screaming. "We looked out for you and you do some grimy shit like that to us? We fed you, clothed you, spoiled yo' bitch ass, and you got the nerve to turn around and be a snake?"

I drove up to them. Foots had his brother with him, an older brother who'd spent a few years locked up. I had my gun on my lap. I looked at Sheila. I looked at Foots. I looked at Ree. I knew I couldn't let the heat of the moment make me do something in broad daylight that I'd regret forever. On impulse, I took the gun and tossed it under the seat, then whipped the car to the side.

I told Sheila to get Ree and back out of the way. "I'll handle it from here," I told her. When I said that, Foots hurried to his car, reached under the seat, and turned and faced me with his hand under his shirt as if he had a gun.

He looked at me and said, "What up, cuz?" I walked up to him and, without saying a word, started to beat the brakes off him in the middle of the parking lot in front of everybody. I didn't know if his brother was going to jump in or not, but luckily a crowd formed. Any thought of him joining in was squashed when someone from the neighborhood shouted, "Ain't gon' be bank out here, cuz. Let them niggas fight one on one! It's gon' be a fair fight, tho'!" After it was over, Foots quickly got in the car with his brother and left as I shouted to him, "Every time I see you, you catching this same ass whipping, Mr. You Ain't Gon' Catch Me!" I looked back at Sheila and told her to go home. Ree was crying.

Putting Up the Mic

When I got back to the house, I had a long talk with Ree and calmed her down. I told her that she had nothing to worry about and that Daddy would always be there to protect her. Some people said I shouldn't have beat his ass in front of her. I say it was therapeutic for her. After that day in the store parking lot, she didn't need counseling no more. *That was her last counseling session!* From that day on, the nightmares were over, and she was no longer scared. She knew her daddy had her. And she walked away with a very important life lesson about what happens where you're grimy to other people!

Due to a combination of things—the Foots thing happening, my streets chapter closing, and my resolve to sacrifice my dream for my family—I ended up putting up the mic. And yes, I miss it, sometimes greatly, but I haven't felt the motivation to either record or write music since. But even though I don't, I still consider myself an aficionado of the art form. I think the dues I paid earned me the right to think of myself as a connoisseur. Hip-hop was a chapter in my life that meant so much to me—and it still does. It's a huge part of what made me "me." I love you, hip-hop! And even though I don't actively practice you, I will forever carry you in my spirit.

20

AGES 21 TO 25: ONE OF THE LUCKY FEW WHO MADE IT OUT OF THE GAME

Y'all hustling tomorrow, I'm hustling like there's only one last second to this hustle ...
—P. Diddy, rapper, record producer, and entrepreneur

AS I STARTED making steady money from hustling, things really began to change. I suddenly had access to resources and options that I'd never had before. While I was gaining greater confidence and more security, I had to learn how to balance my temptations and impulses. Sheila was doing great in school, passing one class after another, one semester after another. Before long, she had her bachelor's degree.

I wanted her to keep going. "Let's take full advantage of our situation," I'd tell her. So she kept going and acquired her master's. I still wanted her to push harder. "Fuck it, get your PhD," I'd say, holding my hands up the way sports fans do when they're signaling a touchdown. "Why not?! Dr. Jones has a great ring to it." She argued with me about this. As a matter of fact, we spent many nights arguing about this one subject.

Buying Our First Home

After a while, I conceded. It wasn't my place to tell her to keep going to school. She was tired of it, and I couldn't blame her. She'd been going to school for most of her life. She wanted to take a break. She'd already enrolled in a postgraduate program and taken a couple of classes after receiving her master's when she decided to stop for a while. She wanted to work, so she got a position with a major insurance company that paid her about $50,000 a year. That was cool in the big picture because we needed some "justifiable" income for the household. Some legally verifiable income. Her job actually enabled us to make better moves in our life, including those that required credit, like eventually buying a home.

I never really had shit in my life up to this point. Then, all of a sudden, I had the ability to get what I wanted. Yeah, I went a little stupid. I was kind of excessive. And me being the extreme person I am by nature, I was almost like an unchecked child in certain ways. I had to learn to self-govern. I had to learn to discipline myself because I had no mentor, no guide to tell me what to do or what not to do. But part of this new experience with money I just had to get out of my system because I wasn't used to having it, so I kind of spoiled myself. And boy, did I spend money—a whole lot of it!

Let's Start with Clothes

I wasn't the most fashionable dude growing up, so naturally I started filling this void first after catching up on bills and saving money. I loved Timberland boots at the time, so what did I do? I bought a pair in every color. My favorites were the premium wheat Tims. Only problem with them was that they were a wheat-tan color. Easy to scratch up. I'd wear them for a couple of weeks and buy another pair as soon as they were scratched up. I'd give my old ones away to people in the neighborhood who needed shoes. They'd feel like I was giving them a brand new pair 'cause, to them, I was.

I bought jeans, shirts, and hats from the hot brand at the time. I believe back then it was Enyce, Parasuco, and Blac Label. At that time,

Gucci and Versace were still out of my league. I couldn't see myself paying $800 for a shirt! You crazy? I still worked hard for my money. You could catch me in an outfit that cost anywhere from $500 to $1,300 dollars from head to toe, including shoes and hat. But I'd be damned if you were going to catch me in a $5,000 outfit. Nope! I refused.

I controlled the clothes. The clothes never controlled me, let alone define me. That was my outlook. You should be able to throw on anything and, as long as it looks good on you, you straight. So even though I shopped at places like DTLR, I also shopped at Burlington Coat Factory. Clothes were clothes. If I wanted a brand-name pair of pants, I'd buy them. If I wanted an off-brand shirt, I'd buy it. Who cares? Even to this day, I'll rock off-brand shit like the world's top fashion designer made it. And that's me keeping it one hundred with you. It kills me how people are so caught up in brand names (what they'd wear and what they wouldn't) even when their cash ain't together.

Now Let's Talk Cars

We got a bullshit el cheapo whip shortly after I first started hustling. A Chevy Cavalier. One of the worst new cars I've ever owned. But I thought I was doing something at the time. A new car? Shit, that was an accomplishment. After I had the means, I copped my first real car.

Here's how it happened. I was at the corner store bodega one day talking to a friend, an Arab guy who owned the store. His family was known to sell cars. They all either owned convenience stores or were car salesmen. Anyway, his cousin came through and, while we were just chopping it up over conversation, the cousin said, "Man, I gotta dump this whip! Yo, Shi, you know anybody looking for a whip, dawg? I got some fly shit I'm willing to offer at a great deal."

The car, a BMW, was parked in front of the store. He tossed me the keys.

When I went outside, there it was: a black BMW 740iL. I hit the key. Boop boop! The doors unlocked. I got in and, *maaaan*, I tell you. That was the cleanest car I'd ever been in *in my life*. I drove it around the block and then I went back in and hollered at my Arab buddy and his cousin. I asked, "How much you want for it?"

"Yo, give me $19K," he said.

Shit: $19,000? That's way too high, Shiloh. But my impulses were speaking to me right then. I wanted this joint. Then I started rationalizing. *I work hard enough. Shit, I deserve to have something like this. Not to drive every day, of course, but when I want to ride out in style. Man, this is me right here!* Right then, I made up my mind that I was going to get this car.

"Homie, I got straight cash for you," I said. "You gotta give me a helluva better price than that, though. What about $12,500? All bills." We haggled and haggled until I said, "Look, highest I am going to go is $15K. And I'll bring that right now to you in a shoebox. You can count it out right here. But I can't go no higher."

He said, "You know what? I fucks with you, Shi-leezy. Go get it."

"Give me five minutes," I told him.

"Who Name You Putting This In?"

So I drove to my crib right around the corner, went to my stash, and counted out fifteen knots. I used to pre-count my money as I made it. I'd separate bills into $1,000 stacks (referred to as Gs) and then fold the bills and put a rubber band around them. I'd spread out the fives, tens, twenties, fifties, and hundreds to make the stacks similar in size. If not, I'd have some overly large wads and some super-skinny wads. I was OCD like that. One thing I did was keep my money neat. The ones? I'd just chuck them to the side like they were pennies. They were bullshit odds-and-ends store money.

Anyway, I quickly grabbed fifteen wads and got my gun. (Never trust anyone, remember?) Then I rode back to the store and made the purchase. He asked me, "Who name you putting this in?"

Shit, I hadn't thought about that. I couldn't put the car in my name. (How could I justify that?) I couldn't put it in Sheila's name. (Nope! Too close to home. That's too hot!) I couldn't come up with an answer quickly so I said, "Look, bro, you got you bread. Go 'head and drive the car home and I'll catch up with you tomorrow sometime and iron out all the details."

"Okay," he said. "You want your paper back, though? Until tomorrow?"

"I'm Gucci," I said. "I trust you." Then I looked him dead in the eye and gave him a look that said, "I know you ain't gon' fuck me. We good!" Plus, I knew exactly where to find him.

That night, I tried to figure out whose name I was going to register the car in. It had to be someone I trusted. I couldn't go to just anybody because I'd be revealing too much about myself. *You know what?* I thought. *Let me holla at Bill Jones.* I called him up and explained the situation.

Before I could finish, he said, "Sure, I got you."

Next day, Bill met me at the car lot and we completed the transaction. It was done! I officially owned a BMW. I took the car home and realized I couldn't park it in front of my house. So I parked it around the corner in front of some random house. That became my official parking spot from that point on.

Never Shit Where You Eat

I didn't tell Sheila about the car until a few days later. One night, we at home watching TV and I said, "C'mon, ride to the store with me." When she got outside, I informed her that I parked the car around the corner.

"Why would you do that?" she asked.

"Why you asking me all these questions?" I answered. As we approached the car, I pulled the key out of my pocket and hit the unlock button. Boop boop! She didn't pay any attention. I had to do it again before she looked over and I stopped. When I told her that this was our new car, she didn't believe me. We had to actually drive to the store for her to fully accept the idea that this was our shit. In that moment, I knew she was proud of me. And it felt damn good to make her proud.

Now here goes the irony: I didn't really get to drive the car as I'd planned. That was mainly because the only time I could drive it was when I was away from my neighborhood. I couldn't flash in the district that I hustled in. That was stupid. Hustle rule number one: Never shit where you eat. Sheila actually drove the car more than I did. When I bought the vehicle, there were 68,000 miles on it. When I sold it several years later, it was barely touching 75,000 miles. So, needless to say, I never drove my money's worth out of the car.

After clothes and cars came all the other stuff. I bought everything I needed for recording music. I bought several mics, high-end wires, high-quality monitor speakers, record players, and a tricked-out computer. I also bought every accessory I needed for producing and mixing music, from a Korg Triton synthesizer to an MPC2000 64-track sampler-sequencer workstation.

Next came the video games. I loved playing them as a hobby. Plus, they got my creative juices going for some reason. So what did I do? I went out to the game store and bought every game I thought I'd enjoy. Then I bought all of the top game systems.

Starting to Attract Unwanted Attention

I spent because I knew that I was consistently making money every month, like clockwork. Before long, I started to attract unwanted attention. As much as I thought I was keeping a low profile, people paid attention, especially my nosy-ass neighbors. Dude, I would come out of the house and these fuckers would be like, "I wonder what new he got on today?" "There go the superstar!" and "Bro, let me borrow a couple of dollars, I know you got it."

Then the dudes I didn't want to fuck with started approaching me. They would ask me about working with them and I'd say, "Nah, bro, I don't be fucking around, man."

"C'mon, Shiloh. Man, fuck with me, bro. I know you got the smoke. Everybody know you got it, cuz. And I supposed to be your boy. Why you doing me like that?"

"I don't know who the fuck everybody is, but they lying to you, homie," I'd tell them. "If I had it, I'd fuck with you. I can't sell you what I don't got, bro."

This happened more and more. I couldn't allow this problem to get worse. It just felt like my environment was getting smaller and smaller.

My area of town was getting way too claustrophobic for me. I was becoming too well known. It was getting way too hard to be invisible (like I needed to be sometimes). I had to do something about it, and there was only one option: move!

Neighbors with Big Mouths

Sheila and I started looking for a place. We eventually decided we'd get a house. I was smart enough that I never bought real assets with drug money—only bullshit. However, there were some pros and cons to that. Part of me wishes that I had been properly mentored, so I would have found a way to actually invest in some assets. But at that time, I was working with the knowledge and understanding that that's not what you do. You stay untraceable.

So I explained to Sheila that she would have to get the house in her name with money from her job. I would get everything we needed for the house with my money. She understood. We ended up buying a house in Northside. We got the fuck outta Church Hill, and I retreated to my new secret location. It was time for me to move away from Church Hill anyway. I'd outgrown it. If I'd stayed there another six months, I'm pretty sure I wouldn't have lasted long because I'd have been arrested.

See, I wasn't scared of my neighbors doing larceny to me. I was scared because people have big mouths, especially them! I was worried about the who-and-what information they divulged about me to God-knows-who. That's where it got dangerous. And I would have been at the mercy of the street. Church Hill was full of snitches. The streets birthed them easily and abundantly because most dudes were scared to do the time for the crime they committed when they eventually got caught.

They just needed a little bit of dirt on somebody and they'd tell on you like that, with no hesitation or remorse. That's the unfair thing about the game and what makes the game so volatile. This is why I highly recommend you choose another lane. The odds are never in your favor. Anybody can snitch on you. No matter how much you do things right, how you treat people, how careful you are, how small a circle you keep, or how out of sight you stay, it just takes one person to have a hunch or to know somebody who knows somebody who deals with you and, poof, you're gone! Just like that.

Who's Gonna Wait for You? Nobody

Depending on the level of drugs you fucked with, you were talking spending months to years of your life locked up. And the sad reality was, who was going to wait for you? Nobody. Life would go on, and people just go on with it. Your connects would move on. Everyone would move on: your friends, your mate, even your kids. But your kids would never understand why you were gone. They'd just see their immediate reality: the fact that you weren't there because you were in jail! (Try convincing them that you did it all for them. See if that works for you after a ten-year bid. See if your wife waits for you. See if your connect holds onto that package for you. See if your girl holds on to the money you stashed in shoeboxes in your closet just five years after you're gone.)

This is what ran through my mind! This is what the future looked like for me if I kept continuing down this path. And it was painful when I journeyed down this train of thought. But this was the reality of the streets. TV glamorizes the game and calls it "the trap." But there's a reason why they call it "the trap": 'cause it's a fucking trap! I had to reground and tell myself, *Don't ever get this fucked up! Don't get comfortable thinking this life will last forever! Don't get content and start slipping! You better wise the fuck up. Your family is on the line!*

Me (left), Kai (middle), and Ree (right) as a teenager.

Paranoia: A Side Effect of Hustling

This is when the seeds of paranoia started to germinate in me. Trust and believe me when I tell you this: paranoia is a side effect of the hustling game. You can ask any hustler on this planet who's been in the game long enough and they'll tell you that's the realest shit I ever wrote on these pages. Stay in the game long enough and you'll distrust anything and everything. You'll start to believe that anybody can turn on you. I mean, you see it happen to other people every day: best friends, your girlfriend, jealous niggas, snakes. I realized I had to come up with a new strategy and change up the way I moved.

Number one, I told myself, *I would have to be ten times more careful.* I'd have to take more preventative measures and stay aware. That meant using disguises and uniforms when moving work. It also meant being smarter about the people I dealt with (my excellent judgment of character came into play here) and watching how I moved. I'd have to stay away from giving the impression that I had money.

I'd meet people at clubs and bars with loud music to talk business in order to protect myself against potential "wires." I'd leave my main phone at home in case it was tracked. As a matter of fact, I'd never talk business on my phone and I'd never give my real number out. I would buy temp cells ("burnouts," we called them) and talk until they ran out of minutes before buying new ones. Basically, if I didn't call you, you had no real way to get in touch with me after I disposed of the burnout phone. This made it easier to disassociate myself from people who were getting too hot and becoming bad for business.

Code Words and Disguises

I could never be too careful. For example, I developed a code system that I used when I talked to my customers—a million codes—so an outsider could never understand what we were talking about. Say I normally met one of them at a food spot. I'd call them, start a general conversation, and then eventually mention how hungry I was. We'd use this premise to coordinate both quantity of work and meeting time. Here's how it went:

Me: "What's up, homie?" (Translation: "You good?")

Him: "Shit. Been in the house all day. Ain't eat nothing. I'm starving." (Translation: "What up, bro? Need some work.")

Me: "Yo, I was thinking the same thing myself. What time you trying to get something to eat?" (Translation: "That's cool. How much?")

Him: "I don't know, I'll probably leave in about ten minutes or so." (Translation: "10 pounds.")

Me: "Okay, wait for me. I'll probably be about thirty minutes. (Translation: "Meet you at the same spot as last time in thirty minutes exactly.")

The code language was just one of my preventative measures. I also rented rooms, apartments, or houses for storing work but only for six months at a time. Secret stash spots. The limits I would go to were endless because I knew what separated the stupid from the smart, the unlucky from the lucky: it was the constant obsession with staying ten steps ahead—twenty if possible. You had to be willing to go the extra mile. One thing I learned is that there's no such thing as being too careful. Matter of fact, the opposite is true in that world. The one time you slip is the one time you get "got," and that means being caught, robbed, or murdered. I spent extra money on infrastructure costs in an effort to protect myself and mitigate risks.

When it came to disguises, I'd go to Lowe's and buy construction accessories like a hardhat and safety vest and then add dusty jeans to make my runs. I'd carry around a big cooler that looked like it was full of lunch, only it was full of work. I knew some people who worked at fast-food joints, so I'd buy their uniforms from them and put the work inside delivery bags like I was delivering an order. Yes! My job was to be incognito—a master of disguises—and I played it well.

A Recession in the Streets

Then it happened: the first drought I ever experienced. Work just stopped coming through. My connect told me that his connect was dry. WTF! I always had smoke. Even when everybody else was dry, I kept it. That was one of the ways I acquired new customers. Business 104: If you consistently keep enough supply to meet demand, then you'll keep your own clients, as well as steal them from the competition. Anyway, the drought lasted for almost three months straight. Luckily, I had money saved up.

I promise you, this drought in particular made a lot of people fall off. They were forced to spend their re-up money. It's similar to a recession in the streets. Even when I got work in after the drought was over, I had to front a lot of work out to help my main buyers get back on their feet. This is when I learned about contingency planning because there is never a sign that a drought is coming; it just comes. And even though I successfully recovered, it drove the point home that I should always save for a rainy day. Even squirrels put nuts away for the winter. This is another principle that lived with me and that I was able to carry into the corporate world.

A Change in the Market

What I didn't know was that a transition was happening in those three months. When smoke came back around, it was no longer regular weed. The market had changed. A new type of weed had hit the scene. It was called "lob" and was a mid-grade weed. A stronger weed than before and more expensive. Everybody had to adjust to this shift. And the transition was a little rough for most. Now, instead of getting $600 per pound, I was getting $1,000 to $1,200. The market price for this was up to $1,500 for retail per pound. I still got my batches of fifty, but now it was costing $50,000 to $60,000 for my inventory rather than $30,000.

Every industry has unexpected market shifts. You must make the proper adjustments if you want to survive.

I decided I'd keep my net profit goals the same at approximately $150 per pound. That way, I could still undercut the market and allow my middleman customers to make their money and have a place in the market. I had a few clients buying fifty straight up, in which case I lowered my price point because it was bulk. In those cases, I aimed to make a net of $75 to $100 per pound or, in rare cases, $50 per pound. The way I saw it, it was still a $2,500 profit for an hour max of my time. To me, it was still a phenomenal profit margin for the time I invested. I got to the point where it would take me no more than two days to move an entire batch. I would still sell half and front half and then I would chill for the rest of the week while I waited for my money to return. From a business angle, not too bad. Once I streamlined my processes, I had my thing down to a science.

Dealing with the Bullshit

In any industry, any business, any venture, you will take losses. That's just a part of the game. It was no different for me back then. I had to find my resolve with the setbacks, 'cause I hated to take losses. Mine never came from being stuck up. Mine came from a small percentage of the people I fronted work to. In this game, you distrust before you trust, so I never believed the excuses when somebody took a loss with my shit. I always had the money to cover the loss, though, because remember the golden rule: never front work out that you can't cover with your personal money. I handled some situations differently than others, depending on the track record of the people I was dealing with. For the majority, I had a strict rule: if you cross me, I cut you off! You can't default on a loan with the bank and expect it to give you more money, can you? Hells no. So, consider me the bank. It's going to hurt you more than me if I cut you off. I can easily recover, but you will have burnt a valuable bridge.

Back then, I always applied this analogy: why try to fuck me over for one slice of pizza when you can have an infinite number of pies if you do clean business with me? The immediate greed is what fucked people up with their connects. Or them trying to get over. That's why a legitimate connect was priceless. It was golden. Sometimes, depending on the extent of the work that was fucked up, I would take more drastic measures. I remember one time when my supposed homie had a dude who wanted 10 pounds. I gave him the work and told him to bring back the money the next day. When the next day came, he called and said, "Man, I gotta holla at you."

"What's up?" I said. "Holla at me."

"I can't talk over the phone," he said. I knew what that meant. Here comes the bullshit. So we met in person. He told me the dude he'd sold to had robbed him. (*Oh yeah?* I thought.) Right then and there, I walked him outside and made him sign the title of his tricked-out car to me. You damn skippy I did! And here's the thing: his car was worth more than the work.

I told him, "I'll give you a week to get my muthafucking money and you can get your car back. By week's end, if you don't have my money, this car is officially mine." He couldn't make the quota, so I absorbed his collateral. Fuck him! You shouldn't have grabbed my work if you didn't trust *your* man! That's your boy. You're grown enough to know what it means to vouch for a person, so that falls on you! Never gamble with someone else's work or their money, for that matter. Or if it was an actual setup, you're not just gonna make some quick, easy money off me. A week later, I changed my number and never talked to him again. I cut him slam the fuck off.

Paranoia Starting to Escalate

As time went on, my paranoia grew—and badly. A few events escalated it to new levels.

Event One

A customer came to get some work from me. I gave him 3 pounds. He was going to take it to Chesterfield to someone he regularly dealt with. He would usually make the run, bring me the money right after he finished, and go on his way. This time, he didn't come back. I called him several hours later. No answer. This was weird. We'd known each other for a few years. He was kind of close to me, like I knew where he lived, he knew where I lived.

A week later, he showed up, telling me that he'd been set up. His customer had done a sting on him and the police had locked him up. He came and brought me my money anyway as he was telling me this. Fuck! Were they watching him now? Did they follow him to my crib? Did he snitch on me? Why was he out so fast? My thoughts were racing. He swore that he didn't snitch and wouldn't ever snitch on anyone. He did admit that they pressed him and tried to get him to snitch. I switched up my whole situation. I changed stash spots, switched phones—the regular damage control shit. I took all the cash I had in my house to my mom's house and put it in the attic. (Paranoia level: 8.)

Event Two

My main connect called me on the phone I used to keep just for him and told me a new shipment was in. He wanted to drop it to me the next day. I did my regular routine. I gathered my money, called my folks, and told them to expect me to holla at them the next day and to be ready. (As soon as a shipment dropped, I liked to move it immediately.) The next day, I didn't get a call from him. I didn't stress it, thinking I'd give him another day before reaching out. I still didn't hear from him the next day. My people started calling me, asking when they were supposed to move.

When I tried him, my call went straight to voicemail. Tried a few times the next day. Voicemail.

A week later, I saw him on the news! He'd gotten caught with over 1,000 pounds. WTF! The feds had gotten him. You don't play with the feds. I'm thinking, *We all going to jail!* Was he going to fold? Was he going to snitch? Or maybe they'd been watching him all along. If so, they could have been watching all of us!

I was on my way home a week after that. As I turned the corner to my street, I saw what had to be about twenty unmarked vehicles on my block. Cops were everywhere with ATF jackets and vests on. I immediately got nervous. This was it! In a moment of panic, I drove right past my house. My homegirl Keisha was on the porch with Sheila. I didn't even look over, but I heard, "There go Shi right there," loud as fuck from Keisha's mouth. "Aye, Shi!" she shouted as I just kept going down the street.

Sheila called me two minutes later and said, "Why you ignore us?"

I said, "The fuck is going on at the house?"

She started laughing. "Nigga, these police ain't here for you, dumbass! The boys across the street apparently stole a string of cars and are caught up with some other shit. Boy, bring yo' ass home!" (Paranoia level: 9.)

Event Three

I laid low for a few months after that. Then I got a new connect and started working again. My stepbrother knew a guy who bought between 8 and 15 pounds from him at a time. Of course, my stepbrother would get the work from me, sell it to him, and bring the money back to me and I'd give him his cut. So normal routine run, he makes the sell and comes back. The next day, when he was driving home, the police stopped him and "randomly" searched his car. They told my stepbrother that this was just a routine training exercise and thanked him for cooperating. Halfway through the search, the officers got mad because they couldn't find anything in his car. They made a big ordeal, held him for a few, and then let him go.

The very next day, undercover cops showed up at his house and questioned him about the guy he sold the work to. They informed him that they'd locked the guy up and had my stepbrother's visit to his house on camera. They asked to search the house. My stepbrother denied the search. They told him that they knew he was involved and their plan was to get him indicted once the boy snitched. (Paranoia level: 10.)

> **BITCH NIGGAS SNITCHING,**
> BRINGING COPPERS TO YOUR HOME FRONT,
> **STAY PARANOID,** I CAN'T EVEN ENJOY MY OWN BLUNTS,
> DON'T CALL ME TALKIN' 'BOUT SHIT, THEY **TAPPING TELEPHONES UP,**
> SPYING ON NIGGAS, IN UNDERCOVER TELEPHONE TRUCKS.
>
> —EXCERPT FROM HIP-HOP SONG BY SHILOH JONES

NIGHTMARES ABOUT THE FEDS

I'd reached the highest level of paranoia my system could handle. I started having nightmares about the feds coming to lock me up in front of my kids, my family. For months now, I'd been fighting off visions of me getting sentenced to lengthy jail time. How could my kids ever forgive me? They wouldn't. They wouldn't understand this. And I'd end up another statistic, a sad story of another hustler being hauled off to prison while the world—including his kids—moved on.

By the time I got out, they would probably look down on me, be ashamed of me. But I did all of this to provide a better quality of life for them, to shield them from all the struggles that I went through. That was my promise to both of them when they were born. By any means! By any means? Be careful what you wish for. I had this secret life that I'd been hiding from them. Was this the way they were going to find out? By me getting locked up?

Time to Get the Fuck Out

I just knew I was being watched. I started to see telephone trucks randomly parked in my neighborhood. They'd sit there for days. I would see people parked down the street, sitting in cars and systematically watching my block for hours at a time every day. Who the fuck else were they watching but me? I assumed my phone was tapped and even tracked, for that matter. What the hell was I supposed to do now? I pulled out all my tricks, all my techniques. I couldn't play the game any smarter than I had been.

I realized that I couldn't hustle again from that day forward. My time was up. It was expired. I was too smart to miss the signs. I truly felt that if I touched one more grain of work, I was doomed. But shit! What was I going to do now for money? For survival? How was I going to feed and sustain my family when my savings ran out? (*You better hope all those nuts you put away will pay off, Shiloh.*) I was stressed out. I didn't have any answers. I needed to get away and clear my head.

21

AGE 25: WE'VE ALL GOT DEMONS

THROUGHOUT THIS TIME, my mother and I stayed estranged. It hurt, but I thought I had too much going on to deal with her bullshit until, one day, I realized that the situation was vastly bigger than me and would work against me no matter what I did. As I mentioned earlier, my mother's mother had mental health issues. And it became apparent to me that my mother did, too. She was dealing with serious depression and bipolar disorder.

I'd thought she was behaving irrationally when she was actually displaying symptoms of mental health issues. And as anyone who's ever dealt with someone with depression knows, the things they desire are only Band-Aids on a wound that will forever bleed until the true problem is addressed. For example, this explained why she wanted me to heap gifts on her. It was her attempt to fill a bottomless hole. And no matter how I responded, no amount of giving would have filled it. It would have never been enough. It's like an itch you can't scratch.

THE MISERY-LOVES-COMPANY THING

Depression often carries the whole misery-loves-company thing with it. That was the reason for the constant arguing with my mother. It was also the reason why, when she felt wronged by me, she would take it to everyone in the world because she literally wanted everyone else to "feel" her pain the way she felt it. Her depression also kept her from accepting the true reality of our past because it was too much for her to bear. To face the demons we had between us would've led to tremendous guilt, so her mind built a delusional reality to protect itself.

The even deeper thing with depression? Until the individual accepts that their behavior is the result of impaired mental health, you can't make any headway with them. They'll just continue to warp and distort reality so that they can digest it the way they want to, even if their version is a million miles from the actual truth. With what I now know about mental health, I would do things a lot differently. I would've had better tools to help me deal with my mother more skillfully. But back then, I didn't, so I reacted the best way I knew how. Little did I know then, but this would later lead to my passion to make such an impact in the world of mental health.

What happened was that we stopped speaking for a while. Then, after I'd dealt with my anger, I forgave my mother. I still kept a cautionary distance between us to protect myself, though. So we only spoke once or twice a week, some hi-and-bye shit. But every time we talked, I made sure to tell her that I loved her. It was better to leave the past in the past—for her and for me. We stayed in this state for a few years until …

"I Can't Live Like This. I Can't."

One day, my sister called me and asked, "Have you heard from Ma? I haven't heard from her in a couple of days, and I usually talk to her at least once a day."

"Nope," I said.

"This is strange," Brandi said.

"Just go by her house," I told her.

"I did, and nobody's seen her," she said. "I'm starting to get worried."

I didn't think too much of it. My mom was probably with one of her friends or something. Or maybe my sister was bugging. The next day, I checked in with Brandi to see if she'd heard from Mom. She hadn't. Then the next day, I started to get worried myself. Had she been in an accident? I called her phone a few times and couldn't get through. I suggested that Brandi put out a missing persons report, since we were a few days in at this point. The next day, my sister called me, crying. "Shiloh, they found Mommy."

"What do you mean 'found'?" I asked. "What happened?"

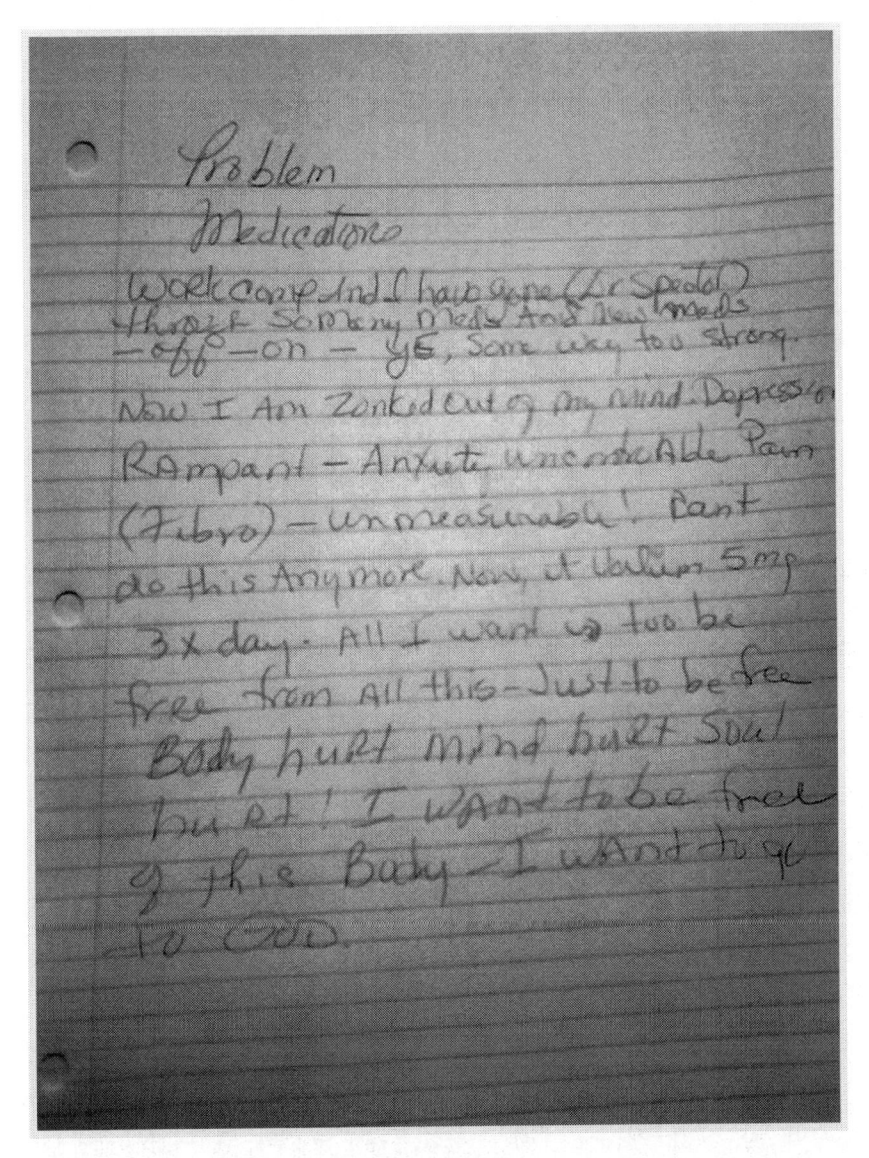

> Problem
> Medications
> Work comp. And I have some (Dr. Speedol) throat so many meds And new meds — off — on — yes, some way too strong. Now I Am Zonked out of my mind. Depression Rampant — Anxiety uncontrollable Pain (Fibro) — unmeasurable! Can't do this anymore. Now it Valium 5mg 3x day. All I want is too be free from All this — Just to be free. Body hurt mind hurt Soul hurt! I want to be free of this Baby — I want to go to God.

My mom's suicide letter.

The police had found her in a room at the Wyndham Hotel in the Short Pump area of town. She had checked herself in, stayed for a few days, written a suicide letter, and then ingested an entire bottle of pills. Housekeeping eventually found her. She'd been in that room for days, lying in one spot, some body parts blue. When the paramedics arrived, they could barely detect life. She was in a coma. If the housekeeper hadn't come along when she did, my mom wouldn't have even had the little life that they detected. The paramedics rushed her to Henrico Doctors' Hospital, along with several suicide notes she'd written.

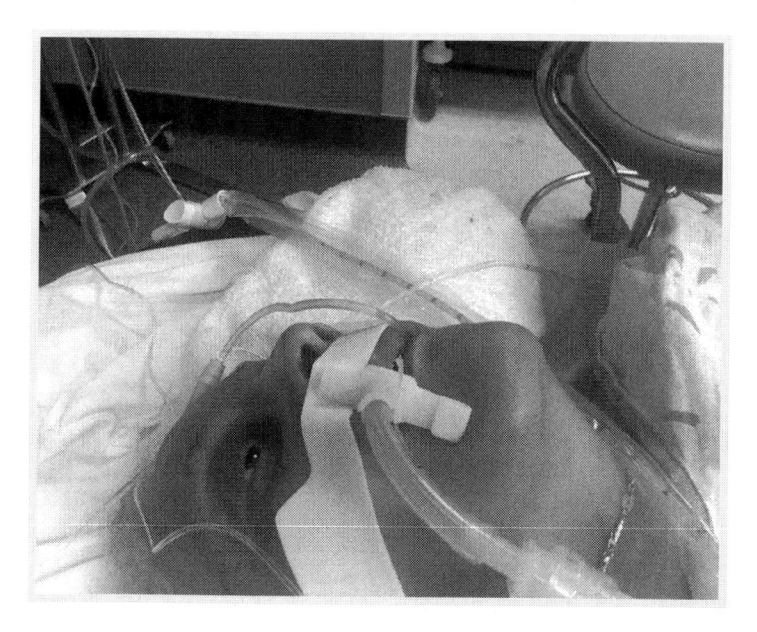

My mom in the hospital.

The first note wasn't written to anybody in particular. It painted a picture of her struggle, including her depression, her extreme anxiety, the pain of fibromyalgia, and the lifeless feeling her medications gave her. It read, "Body hurt, mind hurt, soul hurt. I want to be free of this body. I want to go to God."

The second note was to Ross, her girlfriend at the time. "I can't live like this," she wrote. "I can't. I love you, but I can't do this. I am so very sorry."

The third note detailed a credit union account, which she had left to my sister. She also wanted Brandi to have her car and the things in her apartment.

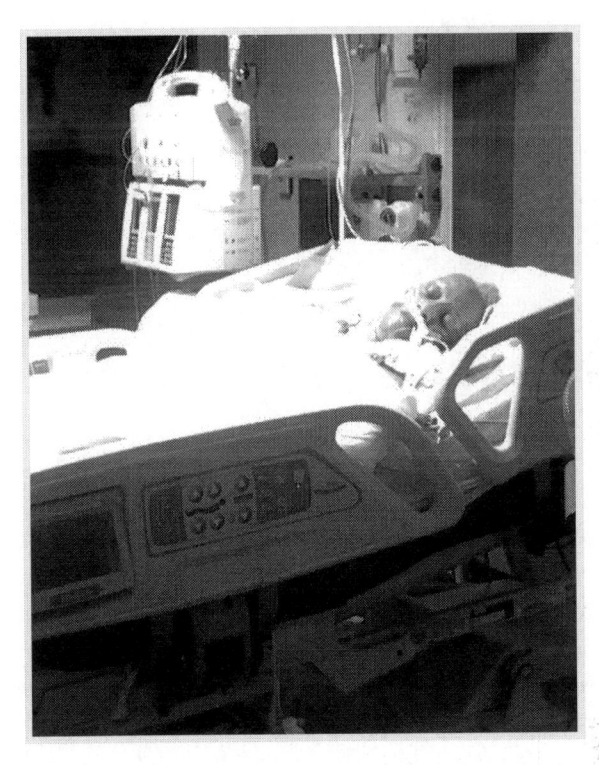

This image really messed me up. It felt surreal.

"Can't Tell You What I Lost When I Lost You"

The fourth note was to me. This is what it said: "Shiloh, can't tell you what I lost when I lost you—unspeakable. Take it to my grave! Can't live life like this. Head all messed up. Can't focus. No purpose. Too messed up to have a purpose. No hope—just existing. Can't do it no more. Fibro is a big part of it. Memory going—gone. No interest in life. Afraid! Hate it!! Not your fault! I love you, but I don't want to be here anymore!!"

Hard to read, right? When I got to the hospital, what I saw was even worse.

My mother was on life support. Her eyes were wide open, she had tubes coming out of her mouth, and she wasn't present at all. She looked dead. All I could feel was the pain that she had felt all through her years growing up. The trials, tribulations, and struggles she'd been through. How hard life had beaten her up. How heavy her depression must've been. I felt extreme sorrow for her. Extreme sorrow for myself for not really getting it right with her before now.

This was one of the saddest moments of my life. I thought about how petty everything we'd gone through was. How precious life is. I talked to my mother and apologized for the life we had, the life she had, even though she didn't hear me. I told her that I loved her and kissed her on the forehead. If only I could talk to her one more time. See her smile just once. Rewind time. If only I'd picked up the phone when she'd called me. If only I could take those years back when I wasn't speaking to her. If only …

I left the hospital. It killed me to see her like that. I couldn't eat. I couldn't think. My head was cloudy, and everything felt surreal. At night I could barely sleep, and every morning I'd wake up hours before my normal waking time. I couldn't stop thinking about her. And all I could think was that she was about to die any day now. Sheila tried to comfort me, but it didn't work. I didn't want to be around her. I didn't want to be around my kids. But I didn't want to be alone.

It was strange and awful, all at the same time. When I'm really stressed out, my go-to has always been work. So I dove into work so hard that it was all I did. Losing my parent was something I didn't want to accept. I just wasn't ready.

I Decided to Leave It in His Hands

Mom stayed on life support for a week straight before the doctors asked for a conference with me. I knew what this meant. When we met, they told me that a decision had to be made soon about whether or not to take her off life support. The doctor then closed the door, leaned in, and said, "Your mother has been dealing with mental health issues all her life. She attempted this twice before, when she was younger. I saw the suicide letter. Maybe, just maybe, we are giving her what she wants if we take her off life support and let her go. She has had a very rough life. And this is what she wanted."

What he said made sense. What if we did keep her on life support for a couple of months and she came back "to" and cussed me slam the fuck out for bringing her back? This was her wish. Nobody knew the level of pain she was going through on a daily basis. I read her suicide letter again. Then I called the doctor back in and said, "Doc, give me one day to make up my mind! I want to make sure that this is what I want to do." He agreed and set another meeting up for the next day at 5 p.m. I went home that night and talked to God. In that talk, I found my resolve. I came to the conclusion that I would leave this in His hands.

The next day at 5 p.m., I went to the hospital. I gave the doctors my consent. I said some words from the heart to my mom, and then they turned off the life support machine. They explained that she might keep breathing for a few minutes, hours, or days, depending on her physical condition. She kept breathing, as they had said she would.

Then the next day, I went to check on her, and the most miraculous thing happened. She was still not conscious, but she was mumbling and making sounds. I started to talk to her and, seconds later, a mumble of sounds came back to me. A day later, her arms and head started twitching. Her mumbling turned into incoherent sentences. A day after that, she opened her eyes and started talking. My father was with me. She looked up and said, "Is that Bill Jones's voice I hear? Wait a minute, nigga, you in heaven, too?" We all started laughing. Laughing with joy. She had fully come "to." She started joking, "Ya mufuckas don't look like angels to me. Where the hell am I at? And how in the world did I get here?"

Then, as her memory kicked in, she immediately recalled the suicide event up until the moment she took her pills. She said everything went blank after that. She saw me and said, "Shiloh, it means so much to me that you're here! I couldn't ask God for anything more! I'm so sorry!"

We talked, and I made a promise to her. I told her that, no matter how long we lived, from this moment forward, we would never argue about money again. And I would make sure that I spoke to her every single day. I promised that our relationship would be as good as we could possibly make it, starting right then.

"But you have to promise me one thing," I said.

"What's that, son?"

"That we will address your mental health issues more aggressively."

"I will do whatever it takes to fix this, and fix us, and not live life like this anymore," she told me.

God puts us here for a reason, and my mother's time wasn't up yet. We forced the hospital to deal with her mental health issues. The doctors moved her from one hospital to the next, trying to put Band-Aids on the problem. She ended up at Piedmont Geriatric Hospital in Burkeville, about ninety minutes west of Richmond. And I want to express this clearly: the people there were the *only* ones who took the time to tend to her properly and to find the right cocktail of medications for treating her mental health disorders.

The problem for my mom—and many people who suffer from mental health disorders—was the fact that she couldn't get "focused" treatment, as doctors just prescribe without truly monitoring a patient's condition. There is no one-size-fits-all solution when it comes to mental health. Each approach must be person-centered, with the proper amount of individualized treatment and close medication monitoring to help them properly cope in the healthiest way possible. You have to find the right mix of medicines that best respond to each individual's condition. And they did that successfully at Piedmont, without trying to rush her out of the hospital.

A New Person

She came home a new person. Totally balanced. For the first time ever, she was finally ahead of her mental health. And she was genuinely happy! Instead of seeing all the darkness in life, now she could see the smallest beauty in the simplest of things. I stayed by her side through the whole process and watched the transformation unfold with my own eyes.

Today, my relationship with my mother is more beautiful than I ever imagined it being. Yes, I do shower her with gifts. And, yes, I give her money any time she asks me for it. And I *want* to. She's my mom. And you only get one of those. She had to grow, just like I had to grow.

She just had a different set of challenges that she had to work through and address.

She is a beautiful person today—and I can confidently say this—inside and out! That woman can call me for anything and I'll say "yes" before she can get the question out of her mouth. She is also 100 percent drug-free and has been that way for years. You go, my beautiful queen!!

22

Ages 25 to 38: God Works in Mysterious Ways!

> I was raised in the gutter but,
> Saved in that gutter stuff,
> Didn't pay my mother much, never really gave a fuck,
> Off and on praying but,
> Never really made it much ...
> I think it's 'bout time Shiloh push the wager up!
>
> — *Excerpt from hip-hop song by Shiloh Jones*

ONE OF THE beautiful things about life? You never know what the universe has in store for you. By now, I'd gotten out of the business because I knew my time was up. But what the hell was gonna happen now? After gathering my thoughts, I started to work on a strategy. Math board: totaling all the money I'd made, spread out among all the places I kept it, I had enough to survive for three years. I knew this safety net was large enough to keep me out of panic mode. I had time to think. Time to survive without making any rash decisions.

A Whole New Direction

I found out about a life coaching/counseling job from one of my friends at the time. He explained the details of the job to me and I was interested.

It involved helping impoverished inner-city kids with severe behavioral problems. Now this was something I could do and have a passion for! After all, I'd been one of those kids myself. My boy told me that he could set up an interview with the company for me ASAP. I told him no, that I wanted him to give me some time. See, as an independent self-learner, I wanted to explore as much as I could about that industry. So I read every book I could get my hands on. I went on the internet and found clinical case studies, researched articles—whatever I could find.

After about six months, I felt I was ready for an interview. When I had it, I killed it! The director thought I'd be extremely valuable to the company and wanted me to start right away. He was impressed with everything I'd learned on my own about the field of mental health counseling. He liked my outlook and the fact that I had a relatable street side to me, since the work involved building a rapport with clients, including lots of kids from the projects. I started at $18 per hour. In three months, I got a raise to $20 per hour. I was naturally gifted at the job and fit in perfectly. I opened a bank account and deposited every check I made into it. I didn't spend one dollar. I just lived off my old hustle money until it ran out. Just a few years later, I had close to $90,000 in my bank account from my paychecks.

I decided to take the money I had saved and open my own life coaching/counseling firm. I studied the business. I researched the hierarchical structure that needed to be in place from a clinical perspective versus the business verticals versus the measures I needed to take to survive in that industry. I built a blueprint for myself to follow. I became an obsessed student of the game.

Welcome to the World of Business

As I worked to build my new business, something rapidly became clear to me: only when I began focusing on the future could I start building for the future and seeing my life in the future. I'd learned much about business up to this point, but I knew I needed to know more. As I've mentioned, you have to be willing to learn if your desire is to survive and grow. So I did just that. I kicked up my research. I examined business case studies. I invested in myself and signed up for every business seminar I could find. I took free business classes online. I went to my local community college and paid for business and management classes. I wasn't concerned about stacking up degrees; I was concerned about the immediate, relevant coursework that would help me get where I wanted to go.

I became an avid reader of anything pertaining to business. I subscribed to business magazines. I started to look at every establishment I went into differently. I would analyze the businesses I patronized to see how they ticked, like a watchmaker would do with an unfamiliar wristwatch. I studied companies in my immediate environment, noting how they were structurally organized, how they profited, how they stood resilient in the market, and how they advertised. I became a connoisseur of the business world. This became my new hobby, my new obsession.

One Step Forward, One Step Back

Eventually, I knew I was ready. So I submitted all the documentation required by local government entities to officially start my life coaching/counseling business. I was pumped up and ready to take on the world, but there was one problem: there was a two-year waiting list to get the city, state, and federal licenses I needed to own the type of mental health practice I wanted to in Virginia at that time! Fuck!

I had jumped the gun and already rented office space for my agency, not anticipating that there would be a waiting list. So what was I going to do now with this fresh new office and no business?

When you move toward the universe, the universe moves toward you!

Time for Plan B

For a couple of years, my father and stepbrother had been working with a company as independent contractors, pushing residential alarm systems. My father would sell them, and my brother would install them. They made decent money but wanted to get out of residential sales for a lot of reasons. The biggest was chargebacks, which were a major hassle and expense for their business.

Here's how chargebacks worked: when a residential client purchased an alarm system, they had to sign a three-year service contract. Police/fire monitoring was part of that service. If the client defaulted on their monitoring bill within the first year of service, the alarm system parent company charged the money back to the contractor—in this case, my pops and brother. Companies like theirs can write thousands of deals during the course of their time in business. A significant portion of those thousands result in chargebacks, which are beyond a contractor's control but still seriously impact their income. This was tough for companies like theirs, but it was the way the industry was structured.

My pops and brother decided that commercial clients, with bigger jobs and bigger profits, were the way to go. The problem was that they lacked the proper capital and financial management skills to become an official corporate structure. So they came to me. I had both the capital and the financial skills. Plus, I had an office that I could make our headquarters. I wasn't doing shit with it and was forced to pay rent on it, so why not?

They pitched, I accepted, they made me an equal partner, and we officially shook hands. We got incorporated and obtained all the necessary business licenses. Then we got a contractor's license, Class A, doing low-voltage electrical installation with a concentration in installing commercial security alarm systems. Now we were cooking with gas! We defined roles. Angelo would handle operations, my father would handle sales, and I would handle back-office functions like finance and payroll. We accepted our new roles and immediately went to work.

We started in July 2006. By the time December 31 came around, we'd grossed over $675,000! Not bad for our first six months in business! In fact, it was excellent.

The next year, we hustled hard, experienced 50 percent growth, and made $1.2 million. The following year, in 2008, I finally got licensed with all the necessary government entities for my counseling agency. I made about $30,000 through my counseling business, and our construction business grossed another $1.1 million.

Eating, Shitting, Sleeping, and Breathing Business

Here's the way people think about security: when everything is good, economically speaking, people want to protect their shit. But when things go bad, people *really* want to protect their shit. They want more high-level security options. That's why we diversified our company's skill set when the 2008 recession hit. We added camera installation, fire alarm systems, and electronic and biometric access control to our services. I rapidly grew my counseling agency at the same time, grossing over $450,000 the next year, in 2009. That was 1500 percent growth just my second year in business!

Sooo, how did I build the business so rapidly? Remember, I didn't take a paycheck for nearly three years. Well, I sacrificed. Since I had already learned sacrifice from the street, I was able to put this principle to work here. I equated it to fasting. The streets actually made me good at this. I didn't take any money from the business to reward myself or take care of myself.

I took every single dollar I made in the business and put it right back in the business. I 100-percent reinvested every penny to supercharge my growth through the power of compounding. There are a lot of business books out there and ideologies that say "Pay yourself first." I don't believe in this philosophy when you are first starting a business. If you can starve yourself to expedite the growth of your business without greatly affecting your mental health and your basic needs, then fucking do it! Your future self will thank you later.

It didn't come without a price, though. I would work what felt like twenty-four hours around the clock. I would eat, shit, sleep, and breathe business. But it didn't feel like work because I was loving every minute of it. Over the next few years, I kept adding businesses to my repertoire and portfolio. To date, I have grossed several millions beyond what I ever knew was possible for me! How's that for a boy from the hood?

Part II
NOW

Beyond the days of hustling, embracing a new vision.

As my outlook grew vast, so did my opportunities,
New ways to grow financially, spread love
And foster unity,
Ashamed of my past at first, I speak this truthfully,
Till I realized my hustling background was like a school to me,
And all the codes and morals along
the way that was instilled in me,
To the pain I sustained made way for my resiliency,
Coupled with the discipline,
It set me off from average,
Now add in my vision, and you'll see why I'M A MAVERICK!

—Excerpt from hip-hop song by Shiloh Jones

23

One Mistake Away from Prison to Successful Businessman

It is not a lack of time but a lack of focus that separates the winners from the losers.

— Unknown

HOW DID I do it? How did I go from a hustler who was one mistake away from prison to a comfortable, successful, passionate businessman? I grinded, sacrificed, strategized, planned, went without sleep, made mistakes, got some things right, got some things wrong, lost money, and made money. Everything I just named is the cost of evolving, the cost of transforming, and the cost of doing business. And every businessperson on earth has gone through these very same things. I'm no different. The thing is, I was willing to do those things, learn those lessons, and take those risks. If I'd been scared, I wouldn't be who I am today.

The same courage it took for me to be who I was in the streets is the same courage I use today to be who I am in business. I needed that same *Braveheart* attitude to enter the business world. I was afraid, but I've learned that it's okay to be afraid. The problem comes when the fear halts your legs from moving forward. Courage is being nervous or afraid and having the strength to keep going, to keep fighting. This is what has to make you "you" and separates you from them! Straight up! If business was easy, everybody would be doing it. It takes a special person to succeed in the world of business.

Cocky and you knows this,

                                                             Shi up on his own dick,

                           Somebody gotta pat my back,

                                      I came up from homeless,

Seeing is believing, we put here for reasons,

God in my corner, dawg, a nigga still breathing.

                             —*Excerpt from hip-hop song by Shiloh Jones*

Eliminating the Distractions

True story: my office manager, Amy, came to me the other day and asked, "Mr. Jones, how do you have time to do and accomplish all the stuff you're involved in?"

"Simple," I answered. "I eliminate all distractions."

And that's exactly what I did back then. See, distractions end up forming themselves into these things called excuses. And excuses are the enemy of any goal that you want to achieve, project you want to complete, or vision that you want to bring to reality! Excuses will limit you and stop you from becoming the best version of yourself. The enemy of excuses is discipline. *You have to have the discipline not to make excuses!*

That's why the phrase "by any means necessary" is so powerful to me. It means that you will die before you allow an excuse to stop you from accomplishing whatever it is you're trying to achieve! And it means that you're willing to sacrifice everything to get there! Like a man possessed. This is the very thing that makes people call us business folks crazy! To bring this point home, I'll share a great quote by entrepreneur Jim Rohn: "We all must suffer from one of two pains: the pain of discipline or the pain of regret. The difference is discipline weighs ounces, while regret weighs tons."

Discovering My Purpose

Why did everything I've been through in my life happen? Through the years, I've often wondered about that. What is my purpose? What am I supposed to be doing in this life? Eventually, I found my resolve, my true north. I settled on a few reasons for my existence and purpose that I know to be true:

1. **To create impact through influence:** Looking back at it, I realized that everything I went through was for a reason. Having a rough life led to my understanding of exactly what it takes to evolve from a rough life so I can show others. From my mother having mental health issues to making a hell of an impact in my own community through organizations that I have built that deal directly with helping those with mental health and substance abuse issues. From me going through phases of negatively affecting my community to now positively affecting that same community in ways that I can never imagine. From me not having role models growing up to now having the privilege of serving as a great role model to others in my community and even outside of my community. That's what I mean about influence! If one major problem was that my community suffered from a lack of positive influence, who is responsible for creating it? The answer is us! We are! Starting with you! (If this is applicable to you.) If not you, then who? If not now, then when? I truly believe that era in my life set me up for this stage of my life I'm in now. I can understand the street dude because I WAS HIM! I can understand what it is like to not have because I WAS THERE! I can also relate to the business mind because I AM HERE NOW! And so much more. I learned so many different sides of the coin, so many different perspectives, and so many schools of thought that all contribute to me being well rounded enough to touch people from all walks of life. I'm very grateful for this, but I wouldn't have been able to predict that all that was for now and would be beneficial for my present stage of life.

2. **To be great at business:** I have an insatiable drive for business—I openly admit that. I can literally work for twenty-four hours straight with no sleep. But in that obsession, I found a greater purpose, and that's affecting people. The more I add on businesses or grow any business, the more people I have to hire. By offering stable jobs to these people, I help them provide for their families. I also help them achieve financial security. In a larger societal sense, this helps the economy: more taxes are paid into the system, which helps government programs assist with poverty and fuels government jobs. Bottom line, by doing business, I play my part in adding value to the world. Talk about purpose! How can I not see the joy in this? I receive a certain amount of happiness and completeness in my life simply by being the best business person that I can be.
3. **To share my story with the rest of the world:** By sharing my story, I can do something pretty amazing: I can connect to those who have been through what I've been through or similar, want to achieve what I have, or want to end up where I want to go!
4. **To be the greatest father I can be to my kids.**

Release Therapy

The way I grew up has made me a very private person. It's more challenging for me to open up to strangers than it is for the average person. That's why this book isn't just for you; it's for me as well. It has served as a much-needed release therapy for completing part of my life. It's helping me explore certain chapters that I closed a long time ago and others that I'm just starting to open on this journey called life.

As I tell my daughter Ree, pay attention to what you learn in school now. You never know when that same information will be needed later in life for a specific purpose. That's the funny thing about life: every place you've been, everything you have to go through, and every so-called random situation you were placed in are all for some bigger purpose. My experiences were a form of schooling for me, and I pull from them often in my life today. One can say, for that matter, that life itself is school, as we're constantly applying the elements of learning and development.

> I'M NOT WHERE I WANT TO BE,
> BUT THANK GOD I'M NOT WHERE I USED TO BE!
>
> —JOYCE MEYER, CHRISTIAN AUTHOR AND SPEAKER

I do more than coach people with their businesses; I help them to actually start businesses from scratch. And this is what I love to do.

Raising Your Expectations of Yourself

One of my favorite quotes ever is by Eric Thomas, aka the Hip-Hop Preacher: "Be willing to sacrifice what you *are* for what you will *become*." Hopefully, my story is a living testimony to this life philosophy. At each stage of my life, when I wanted to become more, it was because I was tired (of feeling the pain) of settling for less. You have to consistently raise your level of expectation for yourself.

I stopped competing with people a long time ago because you can never win. There will always be someone bigger than you, badder than you, and sharper than you. There's only one person you're sure to beat if you put the right amount of energy into it: yourself! You are your own best competitor because, more than anyone on the planet, you know exactly who you are and what capabilities you possess. That makes you the perfect opponent because you know exactly where you need to become stronger if you're gonna defeat your past self, the one who is less than your best.

What I'm saying in a nutshell is this: try to outdo the old you, the person you were yesterday. This is the easiest way to constantly improve both internally and externally. I practice this myself and make it a point to do better each year by being better than the guy I was last year.

24

Coming to Terms with My Anger and Finding Forgiveness for My Pops

Question: There are two wolves that are always fighting each other. One is darkness and despair; the other, light and hope. Which one survives?
Answer: The one you feed!
— *Native American folklore*

One of the Most Powerful Things I've Ever Done

I WANTED TO dedicate an entire chapter in this book to the subject of anger because coming to terms with my anger in my mid-twenties changed my life. It's one of the most powerful things I've ever done. It also led to my biggest transformation.

From reading this book, one thing is clear: I have been through a lot. A lot of it was painful, sometimes hurtful, sometimes depressing. And no secret about it, I have openly and honestly admitted that it resulted in me having anger toward the world, anger toward my parents, and anger toward my environment. Eventually, I allowed myself to feel like a victim. A victim of circumstance. The result of a series of wrongdoings by other people. I allowed myself to feel like an outcast, as if I didn't fit in anywhere.

Sometimes I'd even blame myself for things I had no control over. This led to me being mean to people, sometimes shutting them out and not letting them in when they genuinely cared about me. This hate I had for everything around me did give me a fire. I used that fire as a motivation to build self-strength and self-dependency. Eventually came self-realism, self-awareness, and self-recognition. But while the fire fueled me in the beginning, it started to hold me back in the long run. I came to realize that the anger was hindering me. Stagnating me. Preventing me from progressing and evolving. Sometimes you can be in the same zone for so long that you start to run on autopilot. That's what was happening to me.

It became very clear to me that I was going to have to deal with this inner demon known as anger. And it wasn't going to be an overnight thing. It was a huge thing to tackle. I had to deal with it in stages. But here's a question: how do you eat an elephant? The answer: one bite at a time.

Opening Myself up to Blessings from the Universe

As I dealt with the pieces of my anger, I learned so much about myself. And I opened myself up to receiving more blessings that the universe had waiting for me. One huge blessing—and the very reason I'm writing this book—is that I can show people with stories similar to mine that everything can work out. The same thing is true for you. There is a beautiful ending for you, if you *choose* it to be! (The key word is "choose"!) I kept responding hatefully to the cards life dealt me and felt at a disadvantage when I could have empowered myself to change my hand a long time before I did.

If you don't like the hand life has dealt you, simply get the deck of cards and deal yourself a new hand!

If you look at my story in totality, you'll see that it wasn't until I was able to let go of anger and hatred that I was truly able to flourish. Truly able to dream. Truly able to progress. What I had to realize was that I had the power to control my own destiny. I'm not saying it's going to be easy. It will take work. Hard work! Dedication! Focus! It may take some good old-fashioned elbow grease. But with enough determination, you can work *with* the universe on morphing your reality into whatever you want it to be. Don't be like I was for so long. Learn from me. Let my later years inspire you. I am no different than you, other than the lessons I've learned. I'm sharing them with you so that what I've learned can be converted into wisdom in your own world.

I know I'm driving this point home, and I'm intending to. I had every reason to be angry, but that didn't mean *I had to be*! I realized that anger was crippling me, rendering me handicapped to love. It's hard for both anger and love to truly exist in your system in unison. The more you hate, the less ability you have to love. And on the other hand, the more you love, the less ability you have to hate. Think of yourself as a circle that can't change in size, as there is limited space in the circle. The more you fill the circle with anger, the less room you have for love, and vice versa. At each stage of my life, every time I let go of an ounce of anger, I opened myself to make way for an ounce of success. The moment I let go of all the baggage was the moment I truly began to prosper. It was the equivalent of breaking heavy chains that did nothing but shackle me to the bottom.

And what's absolutely crazy to me—and still baffles me to this day—is that I never really had anyone to serve as a backbone or safety net for me. But it's a truly beautiful thing and a blessing that I can serve as a backbone and a rock to my family and so many people around me. Somehow I learned to tune in to gratitude with this: *To hold a grudge against someone is to allow them to live in your head rent-free!*

I had to learn what forgiveness meant and acquire the art for practicing it.

OBSTACLES CANNOT CRUSH ME.

EVERY OBSTACLE YIELDS TO STERN RESOLVE.

HE WHO IS FIXED TO A STAR DOES NOT CHANGE HIS MIND.

—LEONARDO DA VINCI, PAINTER, SCULPTOR, MUSICIAN, MATHEMATICIAN, ARCHITECT, WRITER, AND ENGINEER

Defining Who I Was, and Who I Am

Everything I went through was a step in me defining who I was. Sure, I went left, sometimes too far to the right, but that's similar to target practice. At a shooting range, the first shot may be off to the right of the target, so you adjust. The second shot may be a little to the left because you overcompensated, so you adjust. That third shot is where it's at. You aim, taking into consideration the last two misses (mistakes), and then you squeeze. Bullseye! Who cares that you missed the mark twice? No matter how many times you shoot, you only have to hit your target once for it to be a bullseye.

As long as you have the ability to keep shooting, you keep aiming for the bullseye. That's what life's about. Like the old saying goes, it's not about how you fall; it's about how you get up. Nobody's perfect. The moment you embrace this concept is the moment you start to look at your mistakes/misses as learning experiences. This is where one begins a journey toward wisdom. I am a firm believer that wisdom trumps knowledge in life, for knowledge without wisdom is the equivalent of theory without practice. But true application is when theory meets practice, when knowledge marries wisdom.

I had a conversation with one of my close friends just yesterday, talking about what we would change about our childhoods. After I gave it some careful thought and back and forth, my friend stopped me and said, "If you were to alter anything you've been through in the past, it would change the person you are today. You might not have hustled as hard, might not have learned how to be as focused as you are now, might not have gathered the strength you possess today. So, for that reason alone, I wouldn't change shit about your past because your path had to cross with my path. You've been an inspiration to me and made me work to elevate my own self. You take that away and I wouldn't be who I am!"

Gratitude Propelling Me Forward

Conversations like this remind me of something important: each stone that I had to cross along my path helped me build the bridge to the life I have today, the one I'm so grateful for. Even though I didn't like everything I went through and, at times, endured very painful experiences, I am truly grateful. It's the gratitude that propels me forward in the morning.

As a matter of fact, a few of the seventy-five affirmations that I say to myself every morning focus on gratitude, including these:

- *I have great gratitude for everything around me!*
- *It's an honor and privilege to have this great health, wealth, intelligence, emotional control, and spiritual sight.*
- *Every morning I wake is a blessing, and I will serve the universe and God by putting my best foot forward among the beauty that I'm granted, the beauty that surrounds me.*
- *I will treat people with respect, and expect respect in return. I like myself. I love myself!*

Remember that great things take time. That's why it takes six months to build a Rolls-Royce and thirteen hours to build a Toyota. As I dispelled my anger, I saw my relationships with people become richer, my quality of life greater, and my outlook on the world broader. My entire being became more optimistic. I had the capacity to envision a great future for myself. Tomorrow started to become more important to me than today, and I gained the resolve I needed to let go of yesterday. And with that came a shift in my priorities. The way I treated people, even strangers, became more important.

Life became more meaningful in every way.

OUR PARENTS HAVE TO EVOLVE AND GROW

Once I'd dealt with the anger inside me, I had to face something else: how I felt about my pops. And that journey had to start with forgiveness. When there are negative emotions attached to a situation, you have to have sincere forgiveness in your heart and then move forward with understanding. I realized that the anger I was holding against my father was only hurting me. And what's crazy is that *I* was holding the grudge; *he* wasn't. He ain't have nothing but love for me. He showed me that a number of times when he seriously stepped up and had my back. When I got older, we talked about his leaving in detail and he expressed how deeply he regrets it. So how long was I going to feel justified in beating him down about it?

When I let go—truly let go—he started to hold a different place in my heart. Maybe not one as a daddy because that place has been damaged. Now he holds a place more like a brother, even though I still love him as a father. I feel blessed that we were able to patch things up before time took the chance away. And when we did, I thought how petty I must've seemed for holding a grudge for such a long time. Again, he had to learn his lessons in life at the same time I was learning mine. And the consequences and chain reactions caused by his decisions back then made him who he is today. Made me who I am today. One thing we have to realize as children is that our parents have to evolve and grow the same way we do. They're subjected to the same life lessons that we are, just in different forms. There's no handbook of life to teach them how to be parents, just like there's no handbook for being a kid.

There for Each Other Now

See, until I resolved my extreme anger, I couldn't see the great qualities that he possesses. He is a great and wonderful grandfather. He isn't unstable anymore, and he tries his best to have his priorities in the right place. And I'm super-proud to announce that he is drug-free. He's more responsible now. And he's there for me any time I need him. So I'm there for him, too. I even took the opportunity to start a business with him when we opened our security company together back in 2001.

My dad, as a changed man.

By any definition, that's a changed man! That's a guy who's taken his faults and mistakes and learned from them. That's a guy who's confronted the demons in his closet and used them as motivation to evolve. They say *it's not where you're from that's important but where you're at!* If you stood the person he is today beside the person he was yesterday, you'd think you were looking at two completely different people. In fact, my pops probably wouldn't be able to recognize that guy from the past either. I am very grateful that we were able to get this relationship we have in this thing called life while he is still alive! That's a blessing! And I've had the opportunity to have many powerful lessons with him along the way.

25

Evolution

WHEN YOU GROW up poor, you tend to think that money fixes everything. As they say, money is not the root of evil; the lack of it is. And I can see how this statement holds true. Most of my problems in life came from not having money. The immense amount of stress I felt when I couldn't pay bills, the threat of ending up homeless, and the instability of not having it led to some serious security issues. Therefore, it was easy for me to believe that money fixes everything.

When I got older, I learned a huge lesson: while money does fix many things, it doesn't fix *everything*. Even after achieving some financial security in my twenties, I didn't feel complete. I'd been so focused on making money that I wasn't prepared for something that happened after I got it: I started feeling sort of empty, as if I was missing something in my life. When I started to understand that completeness comes from other things in life, I started evolving as a person again.

This is my truth. It may be different for you. But here are some things I suggest you do for the inner peace and, more importantly, the balance that money won't give you. I want to point out that I am still young and have a lot of growing to do, so this list may evolve as I get older.

Help Others

I grew up in a community that operated from a crab-in-the-bucket mentality. (If you don't know what this means, here's how it works. When a bunch of crabs have been caught and put in a bucket, any of them could easily escape. But none of them do because they pull each other back down, sealing their collective fates. They don't know any better.) When you see this mentality all around you, you start to believe that you have to look out for you! And this was very true for me.

As a kid, I had to learn how to be my own backbone, my own safety net, and my own checks-and-balances system. While growing up this way will rapidly develop your inner strength and independence, you can't lose sight of why we are here on this planet, surrounded by other human beings. There's something about helping others without any expectations that truly fuels the soul. It's a feel-good sensation that not only affects the spirit but also warms the human heart.

While it is wise to be selective about the people you help and why, you should make it your spiritual and community duty to complete random acts of kindness (RAKs) on a regular basis. These acts don't always have to be about money. They can be about giving information when someone needs it, guiding someone, sharing wisdom, or simply giving a helping hand. I'm going to go one step further and say that some people come into your life for a reason, season, or lifetime. Sometimes the mission is to help them, sometimes it's for them to help you, and sometimes it's to help you by helping them. And since universal energy travels in infinite loops, I promise you that by seeking to help others, when you are in need, the universe will surely return the favor without thinking twice.

Feed Your Mind

The mind is something that never stops going, and it can be quite turbulent at times. Stillness of mind is critical to a feeling of completeness. Here are a few ways to achieve it:

- **Read:** I've said it over and over in this book and will probably mention it a few times more: read, read, read! I wouldn't be who

I am today if I didn't read. Somehow I learned to tune in to gratitude with this. The mind is an organism and, just like plants need water and sunlight, the mind's food is knowledge. Every time I feel stagnated mentally, I can attribute it to the fact that I haven't read in a while. Reading helps you expand past the plateau of your own perspective and broaden your perception.

- **Be careful about your mental diet:** By the same token, be careful what you feed your mind. You know how the food you eat affects your physical body? Well, the things you expose yourself to feed your mind, either positively or negatively, in the same way. It's up to you to filter what your mind takes in because what you think shall be. You know how some people seem to have the worst luck, with negative things constantly happening to them? Well, this can almost always be traced back to their way of thinking. Here are three powerful quotes that show the power of the mind and its influence on you and the universe around you:

> WHETHER YOU THINK YOU CAN,
> OR YOU THINK YOU CAN'T, YOU'RE RIGHT!
> —HENRY FORD, FOUNDER OF THE FORD MOTOR COMPANY

> WE BECOME WHAT WE THINK ABOUT MOST OF THE TIME,
> AND THAT'S THE STRANGEST SECRET!
> —EARL NIGHTINGALE, RADIO PERSONALITY, AUTHOR, AND SPEAKER

> PEOPLE WHO SUCCEED HAVE MOMENTUM.
> THE MORE THEY SUCCEED, THE MORE THEY WANT TO SUCCEED,
> AND THE MORE THEY FIND A WAY TO SUCCEED.
> SIMILARLY, WHEN SOMEONE IS FAILING,
> THE TENDENCY IS TO GET ON A DOWNWARD SPIRAL THAT
> CAN EVEN BECOME A SELF-FULFILLING PROPHECY.
> —TONY ROBBINS, WRITER, BUSINESSMAN, AND PHILANTHROPIST

You can achieve being complete in the mind by controlling the mind. It is your garden, so tend to it with care. Money and success are just byproducts of what's in your mind and what's in your heart. One of my favorite business mantras is about focusing on opportunities over obstacles. When you understand the power of controlling your thoughts, you move closer to manipulating the universal law of cause and effect, which states that nothing happens by chance or outside of the universal laws. Every action (including thought) has a reaction or consequence. Thinking negatively will attract negative things into your life. The same is true with thinking positively.

- **Keep your intentions pure and your conscience clear:** I don't want you to think I'm getting all "hippie" on you, but I am going to get into a little about karma and keeping a clear conscience. And I'm just going to be straight and to the point! To be complete, your mind must be at peace. But it's impossible for your mind to be at peace if you are doing fucked-up shit to people. I am a firm believer that God protects and blesses those with pure and positive intentions. There are many experiences in my life that have proven this to be true. If you do a bunch of dirt and carry larceny within you, it will surely rob you of being complete. So drop all negative intentions toward people and live in the most righteous way possible so that you can sleep well at night! Be sure that however you conduct yourself, you can live with it. Don't compromise your long-term peace for short-term impulse or gain.

Spend Time with Family

Some people get this, some don't, and some never will, but I will stress this important area anyway. Appreciate family, for they love you the most. And hold them close. It is your job to teach, guide, and support them in all types of ways. My family doesn't just love me for what I do and who I am to them; they love me simply because I am me. It's precious and rare for someone to love you unconditionally in this way. The world can turn its back on you, but true family won't. Once I truly grasped this concept after letting go of my anger, my capacity to love increased tenfold. On the flipside, know what family you need to keep at arm's length or distance yourself from, especially if they are energy vampires.

Have Friends and a Social Life

It's very important to keep friends—true friends—around you. Yes, they are hard to find, but when you do find them, hold them close as you would family. Balancing your social life helps build a well-rounded you! Eliminate negative friends from your circle, as they can be the equivalent of negative thoughts. They ultimately pull from your inner peace, not to mention your positive aura. Avoid friends who always have drama in their lives, as their drama will surely become yours. I cannot stress this enough: avoid energy vampires!

Focus on Health

This area is one that pertains to all. As for me, I didn't really put too much focus on my health for the first half of my life. But as I started to grow older, I realized that this is one of the most important areas of your life. If you're not doing your best to be as healthy as possible, you'll greatly impact the quality of your life. What good is being successful, making money, or having all the wealth in the world if you can't enjoy it?

This also ties back into your "why." You are doing everything you can to have financial security so that you can have a wonderful, long, and stress-free life, right? What if when you get there, health problems from not taking care of yourself hinder you from enjoying the fruits of your labor? Who would want that horrible irony? Think of all the things you want to do once you get where you want to be financially. One of mine is to travel the world and experience every culture that I possibly can. That would be pretty impossible to do if my health was in poor condition. Shortening your life affects the other "why," and that's family. I have daughters, and I would like to be here on this planet as long as I can for them.

Remember that success can't replace health. There's a mathematical equation that I once read about. I may get it a little wrong, but bear with me. It goes something like this. Write down the number "1" on a piece of paper. (This represents you.) Then list everything that is precious to you—from houses to cars to cash—and assign it a "0." Now add each "0" behind the "1." Your number may look like this: 1,000,000,000,000,000. This is a great number! But if you take away the "1," it has no value. The biggest investment you can ever make is in self!

With this in mind, I started to work out (avidly!). I kept in mind that if the universe blesses you with something—in this case, a healthy body—you should work hard to maintain it. At first it seemed like hard work, but now I'm addicted. I work out six days a week on average.

Transformation didn't happen just in my mind; it happened physically in my body as well.

Once I started working out consistently, I started to really see the benefits of it. Working out:

- **Relieves stress:** With all the work I do on a daily basis, it serves as an excellent way to blow off steam.

- **Recycles energy:** Some people misunderstand the concept of hitting the gym, thinking that it steals your energy. It's quite the opposite. It actually gives you more energy. It equips me very well with the energy I need to complete the work of two people in one day.
- **Keeps you looking good:** Hey, you don't believe me? Look it up. Working out is the fountain of youth.
- **Maintains your strength, which, in turn, impacts your quality of life:** Did you know that as we age, the first thing that starts to deteriorate is our strength. Take a look at any old folks home. Most of our elderly folks have had their strength compromised, impairing basic activities such as walking, dressing, and living independently. My aunt is a retired RN. She once gave me these wise words: "Shiloh, whatever you do, make sure you hit those weights. And don't give them up. This will give you the best chance of being independent when you're my age. I hit the weights currently, and it's a shame to see so many of my friends in wheelchairs because they didn't tend to their bodies and lost so much muscle and bone density." Say no more! I bang the hell out of them weights!

My mother is temporarily using a wheelchair because of health issues. She's said to me more than once, "If I knew then what I know now, I would've been in the gym every day like you are." I heed those words of wisdom. Remember, wisdom is experience, and a truly wise person learns from the experience of others.

Bottom line: Enjoy the fruits of your labor, and aim for a long and prosperous life. I know no one is guaranteed tomorrow, and I know we have a lot of obstacles in our day. Still, don't let what you *can't* do stop you from what you *can* do. Hit the gym!

Just a random-ass pic. LOL. I thought it would match the context.

Have a Spiritual Life and Believe in a Higher Power

Acknowledge and respect the higher power, whatever you choose to call it. It might be God, Allah, the all, Yahweh, or the universe. Have the humility to recognize that something else is greater than you. None of us knows what the afterlife will bring us, if anything at all. But coming to terms with yourself spiritually while on this plane will make you feel more complete, no matter what belief system ends up guiding you.

Practice Gratitude Daily

Here's something I believe strongly: gratitude helps maintain all the blessings in your world and allows you to get continually blessed with more. Arrogance is a fool's downfall. In my late twenties, I started to wake up every morning and thank God and the universe for all the blessings around me. I still do. I also think it's important to repay the blessings I receive by applying myself, being thankful, and working hard. (I've seen so many people bust their ass to start a business and, once they were established, they felt they'd made it and started to slack off. Idiots! This is where the journey begins! What they didn't understand is that it wasn't just them working; the universe was working with them to make things fall into place.)

If the universe works hard for you, the least you can do is work hard for it. That means being the best you can be and being thankful for each and every blessing on a daily basis. And don't just think it; speak it. Verbalize your praise. Then show your gratitude in your actions. This is a principle that must be grasped if one is to reach a higher state of giving and receiving universally.

26

Making the Transition from the Streets to the Corporate World

AS I WRITE this, many of you are still in the streets, just getting in the streets, having one foot in and one foot out, or already making the transition out. Here is my truth and advice for those wanting to fully transition. (If this doesn't apply to you, simply move to the next chapter. But I'm certain that some of you reading this need these words right here.)

Number One: Commit

If you're going to leave that life behind, you have to know your reason for switching over. That reason has to be strong enough for you to dedicate yourself to it. Any true life change starts with commitment. Commit yourself to seeing a new you and fully becoming the new you. Know that you are deserving and have the right to abundance like any one of God's creatures on this planet. Then eliminate every other option not aligned with your new you. This is a matter of prioritizing. You have to build a powerful enough "why" inside of you to help develop your "what to" and "what not to" internal directional compass.

Examine all the dangers and amplify the risks you take by doing street shit. Consider how lucky you are now to read this and that you haven't, up to this point, become a total victim of the streets. Remember, most people don't make it out of the streets. This is REAL. Understand that with all of your being. I'm sure there were many times when you took a risk, whatever it was, and didn't get caught. Now imagine how different your life would be if you had gotten caught. What if you'd been randomly searched that last time you moved work? What if someone set you up? What if a stickup boy just happened to choose you?

Now, risks are like gambling. Sometimes you win, sometimes you lose. Sooner or later, your luck meter runs out. You can't keep doing the same shit forever without eventually getting caught. Bottom line: Accept that your days in hustling are limited. Also, know that the only way you leave that life in one piece is to stop before that life stops you!

That creates a new perspective for you, doesn't it? Because deep down, you know I'm right! How many elderly, retired hustlers do you know personally? Ones who saved up enough money that they're able to live out the rest of their years in peace, traveling the world, and taking care of their grandbabies? I can bet you a million dollars you can't name one! Because the streets don't have that design. Either you get out or the streets put you out of here. This alone should be your motivation to get the fuck out of the streets.

Don't believe the hype you see on TV, in rap videos, or glorified in the media and movies. There is no green grass on the other side or golden carrot at the end of the stick. Right now, you should make your reason for committing because you want a long, stress-free life. You owe it to yourself and your family. The idea of prison being monetized is a very real thing! Prison is big business, and the system is designed to be fed with you as the fuel source. Don't allow yourself to be potential fuel for this heartless beast! The system does NOT give a fuck about you, your kids, your mother, your goals, or your freedom, for that matter. Find yourself the right reason for committing to getting the fuck out, and stay committed!

Number Two: Prepare

Build a plan. This is important because, no matter what you do in life, *if you fail to plan, you plan to fail.*

This is true for everything—working out in the gym, earning a college degree, starting a business, starting a family, conducting a scientific experiment, planning a military offensive—including leaving the streets. Your plan doesn't have to be elaborate. It can have options, backups, and several potential strategies. Shit, even football plays have audibles! It's insane to think that life can't. Be comfortable having several strategies. But the point is that you have to think it out. Think it out as much as possible and try your best to see it! Visualize your plan, and become a man possessed with making it happen. Remember, the future doesn't have to be something that just happens; it can be something you make happen! Take control of your destiny, your fate. Get in the driver's seat of your life. The same way you made things happen in the street? Make them happen in the corporate world, the industrial world, or the service world.

Number Three: Increase Your Value

I keep saying, the best investment you can ever make is in yourself! Make yourself of greater value to your mission or someone else's. This is the key to giving life to the new you. Don't be scared to increase your skills by going to school, researching, learning a trade, or being an apprentice. The key is to be willing to learn. If you're going to make it in this world, you have to build value in yourself. Some of you already possess great skills to offer business owners and corporations. And some of you have enough skill, even if it needs some tweaking, to be sole proprietors with your own businesses. Find a passion and pursue it. If you don't have one, be willing to try different things until you find one. Mine was business. I like the way it ticks. It fuels me. Find yours. Don't be afraid.

Here's a secret: even the most successful people in the world have to constantly learn if they're going to grow. This applies to business owners, highly accomplished managers and directors, CEOs of the world's leading corporations, and even billionaires. Every industry is constantly changing. They know that if they are to survive market shifts, new technologies, global market takeovers, and fierce competition, they have to constantly be learning. What makes you any different? To be successful like these guys, you *must* practice what they do! Period.

I'm going to be straightforward with you here. Don't be weak. Get the bitch out of your system! Marry your motivation and have the discipline to stay faithful to it. Some of ya, as soon as the going gets tough, you fall and crumble. The moment things look a little tough, you quit and go right back to the street or give up on whatever goal you are working on. That's one-foot-in-and-one-foot-out bullshit. And I don't mean no harm, but that's the bitch in you that makes you do that. That's being scared of failure, so you quit! You fold! Another secret: I'm scared of failure, too, and that's the very reason why I don't quit. Because if you quit too soon, how do you know if you could've been successful or not?

I'm going to share a story that came from Napoleon Hill's *Think and Grow Rich*.

THREE FEET AWAY FROM GOLD!

There once was a man who had a dream of building a business mining gold and striking it big. So he read all available research pointing to the geographical area with the highest probability for containing gold. He put his entire life savings toward his goal. He also secured bank loans so that he could buy everything he needed to make his dream a reality. He got everything he asked for and went to work. He dug and dug and dug but couldn't find gold. This went on for three years. He then went back to the drawing board and reworked his calculations about the area. They worked out to be the same as before. So he stayed in that area and kept digging.

This started to take a toll on him as he grew more frustrated and stressed. He still didn't strike any gold. He started running out of money, so he went back to the banks and his private investors and requested more. Two years later, still no gold. Feeling defeated and like a failure, he gave up! But what was he to do with all the equipment he had? He met with a young businessman who had fresh ambition to get into the business of finding gold. They spoke about the area and how there was a high probability that gold would be found there.

The man, confidence broken, sold the equipment to the young businessman, asking only for enough money to cover his debts. They made the deal and the man went about his life. On his first day on the job site, the young businessman ordered the laborers to continue with business as usual. He instructed them to follow the same path they were already digging. Three feet in, they struck gold! So much of it, in fact, four generations of his offspring would not have to pick up a screw or a hammer in their entire lives.

When the going gets tough, remind yourself of your purpose. Reground yourself with the same "why" you initially used to commit yourself to a new life. For me, it was my kids. I had to look them in the face every day. I needed to show them a few things while also proving to myself:

1. I would not go back to the streets and risk everything.
2. I would not go backward; instead, I'd make every year better than the last.
3. I was not a failure.
4. I was more than just talk and was ready to stand for and put exceptional energy into everything I believed in.

More important than what you *tell* your kids is what you *show* them. I've always told my girls that they will be great in life. I knew if I wanted to prove that to them, I had to be a living testimony to that idea. Otherwise, I would be all talk—just words. By challenging myself on a daily basis to be the best version of myself that I can be, I set the bar for them.

To reach the goals I set for myself, I had to be willing to run on the track of life as fast as I could. Don't be scared of hard work! The only place success comes before work is in the dictionary. In life, you have to grind for it. Ain't nobody going to just give you shit; you have to take it! And what I have honestly learned is that it's not just about paying your dues; you have to constantly prove yourself to yourself.

It's so easy to fall off and take the easy route. But history shows that those who choose the harder path, the unbeaten path, are those who get rewarded the most! Be willing to do what the average person isn't willing to do, to get to where the average person is not. You got this! Commit yourself, build a plan, increase your value, and don't go backward. Take the time to dedicate yourself now.

27

How to Maintain Success

Persistency will get you there;
consistency will keep you there!
— Unknown

MY FRIEND ROCSTAGIS was one of the people who bugged me to write this book. And when I did, he wanted me to address this question for him: "How do you maintain success?"

I've chosen to break the most important factors in maintaining long-term success (in my experience) into several categories. These are traits that all people with a track record of five or more years of consistent growth and development in their businesses must possess. They're essential to those who want longevity in the world of business. Remember, most businesses don't survive their first two years. Given that fact, those who have been in business for at least five years are doing something right! Ten and they are doing amazing! And they deserve a pat on the back.

Resiliency

Do this exercise for me. Write down everything that is currently a threat to your business. Each threat has the potential to cripple your business or put you out of business entirely. Think about what other companies in your industry are doing that you are not doing to threaten your position in the marketplace. Put the threats in numerical order—least damaging to most damaging—as you list them. Now, on another sheet of paper, think of a strategy to address each threat if confronted with it. It's okay if you have more than one strategy per threat—it's good, in fact. The more, the better. Now, be proactive and act on these strategies in advance, whether you implement a new oversight process, a contingency plan, or even an exit strategy.

You have just created situational awareness for your business. This is a perfect example of resiliency. You must be willing to stay one step ahead of the competition, two steps ahead of all threats, and three steps ahead of obvious oncoming obstacles. If you don't, you will find yourself in one or more spots behind the eight ball.

GOOD FINANCIAL MANAGEMENT SKILLS

If you've already achieved a level of success, great! But you need to maintain your success and build on it. Luck can get a person a few thousand dollars—even a few hundred thousand dollars. But there are certain skills that you need if you want to make million-dollar money and keep that money while making it grow. Financial competence is one of them. I see extremely talented guys all the time who can't stay afloat because they refuse to educate themselves in financial matters. So they end up in a cycle of purgatory—ahead this quarter, behind the next—and running in what I call a tortoise-and-hare race with themselves, sometimes as the tortoise and sometimes as the hare.

I can't stress this enough: learn everything you can so that you'll always be in tune with your finances. You can be the most talented person on the planet, but if you don't handle your finances properly, you will be the most broke talented person on the planet. Go hire a competent accountant and work with them on a monthly basis. Or, depending on your level of success, it may be wise to go one step further and find a financial coach you can trust.

Mike Tyson, for example, was a very talented guy who went broke because he was financially incompetent. MC Hammer, super-talented, ended with pennies because he had no clue what was going on in his financial world. Even if you have people you pay to watch over your finances, it doesn't mean you shouldn't educate yourself anyway. Shit, even Oprah has a separate accountant to provide checks and balances for her primary accountant.

Review your bank statements monthly or weekly. Audit yourself regularly to determine how your overhead has changed from one month to the next. This is where you can eliminate waste. Double-check your gross profits against your net profits and compare the difference between your expenses, payroll, and total overhead to see if everything balances out. By auditing yourself, you may find that *you* are the problem and spend carelessly at times when you shouldn't.

For example, are you paying too much for a leisure service? Do you have double the insurance coverage you need just because your agent sold you an inflated policy to get a bigger commission? Are you paying your employees too much? Does it make more sense to hire independent contractors? Are you eating out too much? Is a monthly recurring bill still charging your account when you no longer use that service? These are questions you have to continuously ask yourself to ensure proper maintenance of your financial health.

I want to take this one step further and tell you that it is your responsibility to know exactly how much you are worth at any given time. The actual term for this is your personal financial statement (PFS). It doesn't have to be fancy! Get on your computer, open Excel, and build a spreadsheet to help you calculate your net worth. The easiest way to do this is to list your assets. (This is what you own, including cash accounts, equity in your home, cars, accounts receivable, notes receivable, inventory, and supplies.) Attach positive dollar values to your assets. Next, list your liabilities. (This is what you owe, including what you owe on your home, accounts payable, notes payable, car loans, other loans, and so on.) Attach negative dollar values to your liabilities. The difference between your assets and your liabilities is your net worth. Do this monthly, quarterly, every six months, or once a year. I choose to do this exercise quarterly as it helps to give me a good view of my financial health. It also helps me determine if I need to make any adjustments.

If you don't know exactly where you stand financially, how can you determine what moves to make at the right time? Essentially, you're limiting your options or allowing yourself to gamble blindly. Get financially fit! It's never too late, so start educating yourself now!

Solid Leadership

The days of autocratic leadership are pretty much over unless you work in a low-skilled-labor industry, which may warrant that style of leadership. But in general, nobody wants an Adolf Hitler as a boss. The more skilled, educated, and corporate your labor force is, the more it will resent an autocratic leadership style. The autocratic leadership style is "Do as I say because I say it and you don't need a reason. I am telling you to do it and do it now!" Autocratic leaders make decisions with little or no involvement from their employees. This disconnects the owners or bosses (the head) from the rest of the company (the body). While this may have worked in the old days, times are changing. People are changing. If you want to be a resilient leader, you have to be more diplomatic than your predecessors.

There are many leadership styles in today's business world, and you should spend some time researching them for yourself. In my opinion, the smart leader will employ different styles at different times, depending on the situation. Monotone leadership won't win the favor of a colorful workforce, as people are as different as fingerprints. This means adapting to your environment like a teacher does with students in a classroom, as some students are visual learners while others are auditory or kinesthetic learners. The best teachers know this and will engage all three types of learners, depending on the situation in their classroom.

Business leadership is the same. One great example of leadership style is "situational leadership," a style developed by Kenneth Blanchard and Paul Hersey. Situational leadership applies when a leader in an organization must adjust his or her style to fit the development level of the followers they're trying to influence.

Another person to study is Jack Welch, former CEO of General Electric. He believed the people on the front line performing a job know the best way to perform it as compared to a manager who knows "of" the job. That's also true of the boss who knows the "concept" of how the job is performed and may design eight steps for the front-line person to perform the work. By listening to the performer and giving them a voice, a manager might discover that the job can be performed in just three steps instead of eight. This approach will save you time and money and move you from being merely efficient to being more effective. Remember, efficiency is doing things right, but effectiveness is doing the right things! If you're going to be a formidable and stable force in your industry, your goal as a leader, manager, owner, or CEO is to be as effective as possible in every facet of your business.

Develop into a great leader to stop yourself from stagnating in your growth. In my opinion, leadership is something that you can't truly perfect but something you should constantly be improving on. This is very important to maintaining or growing your success.

Critical Decision-Making Skills

In business, you will inevitably face situations, sometimes daily, that require critical decision-making. You'll either have to think fast on your toes or have a short turnaround time to produce a solid decision on an array of matters concerning your business. Of course, some decisions are more important than others. But successful people understand the butterfly effect, as one bad decision can snowball into an uncontrollable series of events. That's why so much about maintaining success is about being skillful with your decision-making.

Critical decision-making skills are based on a few important factors:

1. **Getting the right information to the right people at the right time:** Make sure you streamline communication within your organization or group as much as possible so that you can efficiently and effectively deal with crucial, time-sensitive problems when they arise. Not having the necessary information in the business decision-maker's hands is like a cook trying to prepare a meal for the first time with half the ingredients and only 25 percent of the recipe. How do you think the dish would turn out?

You have to have all relevant information available to you or your management to produce the best possible outcome.

2. **Weighing the pros and cons with the best information available and then acting on them:** Once you have all relevant information, it's wise to think of as many options for addressing the issue as possible before acting. Write down the pros and cons of each option. Try to think of the effects each option will have if you decide to use it. Do a process of elimination to determine your best route, and go with it!

3. **Supporting the decision by applying the proper oversight and management to see it through to its end:** Understand that no decision will work if you don't see it all the way through. You'll want to internalize the famous words "Inspect what you expect" as you take your next course of action. You can't risk having an idea, plan, response to a situation, directive, or decision fail because you don't give it proper oversight. Even if you do make a decision or plan without the proper oversight and it fails, you can't properly learn why it failed without fully analyzing exactly what happened. The end result would be you not learning from your mistake. I believe each failure is an opportunity to learn how to successfully get it right the next time! But you have to inspect what you expect, which essentially means managing and measuring your efforts and follow-through.

4. **Having the proper contingency strategy in place in case Plan A doesn't work out:** Sometimes the perfect plan simply doesn't work. We have to remember that a plan is, essentially, a theory. When put into practice, factors beyond our control can sometimes hinder a plan from developing to its full potential. Be wise enough to know when to hold 'em and when to fold 'em! The point is, you need to have a backup strategy in case the first one doesn't work anymore. Successful people understand that they have to be proactive in anticipating these kinds of situations, especially when it comes to making decisions that can affect the course of an entire company.

5. **Finding motivation:** A car needs gas. A body needs food. A plant needs water. Get the picture? Successful people need motivation! If you are naturally motivated 24/7, great! If not, and you are like the rest of us, it's your job to find sources of motivation to keep you pumped up. Whether your motivation is internet material, inspirational books, or books by successful people, find it! Also, surround yourself with others who either have the same drive as you do or are just as successful. They say your network is your net worth! Find like-minded individuals and make sure to maintain regular contact with them so you can bounce good energy off one another.

6. **Making a commitment to lifelong learning:** I find the only time I feel stagnant or unfulfilled is when I'm not challenging myself. That's why every chance I get, I research materials relevant to one of my industries, attend a seminar, or take coursework on something that sparks my interest at a local college. An idle mind is the devil's playground; it's also detrimental to long-term success. To maintain enthusiasm, you must learn new things. You also have to regularly rekindle the flame that gave you the initial spark to go into business in the first place.

7. **Setting goals:**

> THE TROUBLE WITH NOT HAVING A GOAL IS THAT YOU CAN SPEND YOUR LIFE RUNNING UP AND DOWN THE FIELD AND NEVER SCORE.
>
> —BILL COPELAND, WRITER AND HISTORIAN

It's insane to *not* set goals. That's true for yourself and your business. Setting long-term and short-term goals feeds motivation. It also assists with managing your time, acquiring and applying knowledge, and utilizing resources to keep you on track and aligned with your mission of being and staying successful. Be realistic with your goals and make sure that they're attainable. Larger goals require more time; smaller goals have to be met with unshakable determination. By regularly setting and reaching your goals, you start to build integrity and also establish a pattern of completing tasks, which leads to higher confidence levels. This is important because once you see yourself as a successful person on the inside, you start to appear more successful on the outside as well. If done properly, goal setting will provide a road map to your success. For example, you may have a long-term goal of your business producing $5 million in revenue per year over the next five years. You may have set this large goal today, when you've been experiencing stagnation and only grossing $1 million per year for the last year or two. This is where those beautiful short-term goals come into play. Doing quick math, this means that your business will need to experience five times growth over this period to reach your new long-term goal. So your short-term goal would look something like this:

Short-term goal #1: Each quarter, we need to see roughly 25 percent revenue growth. To experience revenue growth, you may need new customers or increased sales from existing customers, so you make objectives for your short-term goal. Your objectives may look like this:

> **Objective #1:** Sales team will acquire at least two new customers per week.
>
> **Objective #2:** Sales team will contact all existing customers to offer "X" product to them at a discounted price for a limited time.

But hold up, you're not done yet. Now you have to apply oversight to your goals and objectives. Remember to inspect what you expect! That may look something like this:

> **Oversight #1:** Sales managers will be responsible for driving their individual sales teams to reach weekly quotas. All sales managers are to provide biweekly progress reports on Tuesday by noon and Fridays by 9 a.m.

> **Oversight #2:** All reports will be reviewed by the director and discussed in a weekly meeting.

You can motivate your sales force and sales managers by throwing in incentives to inspire them to reach your target faster. Incentives create friendly competition so that your team adopts your mission with extra vigor. One of your incentives may look like this:

> **Incentive:** The sales team with the highest sales for the quarter will receive a bonus of "X" dollars and be recognized in the company's quarterly online newsletter. Public recognition can be just as powerful a tool as money, so use it to motivate the soldiers around you to excel on the battlefield and swing the war in your favor.

This is a very basic example of effective, strategic goal setting. Of course, you should tailor your goal setting to your reality, industry, and overall vision. But always remember that anyone without goals is like a tree without roots, as they are not firmly planted in their foundation!

8. **Being open-minded:** This one is key! Being able to accept new ideas, being creative, and viewing your business from every angle with a fresh eye is imperative. Keeping an open mind definitely leads to greater success and inner happiness. Just by practicing this, you attract new opportunities to yourself—ones that can be beneficial to you and your industry. Enough said!

Hopefully, the concepts I've discussed in this chapter will be of value to you, either now or in the future. If your goal is to build success and maintain it—and if your desire is strong enough—you will.

If you have a big enough why, you will figure out the how!

28

Becoming the Best Version of Yourself

SO WHAT DO I do now that's different from what I did ten, fifteen, or twenty years ago? Certain things have changed about my daily routine, my outlook, and the principles and moral compass that guide me. In my opinion, we are driven by habits. It's possible that you can change your life simply by changing your habits and creating a new set of patterns to follow.

I'd like to share some thoughts on what I consider to be my secret sauce for producing a better me, a more proactive me, and a more efficient me. Applying these ideas will surely put you on the road to being the best version of yourself, which I believe is the true purpose of humankind.

Here is my secret sauce.

Treat People with Respect

Okay, so coming to terms with my anger and letting go of it produced some unexpected benefits. As I've mentioned earlier, I now have the capacity to love at a much greater volume than before. Another milestone for me, in lessons of love, were the births of my daughters. They started a chain reaction that resulted in an extension of my love for other people and a higher respect for friends, associates, and strangers alike.

My point is, treating all people with respect can produce some wonderful things. For one, it enhances your reputation and presence in the community through your social, business, and personal interactions. Your existing relationships also become enriched. Treating people well is also important because you never know when you'll meet them again. There's an old saying that goes like this: "The same people you pass on your way up will be the same people you see on your way down."

Taking it a step further, the people you help pull up while you're moving up may be the same people who lend a hand to prevent you from falling any further on your way down. They may even swing the tide by helping you to quickly recover and go up again. The unseen benefits of treating *all* people with respect are endless and will carry you further than almost anything else in life.

CARE ABOUT OTHER PEOPLE'S SUCCESS

Caring about other people's successes has to be next on your secret sauce menu. The universal law of return applies here. One way to truly start on the road to success, especially for me, is to want success for others. If you wish blessings on other people, you are sure to receive blessings in your own world. Now it's up to you how you seize the opportunity within that blessing, but a blessing nonetheless will present itself to you. *One way to guarantee your success is to show people that it is in their best interest to promote yours.*

But in your core, you have to want them to have it as well. If part of their success means working for a great company and having the best leader possible, then you have to be that for them. In turn, you strengthen the foundation that allows you to accomplish your goals.

Show people the things you learned along the way. One day, I promise you'll need help to get to the next level. We all need help from time to time. Information should not be hoarded but given freely. For us to expand and grow as a nation, as a people, as a race, we must spread valuable knowledge to others who are thirsty for it.

Practice Affirmations

Next up on the secret sauce menu: affirmations. Affirmations serve to reinforce your subconscious and psyche. There will be times when you become weak, and it's natural to not feel as strong some days as others. You have to insure yourself with what I call a "multivitamin" fail-safe for your true north, purpose, motivation, and drive. An affirmation is defined in the dictionary (*Oxford Languages*) as:

> **af·firm·a·tion**, əfər'maSH(ə)n/ *noun*
> plural noun: affirmations
> 1. The action or process of affirming something or being affirmed
> 2. Emotional support or encouragement (in this case, self-encouragement)

Affirmations are powerful, and I don't know any successful person on earth who doesn't take advantage of this secret power. A great way to start an affirmation system is to write down every great quality that:

1. You admire about yourself
2. You aspire to have
3. You want to enforce in yourself daily
4. You want to put considerable focus on

Say them to yourself aloud every morning with conviction. Do this faithfully and work it into your daily routine, just like brushing your teeth in the morning.

Create a Vision Board

A vision board is just as important and powerful as an affirmation system. Creating a vision board activates the Law of Attraction, which states that we create the things, events, and people that come into our lives.

Our thoughts, feelings, words, and actions produce energies that attract like energies.

A vision board plants the seeds of your future trees that are to come to fruition. Remember, when a seed is magically planted, it will bear fruit greater than its weight and original value. You should intend on creating a forest with this platform, so don't just plant one seed; plant many. Literally, go and get a giant poster board and fill it with writing and images that relate to your goals for the next year.

For example, you might have a goal of starting a car wash business. On your vision board, you would either write out your dream or attach a picture of a car wash facility to it. If you desire a brand new, candy-apple-red sports car as a byproduct of your goal, find a picture of that exact car and put it on your vision board as well. You can get as creative as you want. That's the beauty of the vision board: it is *yours*. After you've created your vision board, take time to review it daily, weekly, or monthly and engrave the words and images in your mind. See it, taste it, smell it!

And just to let you know how powerful the vision board is, I was going through my vision board the other day and was surprised to see this:

For the past ten years, friends and family members have been asking me to write a book. (Of course, they all have their own reasons for wanting it to happen.) Writing a book has been on my bucket list, but I didn't plan on doing anything about it until a few years from now. When I was writing out my goals and desires on my last vision board near the end of 2015, I decided to include "write a book" on it.

About nine months later, in June 2016, I had the sudden motivation to write. I promise you this: when the motivation hit, the thought wasn't at the forefront of my brain, let alone on my to-do list with all the shit I got going on. As I caught this wave of inspiration out of the blue, I figured I'd write a few thoughts down just to organize them for later. Well, I ended up diving head first into the project, working on it every single day.

Two days ago, when I looked at the vision board that I'd created many months before, I was shocked to see that writing a book was on it. I was astonished. More than anything, though, the experience was total confirmation of the power of the vision board. Honestly, it's what inspired this chapter. So, I tell you this right now from personal experience: complete your vision board today, plant the seeds of your desires and goals, and watch them come to life over time.

Work Out/Exercise

Fitness is directly correlated with success. I am a walking testament to this, as are many, *many* others. Working out builds confidence like nothing else. For some, it serves as a peaceful way to get in touch with themselves. For others, it's meditation, a stress reliever, or a way to get mentally stronger. Some even look at their workouts as a spiritual experience. Here are the views of some very successful people on working out:

> I go to bed early and get up at 4 a.m. to train. Then I eat, take my supplements, spend some time on my lines, and get to work.
> —Mark Wahlberg, actor, producer, and entrepreneur

> I schedule workouts like they're meetings and make sure they don't get canceled. I make a deliberate plan to fit a workout into my schedule each day.
> —Ryan Seacrest, television/radio host and producer

> I don't always get to the gym or even pack workout clothes if I'm covering breaking news, so I do a lot of workouts in hotel rooms.
> —Jeff Glor, anchor, *CBS Evening News Sunday Edition*

> I stay in my routines and focus on the
> present and on our next opponent.
> I work out at 7 a.m. five days a week before work.
> Then I add workouts at 2 p.m. two or three days a week.
> —Jim Larrañaga, head coach,
> University of Miami men's basketball team

> When I fail to work out, my ability to be effective
> professionally and personally suffers.
> So I work out. Because we're called to
> great service, not great suffering.
> —Cory Booker, former mayor of Newark, New Jersey,
> and current U.S. Senator

Enough said! If these successful folks are doing it, why aren't you? Remember this: the easiest way to be successful is by doing exactly what successful people do.

Eliminate Distractions

> A man can be as great as he wants to be.
> If you believe in yourself and have the courage,
> The determination, the dedication,
> And the competitive drive
> And if you are willing to sacrifice
> The little things in life and
> Pay the price for the things that are
> worthwhile, it can be done.
> —Vincez, football coach and
> National Football League executive

To be honest with you, I believe that distractions are the biggest enemy to accomplishment. Distractions will come at you in any form, at any time. You cannot allow yourself to let distractions knock you off your focus. As I've said before, the fastest way to accomplish a mission is to become like a man possessed, so obsessed with reaching his goal that he can't see anything else. Understand how life works, for there will always be distractions lurking in every corner of every path you travel.

Some of these distractions disguise themselves in the biggest cloaks, presenting every possible excuse for you to stop what you're doing. Beware of this and practice your willpower for ignoring them. The more skillful you are in eliminating distractions, the more you will obtain laser-like focus, an attribute that complements and compensates successful people well. Bruce Lee once stated, "I fear not the man who has practiced 10,000 kicks once, but I fear the man who has practiced one kick 10,000 times!"

Follow the 90/10 Rule

I'm about to put you on the straight game right now and drop a heavy jewel. You want a true formula that I *know* works? Follow this blueprint:

After you establish your mission, goals, and objectives, everything else is about time management. If you spend the majority of your time in line with your cause, you will become unstoppable and your dreams will be achieved at lightning speed. The most efficient way to do this is by following what I call the "90/10 rule." This rule states that you only have so much time in a day to be effective. When you eliminate sleep (an average of eight hours) and needed breaks (2½ hours for eating, clearing your mind, personal hygiene, and workouts), then you have 13½ remaining hours in a day to be as productive as you can push yourself to be. If you're like me—a heavy pusher who will work seven days a week—then you'll take those 13½ daily hours and turn them into 94½ hours to use toward obtaining your goals in a 168-hour week.

Imagine your effective time accrued as a paid time off (PTO) system. Allow yourself at least ten hours each week to recharge your batteries. (You might even want to take a full day off and make Sunday a day of rest.) Do something fun. Allow yourself some irresponsible time—some "me time." This may mean going out and partying, going fishing, playing golf, or spending some time with a friend or romantic interest. Whatever. The goal is to reward yourself for working so hard and truly blow off some steam. During this time, don't answer the phone for business. Be selfish. You owe it to yourself. This will undoubtedly keep you balanced.

This thinking is even used in the bodybuilding world, where bodybuilders will eat a very strict, healthy diet six days a week but allow for an "anything goes" cheat meal or cheat day on the seventh day. It helps them to keep their head in the game and even prevents them from falling off the wagon. This theory emphasizes balance. I wouldn't recommend a more relaxed schedule until you establish yourself in working toward your goal.

The time-and-energy investment needed at the beginning of any venture is immense if you want it to flourish quickly and correctly. But a word of advice: stopping and starting is a bad idea. It's a momentum killer. A 50/50 ratio is too hard to maintain because you have to keep regathering motivation. Plus, I feel it's not sufficient for the motivated entrepreneur who has that fire and wants to bring their dreams to reality.

Prioritize

> DISCIPLINE IS DOING WHAT YOU NEED TO DO,
> WHEN YOU NEED TO DO IT, WHETHER YOU
> FEEL LIKE DOING IT OR NOT.
>
> —ANONYMOUS

The power of prioritizing will greatly define what you do on a daily basis, what you have time for, and what you don't have time to waste on. It will help shape the circles of people in your life and guide your real-time decision-making about whether something is a liability or an asset worthy of spending physical energy and time on. Remember, time is so special, as it's the one thing that can't be duplicated. You must use it wisely. The way you master your time will determine how effective you are in general. And when you find things that are in line with your priorities—things that you should spend time on—do them to the best of your ability. As the saying goes, *how you do anything is how you do everything!*

Handle Situations Differently

Coming from the streets has often affected how I respond to situations. In the past, I was often told that I could be a bit over the top when faced with a confrontation or an adversary. But growing up and evolving is about controlling your anger and your emotions. After all, you have a reputation to uphold. The more you ladder yourself to success, the more you may become a pillar of the community, so people watch your actions more.

I had to learn patience, calmness, de-escalation (for myself and others), and anger management. I had to come to terms with the fact that I cannot handle things as an adult in the corporate world as I would in the street. (As a matter of fact, if I handle things like I would in the street, I could put myself in situations that could compromise all the beautiful things I have going on. I would risk my freedom, publicly embarrass my family and friends, and so on.)

I had to understand that the more successful I become, the more people depend on me. And as more people depend on me, their families depend on them. It's a chain reaction of dependence. Then there are my daughters, who, of course, depend on me. I have a lot riding on the decisions I make and how I react to things. When I had a "fuck the world" mentality, it wasn't this complicated. But with great power comes great responsibility, and that means thinking before acting.

29

Doing the Right Thing Means Doing Things Right!

DO YOU WANT to know why my construction company, in its third year in business, didn't follow the growth patterns of years one and two? As I told you, in our first year, we made over $675,000. (In fact, we did that in the first six months.) Second year, we did $1.2 million in revenue. The third year, though, we only did $1.1 million. Here's why.

A Huge Opportunity

In our third year, we got in bed with a very large, well-known corporation that did fire alarm and high-end security installation. (I'm keeping its name confidential out of respect for the privacy of everyone involved.) The large company was getting leaner, slimming down with the goal of becoming more profitable. Its principals made the decision to sell only high-end security equipment, as well as software management and monitoring solutions. The company got rid of its labor force of installers and started subbing that work out to smaller companies like ours. It worked for us, as we profited from installations. That's the short of it.

Anyway, the company landed all of the hospitals under the HCA Healthcare umbrella on the U.S. East Coast. The project involved upgrading all camera systems, access controls, nurses stations, and so on. Because of our great relationship with these guys, we immediately got dibs on the first hospital in our area. What did the job look like for us? Close to $200K. Even better than that, they said if we performed perfectly on this job, we'd have first rights to the next seven hospitals. That was $1.4 million dollars in HCA hospitals alone. Coupled with our other work, we were looking at closing out the year with $3 to $4 million in revenue. The large company needed the job done quickly, efficiently, and professionally. Our contacts there knew the quality of our work and were confident about putting the job in our hands.

We Had to Think Fast

Our contacts took forever to seal the deal, but when the job came online, they wanted us to move on it right away. The problem was, most of our core workforce was tied up on other projects we had committed to while we waited for the green light. We were faced with a dilemma: we couldn't pull our guys off of active jobs, as they had tight timelines, too, but we couldn't pass up this $200K either. Fuck nah!

We had to think fast. My strategy was to call in some electricians we'd used in the past on wire-pulling jobs and lock them in at a rate of $17 per hour. They'd pull all the wire while buying time for my main guys to get on the job. This was a great idea for a couple of reasons. First, it would satisfy our client that we were making progress. Second, it would save us 25 percent on labor costs. The independent contractors were not only 1099'd but they were also cheaper than the $25-per-hour techs on our regular payroll. (Side note: Our field is specialized and requires licensing and background checks by the Department of Criminal Justice Services. We were in compliance when it came to our regular guys but not with the stand-in electricians who were pulling wire for us. Not with the time constraints we were facing.)

Things Went Downhill Fast

Two weeks into the job, everything was going smoothly. Actually, the electricians had covered twice the distance we expected. Those boys were humping, which meant more profit for us as a company. Couldn't be smoother. So $200K, here we come! We were down to just days before my core team would hit the hospital and get busy. Well, it was a Monday and we got a phone call. One of the stand-in electricians was working on the children's floor of the hospital, where security was very tight. One of the nurses on the floor spotted the guy and knew him from outside of the hospital. She reported to her superiors that she thought he was a sex offender. Hospital authorities hurried to the area, where he was working with another guy. They requested their IDs and took both downstairs for instant background checks. Turns out, he *was* a sex offender! Some shit in his past for statutory rape or something. Wow!

The information traveled uphill fast. Things went downhill for us just as quickly. The issue went all the way to the top of both HCA and the company that had hired us as a subcontractor. To make a long story short, a conference call was held. To protect their asses, our contacts at the major company kicked us off the project. The $200K slipped through our fingers just like that! We did everything in our power to rectify the situation, but, unfortunately, too many people were involved and the problem had become too big. (One thing you need to understand about the corporate world is that people will go into cover-your-ass mode when shit starts to go down.)

No Such Thing As A Shortcut

Everything that happened was my fault. I had to take responsibility for it. I was the one who had come up with the plan. I was the one who'd skipped our processes and procedures. All of it could've been avoided with a simple background check. Fuck! How could I have been so careless? That was a lot of money! When I say that everybody was mad at me, I mean it: HCA Healthcare; the major company that hired us; my partners in the company; and our employees, who would have gained years of job security if the project had gone forward. There was so much riding on this job and I fucking blew it! It felt like the end of the world at the time—it really did. I was so disgusted with myself and was whipping my own ass tremendously.

I learned a no-shortcut lesson, for sure!

But I also learned that in every horrible situation, there is light. The whole yin and yang of things. This is why there's a little black dot on the white side of the yin and a little white dot on the black side of the yang. For me, this was a very valuable lesson. There's no such thing as a shortcut! And trust me, if you do take one, it will always bite you in the ass. Don't be like me and make a $1.4 million mistake. Be careful and do things right because that will always pay off in the long run. Of course, I eventually recovered from that experience and came out a wiser man and an even smarter businessman. Today, I know the value of "trusting in God but tying up your camel."

30

Use Me but Don't Misuse Me

THIS LESSON HITS home. Remember when I told you that money didn't change me, but it changed the people around me? The sad thing about transforming in an environment while the environment stays the same is that people start to approach you in one of three ways. Some will treat you the same as they always did. Others will come at you with the mindset of "You got it, so you shouldn't mind giving it," as if you owe them something. Still others won't know your background and simply assume that you were born with a silver spoon in your mouth.

Circle Constantly Being Refined

I hate that my circle of friends, family, and acquaintances is constantly being refined because of people approaching me for money. Not long ago, for example, a friend from way back came to me for money. Actually, the loan wasn't even for him but for somebody else. I asked for a few days to think it over before I told him I couldn't do it. It wasn't a reasonable risk. Now, this guy isn't somebody I've been in great touch with in recent years, but I look on our history fondly and will always consider him a friend. Still, because I told him no, our relationship will never be the same. He felt that I had it but wouldn't lend it. He was asking for roughly $7,000. I'm not willing to just throw $7,000 out there if I'm not totally confident it will make its way back home. Period.

A lot of the people who will come to you for money have no *way* to pay you back and have no *intention* of paying you back. Some may actually have the intention but lack the financial discipline to set aside even small amounts of money, let alone pay you back. This causes a dilemma. Because I have good financial instincts, it doesn't make any sense to me to lend money to an unstable situation. (The bank won't do it. Why the fuck do you feel I should?) So you say no. And when you say no? Then they ridicule you and label you as selfish or say that you are acting brand new or *that you have changed*. Nope! I'm still the same person. I just didn't have the money before when I told you no, so you didn't take it personally. If I'd had the money back then, I still would've told you no! Believe that!

If you have people around you who have achieved what you're trying to achieve, approach them right. Learn the difference between using and misusing. If you do, you can actively build the people around you to be beneficial to you and, more importantly, you to them. Here are a few things I've learned.

Don't Let People Take Advantage of You

One classic example of misuse to watch out for is "taking advantage." Sometimes people you interact with are more stable than others when it comes to finances. So sometimes, because they're friends or business associates, it might make sense (or, should I say, present less risk) to help them out from time to time. But what do you do when those people misuse you and think they have more leeway *because* they have a bond with you? They end up taking advantage and then destroying or greatly damaging the relationship. So they may take forever to pay just part of your money back or put you on the back burner while they spend the money that should go to you. They wouldn't do that to a payday loan, would they? Nope. Because the interest that would kill them is not in their best interest! Once again, they act in a way they wouldn't if you were a bank. And it kills me how the average human is so quick to give more consideration and courtesy to strangers than to the people in their immediate circle.

As you experience success, whatever that means for you, learn how to preserve your relationships with family and friends by saying "no." In essence, I've learned that I would rather not put myself in that position. Remember, you have a choice! Just because you have money doesn't mean that you have to give it away. Save yourself the headache. And if it gets a little uncomfortable when you want to say no, the truth always works.

Say, "Look, I don't get involved with money and friends and family. I'm sorry, but I had a real bad situation happen a while back and, ever since then, I choose not to. I love you too much as a friend and respect what we have too much to risk being in that uncomfortable space. You can understand that, right?" And leave it at that. The more successful you become, the more you will face these situations. Heed this advice: it's better to be a little awkward now than very awkward later!

Of course, there will be times when you really want to help somebody out—and you should! The key is, do it on your own terms and not because somebody forces you to. In a situation like this, when you want to help, you have two choices. One, simply give from the heart! Two, don't lend any money that you're not willing to lose!

The bottom line is, whether you're already successful or on your way, don't take advantage of people just because you can and don't allow people to take advantage of you.

Transform Yourself Into an Asset

This one goes under the category of "use me, but don't misuse me." It is your duty to try your best not to be a liability to someone else, whether you're successful or not, because people hate liabilities. Instead, be creative enough to transform yourself into an asset to people with the potential to change your life.

Look for What You Can Do for You!

To sum it up, yes, it's very true that God blesses me tremendously. And I am very grateful for where I am in life. But don't think for a second that I don't have to work for every blessing. God blesses the child who has his own.

And the way I honestly feel, the moment I stop having gratitude or stop working for everything I have, I will limit my blessings. Take a look at people who are successful and you'll see that most of them have adopted this way of thinking. You have to get away from the mentality that somebody owes you something! Don't look for what someone can do for you, but what *you* can do for you!

31

Burning the Candle at Both Ends

You can do anything, but not everything!
— Unknown

YOU WILL HAVE ups and downs, failures and successes, on your journey. You'll also learn some lessons in what not to do. I want to share with you my experience with one of those kinds of journeys—in this case, a time when my ambition could not match the speed at which I piled new responsibilities on my plate.

A New Proposal to Consider

A few years ago, one of my closest friends, Jay, came to me with a business idea. At the time, he owned a very successful paint company and a few convenience stores. Needless to say, he had a great deal of business experience. He dreamed about owning a nightclub. It was one of the things on his business bucket list. One night when we were hanging out, he asked me to get into the nightclub business with him as an equal partner. I turned him down. That particular industry had never sparked my interest.

A couple of months later, an opportunity appeared. A four-story building, previously the site of a nightclub, was on the market. Due to bad business practices, the club owner hadn't paid the rent and the landlord evicted him from the space. As Jay told me all this, he asked me to think the situation over thoroughly. He felt this would be a great business move that could make us both a lot of money.

Listing the Pros and Cons

For the next two weeks, I thought about his proposal long and hard. As I do in any situation, I listed my pros and cons:

Pros

- Could be very profitable
- Could be fun (I mean, I do enjoy nightlife recreationally)
- I would have a sound business partner to share the liabilities and burdens with
- I could add another business to my portfolio and create another stream of revenue
- I could build the hottest club in Richmond

Cons

- I didn't know that industry (I'd only seen it from the perspective of a consumer)
- I would have to learn a lot
- I would have to put money into the business until I made money (which is true for any investment)
- I didn't really see Richmond as a great market for nightclubs; the city had no major sports teams—unlike D.C., Charlotte, and Atlanta—which limited high-end partygoers

I took my concerns to Jay and we talked about them in detail. I was still on the fence about the idea, but I was open-minded. After a few long talks and a couple of nights of debates, I decided to give it a shot. As best we could, we built strategies for the obstacles we faced. Working on the cons against us, here's what we did:

- We figured that what we didn't know, we could either learn quickly or hire people who did know.

- We set a larger-than-expected budget aside and each assumed 50 percent responsibility.
- We decided that we would have to go big or go home regarding the market. Be the big fish in a small pond. Yes, Richmond was a smaller city. It had a smaller market for nightlife. But the key was that it did *have* a market for nightlife, so we would have to "Walmart" the "mom-and-pop" competition. With the size of our club, that was a definite possibility.

What Went Wrong? Everything That Could

I started to get excited about the idea once I gave my official buy-in, and I was up for the challenge! Sometimes challenges fuel me, as I get charged up by conquering obstacles. Many people wanted this space, so we had a really small window of opportunity to move on it before the landlord signed a lease with someone else. Jay had an inside connect, so we quickly signed the lease. But we still had time because we'd set aside two months for construction and renovations.

My learning curve was going to have to be condensed. While Jay focused on the renovations, I jumped online and learned everything I could about the business. I also got an ABC consultant to handle my affairs with the state and city. The consultant also coached me on all the legal shit and red tape associated with owning a nightclub and selling alcohol.

So what went wrong? Everything that could. Murphy's Law really had its run with me on this one. First of all, construction lasted twice as long as expected, capping off at four months. The landlord ended up being a sleazy slumlord crook who attempted to gouge us for money whenever he could. He also didn't pay his real estate taxes, which led to problems for us in obtaining a certificate of occupancy, one of the requirements for the ABC license.

There was also a shitload of other stuff we didn't see coming. We ended up going over our budget by 125 percent! (Remember, we started with an overly large budget because we anticipated that we were going to run into bullshit.) Also, our ABC consultant informed us that there was no official thing known as a nightclub in Richmond. Nightclubs fell under the category of restaurants, so we had to follow the same ABC regulations that a restaurant would adhere to. One of the regulations dictated that the food-to-alcohol ratio had to be 55:45. This threw a major wrench in our plans because now we'd have to figure out a way to serve enough food to balance out our projected liquor sales.

The Flyest Club in the City

We ended up triumphing over all the hurdles that were thrown at us. By the time we opened, we had the flyest, prettiest club in the city. We set out to make it look like a D.C. or Atlanta nightclub, and it did! When you stepped in the door, you no longer felt like you were in Richmond. Unlike any other club in town, ours had that big-city feel. Now it was time to get people in the door.

My club with a line out the door.

With everything we went through to obtain our ABC license, we couldn't market the club properly because we honestly didn't know when (or even if, at times) we were going to be open. Opening depended 100 percent on being able to sell liquor because no adult in Richmond was going to come party at a club where there was no alcohol. It wasn't happening. When we finally did receive our ABC license, by the grace of God, we were at a complete disadvantage when it came to our marketing strategy. After a while, we decided that bringing in some promoters was our best tactic. After finally finding the right promoters to mess with, we had our grand opening and things went up from there.

My club while it was poppin'!

We started getting busy—super-busy! Our spot had become what we'd envisioned: the nicest, hottest, and most popular club in Richmond. We had crowds of customers on Thursday, Friday, and Saturday nights. The rest of the week, we would rent our club for all sorts of events, including business gatherings, baby showers, and reunions. We had so many customers on our busiest nights—Fridays and Saturdays—that the City of Richmond sent us a warning about the traffic congestion caused by people trying to come to the club and valet their cars.

We would hit capacity on the regular, which also attracted the attention of fire marshals, who would stand in front of our door to make sure we didn't let any more people in the building. On packed nights, people were willing to spend anything to get into the club. They would offer $100 per person just to come in. We sold VIP sections, and some folks spent close to $1,000 to look like they were the shit. People wanted to be where other people were. They also wanted to attract members of the opposite sex. One way to do that was to stunt in front of them to look like they had the most money in the club. I remember one guy from out of Charlotte who spent over $2,800 on VIP seating and bottles in one night! That was crazy!

Consuming Too Much Time and Energy

The club becoming such a success was great, but the downside was that it posed a new problem for me. Running a nightclub-slash-restaurant meant dealing with security, promoters, DJs, light production, payroll, employee management specific to that industry, inventory control, valet parking specialists, and special events. It also meant maintaining accurate records of food sales versus liquor sales and handling the Mixed Beverage Annual Review (MBAR), which new license holders have to complete every six months with the Virginia ABC.

It was overwhelming and started to consume too much of my time and energy. Remember, I had several other businesses that needed my attention as well—ones that brought me better profits, for that matter. I tended to all my other businesses during regular business hours, from 8 a.m. to 6 p.m. But the club worked on opposite hours, Thursday to Saturday from 9 p.m. to 2 a.m. And those were just the prime hours when I had to be there. There were also a whole lot of behind-the-scenes hours for the club that I had to steal from other things.

I didn't have the option of not completing my daily and weekly to-do lists because if I didn't, there'd be a butterfly effect that would create a shit storm I'd have to clean up later. I could've used more help, but with me not fully knowing the industry, I would've only created more payroll expense and slowed my learning curve. There were certain things I had to do myself until I mastered them. Then I could delegate properly and apply the proper oversight.

What I could delegate, I did. But this was a cash business, and minimizing the number of hands that money floated through meant that less cash was stolen. Even with management, to inspect what you expect, I had to know what to fully expect. The faster business picked up, the more difficult it was to apply the proper oversight. Things just felt like they were going a mile a minute.

"Don't Forget Why You Work So Hard"

I started sleeping less and less. I saw my kids less and less. I mean, I was literally working so much that my family wouldn't see me for days on end. One day, Sheila approached the situation after I got a little short with her out of frustration. She said something to me that was so simple yet put things into perspective. She said, "Don't forget why you work so hard." And that made sense. I was working hard so I could have financial freedom and spend more time with my family. I'd achieved the financial freedom part, but I'd allowed my ambitions to steal away my most important "why": time with my family. I came to the realization that I was burning the candle at both ends.

After that, I felt a growing discontent for my new business and started to dislike the club scene in general. Seeing it behind the scenes had given me a whole different perspective. It was like I was at a constant party where people didn't know how to hold their liquor. It would amaze me how women would come to the club looking elegant, classy, and graceful and then walk out as totally different people, often belligerent, loud, and uncouth.

Took a Loss but Gained Perspective

I made the decision to leave the business and handed it over to my partner. In the long run, I took a loss, but I gained perspective. I realized that the club was reducing my effectiveness with my other businesses. It didn't make sense to become 100 percent at one thing in my world at the expense of becoming 75 percent at everything else. I also realized that I'd started to compromise my own peace of mind and personal life balance.

The moral of this story is fourfold. One, it's important to have balance in what you do, regardless of your ambition. Two, never get lost in the sauce and forget why you do what you do. Three, know when to hold 'em and when to fold 'em. And four, peace of mind is fundamental to happiness, so, unapologetically, never compromise it for no one or no thing.

32

What I Learned from the Club

ON THIS ROAD to becoming the best and most successful that I can be, I constantly learn powerful lessons. Some are jewels in disguise. Others seem to be setbacks at first but end up acting like rudders that send me toward destinations I'm meant to visit. Remember when I opened that nightclub? My biggest reason for doing it was to increase my income and overall net worth by diversifying my ventures. What I got was frustration, lack of time, and financial loss in the long run. Was I capped at my ceiling? Did I already have as much as I could possibly handle on my plate?

After the nightclub incident, I took some time to chill and get my head right. Then I found my resolve again through reading. Thank God I'm an avid reader! After reading a series of books, I found a way out of feeling stuck, like I'd hit my ceiling. I found a new motivation to challenge myself further in the business world. I also found that the answer to building more wealth was in something known as passive income. And here's why.

Active Income Versus Passive Income

Here's something I've realized about myself (everyone is different, so this may not apply to you): I am so hands-on with my businesses that I can't have so many of them without running out of time or experiencing a decline in quality of life. When you look at a business in terms of active income, factors that impact your time include the type of industry, management setup, your active oversight role, and the complexity of your operations.

Once your time is fully committed, the only way to effectively diversify your income is by adding passive income. By definition, passive income is income that is received on a regular basis with little effort required to maintain it or without active involvement in generating it. Now that sounded like something I'd be interested in! It's what the wealthy call "making money while you sleep." It sounded to me like my plan should be to make enough money in active businesses that I could invest in a machine that would yield passive income. So that became my mission.

PIELE AND RETIREMENT

As I looked further into the concept of passive income, I realized a couple of things. One, it was wise to build passive income to generate more money. Two, one day I might not want to work actively and instead live off the fruits of my labor and travel the world. Shit, that's truly the ultimate financial freedom. To have that kind of freedom one day, I knew I'd need money coming in on a dependable basis in addition to my nest egg. I could achieve this through retirement plans, yes. But retirement plans seem so fucking shaky and unstable, and most depend on other companies investing your funds in God-knows-what. I'm sorry, but maybe I'm just old school. Would you give me access to your bank account and let me control your money in hopes of stabilizing your future? After all the scandals I'd seen, including Enron, Bernie Madoff, and such, I just didn't trust that system.

Then I ran into a concept that would stick with me forever. It's called PIELE, and it's an acronym that stands for when your:

Passive (P)
Income (I)
Exceeds (E)
Living (L)
Expenses (E)

When done right, passive income is something tangible that you can build yourself and control yourself. So this concept *became* my retirement plan!

Passive Income

Now all I needed was to find the retirement plan that would work for me. In the long run, my goal was to build many streams of passive income. To keep from becoming a jack of all trades and master of none, I thought it'd be wise to master one first. I started to research as many ways as possible to build passive income. They included:

- Any type of income from selling and flipping properties
- Rent from leasing properties
- Earnings from a business that don't require direct involvement from the owner or merchant
- Interest from a bank account
- Royalties from publishing a book
- Royalties from licensing a patent or other form of intellectual property, such as computer software products
- Earnings from advertisements on websites
- Dividend and interest income from owning securities, such as stocks and bonds
- Franchising a business

Real Estate

As I studied ways of building passive income, I zeroed in on real estate. In addtion to food and clothing, one thing people will always need is shelter. That is guaranteed! I felt like this was my safest bet. So you know what I did next, right? Like I've said over and over in this book, when you want to do something, your first step is to get educated. So I did just that. I purchased over ten books on real estate and read every one of them, page by page. Then I went to people I knew in the field, including realtors and investors. Some were active in the field and others had failed. Why did I seek them out?

- Realtors could give me a perspective from those who consistently sell in the market. (I needed to know how to sell in the market.)
- Investors could give me a perspective on how to buy in the market, as well as strategies for doing so.
- People who were active in the field could teach me what to do right in the market.
- People who failed could teach me what *not* to do in the market, and I could learn from their mistakes.

What I learned is that there are many different strategies in real estate.

1. It's best to build a blueprint you can follow that complements your income and ability to invest. As with anything, study it heavily and find what you gravitate toward most. Here are some of the fundamentals about real estate that I love: if acquired right, it can be a very stable income-producing asset.
2. Real estate can appreciate greatly, meaning your investment increases over time. There are several ways to do this, from forced appreciation (making upgrades, additions, and renovations) to natural appreciation (when the overall market or neighborhood increases in value, bringing up the value of your property right along with it).
3. It has great cash-flow-producing qualities, which pay you frequently like stock dividends yet allow you more control over the payout.
4. It's a great long-term investment strategy and passive-income vehicle.
5. In my opinion, it is a solid wealth builder. Slow and steady at first, but solid.

Whether your goal is retirement, financial freedom, a certain lifestyle you desire, or generational wealth to build and pass down to your kids, real estate stands the test of time. But as in any subject, there is a right way to do it and a wrong way. An ineffective way and an effective way. And the only thin line that separates the two is education and strategy. To this day, I am very much a student in this game, and very hungry to stay that way. And the cool thing is, the better you play the game, the more it rewards you. It has definitely become a passion of mine.

God Always Opens Another Door

See, everything happens for a reason. If I hadn't gone through what I did with the club, I would've never embarked on this path. If I'd never stretched myself thin in active businesses, I never would've considered passive income. If I'd lost my motivation, felt defeated, and accepted that I'd hit my ceiling, I wouldn't have had the determination to keep digging to be three feet away from this gold. God never closes one door without opening another, even if it's hell in the hallway.

33

Advice on a Stick, Wisdom on a Platter

UNDERSTAND THIS: JUST because I don't have to sell drugs anymore and I permanently left the street life behind me doesn't mean I lost my hustle. I have the same insatiable ambition that I did before, maybe even more. It's just that I apply that drive to business now! And while I'm very much still a student in the arena of business, I do have wisdom to share. As we approach the end of this book, I would like to give some dos and don'ts, advice, and rules I feel may be valuable to you.

Love What You Do!

People often ask me how I balance being an owner of multiple businesses, a father, an advice giver, a supporter, an avid gymgoer, a hard-core reader, a traveler, and someone with a social life and multiple hobbies. That's a great question, and it has the simplest of answers. It's because I love what I do! Very rarely do I wake up on the wrong side of the bed, have a stressful day, or have to get my head together because I'm overwhelmed.

When you love what you do and truly enjoy it, you approach it with passion and enthusiasm. The result is that your work doesn't feel much like work at all. This would be my first piece of advice to you about life: find a way to love everything you do or find a way to change the things you don't. I know it's more easily said than done, but you must have short- and long-term goals to ultimately put yourself in that space. I promise you, it will make you ten times happier and your life virtually stress-free.

Dale Carnegie, the writer and lecturer, said it best: "People rarely succeed unless they have fun in what they are doing."

Assemble the Right Team

This may be the single greatest piece of business advice I can offer you: having a successful business is all about assembling the right team. It's about having the "judge of character" to pick the right people. You'll need to find people who possess the skills, knowledge, and leadership needed to carry out the missions and philosophies of your organization to accomplish the goals you set and to embody the vision of the company. It's that simple. It's all about the team. If you put together a weak team, your job is much more difficult and you're less likely to succeed.

The first step in growing a successful organization is picking your players on the basketball court. Sure, it will take some time to find the right people. This is a skill you must develop, and even then you're at the mercy of a variety of factors, including employee market availability, people who have the talent but not the drive, people who have the drive but not the talent, employees with personal problems, wolves in sheep's clothing, and more. The list goes on.

If the first step is finding the right people, the second is getting rid of your key players on the basketball court if they are weak, unfocused, or just not a good fit for your company. The moment you recognize that someone is not good for your company is the moment you need to begin the process of getting rid of them. Don't waste time. Once a person shows you their true colors, be glad that they did. Don't make the mistake of thinking you can change them. You simply don't have the time.

Your time needs to be focused on growing your business, not personally mentoring one employee. You have too many factors working against you (psychological, environmental, emotional) to devote too much time trying to make an employee take a 180-degree turn and keep their head in the game. That's not your job. It's their job. Not saying it can't be done, but this should be strictly avoided when starting out and growing a company. After the company has successfully matured, then you'll have more resources, tools, and time to do that kind of thing if you so choose.

Be Humble Enough to Listen to Other Opinions and Strong Enough to Know When You're Right

As a leader, your people want to know they have a voice with you. I strongly suggest that you promote an open-door policy and an outspoken environment. Nobody likes an arrogant leader. You do damage to yourself and your organization if you don't allow your employees, especially management, to have a voice. But what happens when there are decisions to be made and that voice is wrong? And what happens when there are multiple voices with opposing viewpoints? This is when you, as a leader, must make the final call. Be comfortable doing that *after* gathering all the facts. Also, understand that, deep down, all organizations want a strong leader. So never be weak when it comes to exercising your duty as a leader in giving the final decision, call, answer, or directive.

Realize That Every Problem Does Not Need to Be Fixed Immediately

Some problems need some thinking-cap time for the *best* solution. If it can wait, you're almost always guaranteed to find a better solution with more time and greater resolve. This can be applied in life and in business.

Get the Right Information to the Right People at the Right Time!

Let's use a driving analogy here. When an unexpected obstacle is in the road ahead of you, your brain must identify the object, process that it is a threat to you, and think of a way to get around it. The brain requires that other body parts jump into action and sends signals to the muscles in those body parts to carry out a series of motions that turn the steering wheel to successfully avoid the object. What a symphony of coordination!

Your business is exactly the same when you think of your organization as the vehicle with your employees and management as the "brain" and "body" driving it.

Know That Effectively Applying Yourself Will Determine Your Results

> You got to get up every morning with determination if you are going to go to bed with satisfaction.
>
> —George Lorimer, journalist and editor of *The Saturday Evening Post*

Once you've chosen the path you're going to walk down, you must fully commit. Ain't no half steppin'! You must accept all challenges that come your way and attack them with vigor. You must not get arrogant because of the targets you hit accurately and the things you do right. At the same time, you must not feel down or depressed when you experience failure. You must not feel lost when you don't know something but instead be inspired to seek out the information. Remember, ignorance is simply the lack of knowledge; once you obtain said knowledge, then the term can no longer be applied to you on that topic. Results lie within the journey of commitment, persistence, and consistency!

You must acknowledge your strengths and do what you can to make them stronger. You must identify your weaknesses and employ measures to transform them into strengths. You must find ways to get up and move on days when you are mentally stagnant—rain, hail, sleet, or snow!

Take This Real Estate Advice, If You Can

Real estate can be a very effective way of earning money now and later, generating all-important passive income that you earn in your sleep. The most profitable way to attack real estate is to develop seed money, invest, and keep compounding seed money by reinvesting. Essentially, keep flipping the money to make it as large as you possibly can.

Here are strategies I've found to be highly effective in the area of real estate:

1. **Buy a distressed or dilapidated property for as little money as possible and then renovate or rehab it.** The only challenge with this strategy is that you have to have "good" contractors who will give you excellent work for a great price.
2. **Buy a not-in-such-bad-shape or an in-good-condition property at a higher price if it needs only minor renovation work.** In this scenario, as in the first, the construction costs must be low! They have to be reasonable enough that after the cost of the property and renovations, you still have a comfortable cushion under the comps (comparables) of the neighborhood so that when you sell the property for market value (or close to market value), it will yield an acceptable profit.
3. **Buy an empty lot and build new.** The good thing about this strategy is that there are no hidden costs. You don't have to worry that when your contractors bust open the walls, they'll find damage, mildew, or termites. Once again, make sure that the total of the lot and construction is favorable compared to the comps in the neighborhood to ensure that your market-value sale yields an acceptable profit.

I would stay away from the model of buying a property at market value, having a mortgage on it, and attempting to rent it out. Most times, this model simply does not yield a big enough profit margin. If you own and rent multiple homes, you can find yourself robbing Peter to pay Paul, scrambling to make collected rent cover the properties with empty units or tenants who simply don't pay you.

This tight Ponzi scheme is (1) not sustainable and (2) what helped lead to the 2008/2009 housing crash. I've seen many real estate owners and landlords lose big because they could not balance this model. I highly recommend against it, unless you have a decent amount of money in reserve to cover yourself in times of famine.

In my opinion, it's better to own rental properties outright, which can happen when you reinvest a portion of your profits from flips. But be careful not to compromise your seed money, as it will be needed for more flips. However you choose to do it, playing the game right means playing the game smart! Remember, the object of the money game is to accumulate enough investments so that the income from those investments will eventually support you and your lifestyle.

If you are (or become) a buy-and-hold investor, you should have a heavy focus on cash flow. Always—and I mean *always*—make sure the numbers check out! If you can't make it make sense on paper, you will never make it make sense in the actual physical world. And since the game of real estate is about building wealth, the same goes for obsessive emphasis on increasing your cash flow. Use your profits from cash flow to create more cash flow—meaning that you should pay your mortgages off early with your profits from cash flow. This strategy will give you more cash flow overall from your portfolio performance. With this increased cash flow, you can use it to have a higher quality of life, free your time, or use it to invest in more properties to repeat the process. It's quite a genius strategy honestly but one that takes discipline and consistency.

Close the Garbage Lid on Anger

If you haven't grasped anything else from this book beyond my story up to this point, I want all entrepreneurs and aspiring entrepreneurs to understand this: whatever you're going through, either right now or in the past, you have to let go of your anger! You cannot—I repeat, you *cannot*—be a successful business person with anger. Notice how I didn't start "seeing" opportunities or having the ability to fully use those opportunities until I truly had the inner resolve to lose anger, hate, and self-pity.

Weigh the Pros and Cons of Starting a Business in an Industry You Don't Know Versus One You Do

Some say that for the ambitious, all businesses are virtually the same, with the only variables being the verticals to each specific industry. Others say you can be successful at any business as long as you're resilient enough to endure the learning curves while employing effective business strategies and practices. Still others say that business is hard enough, so stick with what you know for the greatest chance of success.

All of these folks are right. But while each statement can be true, each requires a different mindset, personality, measure of competence, patience, commitment, and level of tenacity. You must find out which scenario will allow you to marry your ambition to the road you're traveling while choosing to be the business person you want to be.

I have a little light to shed on this subject with lessons that come from my confidence and arrogance, my mistakes and learning experiences. Starting a new business in an unfamiliar field, even with great business aptitude, will take more capital. You will inevitably make mistakes while navigating your learning curve; these mistakes will cost a certain amount of money each time, with some larger and some smaller. Also, you'll have to employ more talent to compensate for what you don't know. This, too, will cost you more money. It will take a while to fully gauge the core competencies of your staff. It will also take time to fully quantify their roles and responsibilities in accomplishing certain tasks in acceptable and optimal time frames. You will eventually get it. But feeling your way in the dark in a new industry will be more expensive than establishing a start-up in a field in which you are highly skilled.

Learn the Rules of Starting a Business

Rule #1: Surround Yourself with Great People

Either you have the talent or the gold. The gold can pay for talent, but talent can be expensive, so you may profit less. However, there is very viable leverage in having the gold and employing the talent or partnering with the talent. In fact, this can be a very effective success-yielding formula.

There is a business concept that goes like this: "I don't have to be a genius—just smart enough to either surround myself with them or employ them." Either way, the skill sets of great people get adopted into your organization and give your company considerable leverage in its industry. But after acquiring the talent comes skillfully maneuvering and utilizing it. The more you master this, the more efficient and effective your organization will become.

You can't know everything. With the time it would take to master all the skills needed in your organization, it may not be even feasible, let alone in line with your personal timeline for success and financial freedom. So you have options:

1. If you already have money and business sense, you can partner with the right talent to penetrate a certain industry and create considerable profits; or
2. You can organize and hire the right talent and properly manage it to achieve the goals you've set for your company. For example, take a general construction contractor who may not hammer a single nail in his life but can complete millions of dollars' worth of contracts a year. The contractor does this simply by being a "shepherd" to talent and then employing excellent project-management skills.

My point is, no matter how much talent you have or will acquire, you'll eventually have to employ talent. Company longevity, diversification, growth, and expansion are all reasons why. How, when, and why you apply that talent depends on your strategy, purpose, business structure, and plan.

Rule #2: Never Overpromise and Underdeliver

Man, do I ever see overpromising and underdelivering happen to too many good people with so much potential. But it ends up being the downfall of their company and putting them out of business. Understand this clearly: you're either doing business-to-business (B2B) or dealing directly with consumers (B2C). The easiest way for customers to lose faith in you is by not delivering to their expectations.

They will go to another company to receive the product or service you couldn't deliver properly. Because it's so hard to gain customers in our competitive world, your biggest desire and goal must be to retain your customer base as much as possible. Customer retention is the very foundation of any business. It's also directly correlated with every facet of your business, including the two biggest, which are revenue and profits.

Being in the construction world myself, the most important lesson I had to learn is the one on overpromising and underdelivering. People would much rather that you be honest with them—telling them that you have too much work going on or can't deliver on a certain product—than bullshit them or push them to the side until you can handle their business properly.

So what do you do when you see a sudden spike in business but can't handle it? Pass on it. Say no! It's okay to say no. At least you'll walk away with your reputation. Once your reputation is damaged, it's damaged forever in the eyes of that customer. You only have one chance to make a first impression. Don't blow it!

Rule #3: Embrace Your Fear

We all have fear! Embrace it and counteract it with proper motivation to propel yourself forward. I still have fear to this day. The fear of being homeless. The fear of struggling. I've learned to embrace the fear, as it's the very thing that constantly pushes me past my own limits. It's still the very same thing that gets me up in the morning and gives me fire, day in and day out.

To be honest with you, I think every entrepreneur has some type of fear that comes from their past, defines who they are today, and reminds them of who they want to be tomorrow. It's common for successful people to have a fear of failure. It drives them to relentlessly attack problems until they find the right solutions. This brings to mind the philosophical question: do they succeed because they produce the proper elements for success or do they succeed because they won't accept nothing but success? Learn how to embrace your fears and convert them into the proper "why" to fuel your motivation for the positive outcomes you seek.

RULE #4: REMEMBER THAT YOU CAN FAIL A MILLION TIMES, BUT YOU ONLY HAVE TO GET IT RIGHT ONCE!

> LITTLE MINDS ARE TAMED AND SUBDUED WITH MISFORTUNE, BUT GREAT MINDS RISE ABOVE IT.
>
> —WASHINGTON IRVING, WRITER, HISTORIAN, AND DIPLOMAT

If you experience failure along the way, remember that it's not about how you fall; it's about how you get back up. Keep going, keep pushing! Once you get it right, you get it right! People don't see how many times you fail, but they do see when you succeed. Who cares how many times you failed if by the end of the road you're a millionaire, right? And always remember, you may have to fight a battle more than once to win it!

As Truman Capote, the writer and actor, said, "Failure is the condiment that gives success its flavor."

RULE #5: P = W/T (POWER = WORK/TIME)

Work smarter, not just harder! Remember this universal law of physics: power equals energy (or work) divided by time! Your goal for growth is to find a way to produce better results while improving quality, while increasing production, while doing it with less effort. This concept is what transitioned us from the agricultural era to the industrial era to the service era. Information technology was the catalyst, allowing us to make machines that replaced labor (work) with technology, which got things done faster and more efficiently than slow physical labor (time). Apply this same theory to people in your circumference in addition to using the information technology that we have available to us. Find a way to become more powerful in business without sacrificing effectiveness or efficiency.

RULE #6: REMEMBER THAT DREAMS ONLY WORK IF YOU DO

> TO ACCOMPLISH GREAT THINGS, WE MUST NOT ONLY ACT BUT ALSO DREAM; NOT ONLY PLAN, BUT ALSO BELIEVE.
>
> —ANATOLE FRANCE, POET, NOVELIST AND JOURNALIST

> MOTIVATION IS WHAT GETS YOU STARTED,
> HABIT IS WHAT KEEPS YOU GOING!
>
> —JIM RYUN, OLYMPIC ATHLETE

Lose the idea that you can make this dream of yours work without elbow grease. It's impossible without putting the necessary work into pushing this vehicle so it can move to your desired destination. What you did before brought you the results you had before and was in line with your old habits. To do something new and get where you've never gone before, you have to start moving in a way that you've never done before. You must build a new habit system. Your new habits have to be in line with your dream.

The more you zero in on transforming your old habits into effective new ones, the more you will morph into the dream-producing machine you desire to be. Once again, to master your goals is simply to effectively manage your time and what you do with it. Once you've established where you want to go, then it's time to get off your ass and start moving relentlessly to get there.

RULE #7: EMPLOY UNORTHODOX SOLUTIONS FOR MANAGING MULTIPLE BUSINESSES

Owning and managing multiple businesses can be harder for some than others. But by thinking outside the box, you can find some very unorthodox solutions that can make things easier. It's really all about merging your schedule and workforce appropriately to streamline your time, resources, and processes. I've made managing more than one business easier by employing certain hacks, if you will. In other words, I find creative ways to make my life simpler because simple is better and easier to mentally manage.

Here's an example. Since most businesses have similar back-office verticals and functions (payroll and invoicing, for example), you could find a competent employee or small group of employees, teach them the necessary skills, and then apply them to your multiple companies. Once you've found the right person or people, you can use them for all your businesses, which saves you from having several people carrying out the same functions. By taking human competency and marrying it with information technology and software programs like QuickBooks, you can easily track accounts receivable and accounts payable and perform a multitude of other functions that were once carried out by a team of people.

Of course, this kind of relationship has to be based on trust, respect, and great communication. I used to have a highly competent HR manager named Lisa, for example, who played a role in several of my businesses. Lisa handled most of my invoice management and could tell me at any time in two minutes flat how much money was owed to each of my companies. She was literally an extension of me and could tell you how my brain ticks. That's how close we were. Sure, I'd spot check behind her, and I'm open about it. You must. (Remember: Inspect what you expect!) But this doesn't bother her as she understands the fundamental concept of checks and balances. Unfortunately, Lisa grew a tumor on her brain and barely survived her operation. But the ideology of the "Lisa" concept would live with me forever and would be something I would keep evolving way into the future and even to this day.

Rule #8: Understand Revenue Versus Profit and Don't Get Caught Up in the Hype

Let's start with an example. John and Tom both have businesses. John grosses $1 million annually with his business, while Tom grosses only $250,000 a year. Which one would you rather be? On paper, John is way more successful than Tom, right? But hold on a minute. Let's take a closer look at this situation.

John owns a service company and has twenty employees. He rents office space to accommodate the size of his business. He pays high rent to be centrally located where the action is, in a part of town with many other businesses and where real estate is more expensive.

Tom owns an IT company and has only one employee: himself. He doesn't have office space, because his work is mobile. He prepares his invoices in his home office and travels to his clients' worksites to perform his work.

John's overhead is substantial and includes expensive rent, payroll, employee benefits, company vehicles, and more. Tom's overhead is slim.

All he spends his operating funds on is food for lunch, his car payment (which he runs through his business), and gas to get to his jobs. He charges his customers for his labor for installing and servicing their computers and networks. He also charges his customers for parts and materials. Tom's company is considerably leaner than John's since John employs his talent, while Tom is the talent in his business.

Here's a quick lesson in earnings before interest, taxes, depreciation, and amortization (EBITDA), which is used as an indicator of the overall profitability of a business. According to EBITDA, the stronger company is Tom's! John's EBITDA is about $90,000. Tom's EBITDA is $225,000. Tom's business is two-and-a-half times more profitable than John's. Who would you rather be now? The moral of this story is don't be so concerned with how much revenue you make; be more concerned with profit.

I hope you've gotten something out of the business principles I've shared here. Because the reality is, we're always participating in one business or another, even if we don't own one. Think about that for a second and let it digest. You participate in multiple businesses, whether you're working for someone else to pay bills and survive, getting something to eat (take out, dine in, or grocery), buying clothes, going to college, or even getting locked up! (Yes, prison is big business!) You're living in a world of constant business with each move you make.

Now, you have a choice of ways to become part of a business. (1) You could work for someone else with the simple goal of paying your bills on time and having a roof over your head. (2) You could take it a step further by participating in a business as an invested employee, helping its growth and sustaining your life at the same time. (3) You could take it to an entirely new level by becoming one of the company's top managers or its CEO. (4) You could create your own business and, in the process, affect a multitude of people.

I myself have been put in a position, especially over the past ten years, where I can affect many people. What's amazing is that even my old connects who aren't in the game anymore still come to me for business advice. These people—people I used to go to for work—are now coming to me for my knowledge and expertise in the business world. It's a blessing to not only believe in yourself but also have others believe in you so much that they respect your opinion and look to you for guidance.

I feel very blessed to have experienced so much so far on this road called life. I hope my story has affected each of you in some way. Maybe it's entertained you. Maybe it's given you hope or inspired you. Or maybe you already know me and it's given you a better perspective into who I am. No matter what experience you've had with my book, my wish is that you enjoyed reading it.

34

So What about Sheila?

I KNOW THAT I've mentioned Sheila a lot in this book, and she appears throughout many of my stories. So I know you are probably wondering, *Is she still around?* She is very much still around! In fact, we are—and still make—a great team, although there were challenging moments along the road. Financial growth and newfound freedoms can lead to the luxury of choices that were never at our disposal previously. But some of these options can be toxic if we are naive to their consequences. This set her on a journey where she also had her own lessons, which would later transform into guiding principles.

I would like to share her story of then and now. And I want to, as I have with every other part of this book, be as transparent as possible with you! So consider this a story within a story.

The Paradox of Freedom

Sheila grew up in the projects, as stated earlier. So she also knew what it felt like to live in extreme poverty and definitely knows what it's like to go without. Her rough beginnings taught her the value of hard work, hustle, perseverance, and breaking through the "eggshell" of limitations (environmental and self-imposed), if you will. In time, we started our own businesses and made them successful.

Somewhere along the line, we cracked the code on being successful and started to benefit from the perks of success, such as being able to go where we wanted, eat where we wanted, buy what we wanted, and do what we wanted. (This actually happened twice, in two stages: once when hustling, and then again, collectively, when we transformed skillfully into business.)

We were blessed to just keep growing more and more. But a funny thing happened at a certain point. The more successful we became, the more Sheila started to change. She adopted a viewpoint of "Shit, I worked hard then so that I don't have to work hard now. I feel like I paid my dues!" And with this mentality, she participated in our businesses less and less. We argued about this a lot.

"We didn't get here by sitting the hell around all day!" I would say.

"You fucking *like* working every day," she would tell me. "I don't! Pay somebody else to do that shit! I'm not going into that office every day. I didn't come this far to keep working! Just because we own a business does not mean you have to go to work like you're a fucking employee! Plus, business is *your* passion. That's what fuels you. I've been working all my life, our business or not, and I'm tired of working."

I don't know if it was because of burnout, rebelliousness, or her version of a midlife crisis. Who knows? All I know is that the arguments wouldn't stop. The more I forced her to come to work, the more friction we had. Eventually, the conflict was obvious to our employees. I knew we had to do something or our relationship would suffer, along with our business. I decided to take the route that would cause me the least amount of stress. I took over the businesses while Sheila stayed at home and enjoyed what she considered to be freedom.

In a few months, Sheila's habits started to change. She didn't wake up at 7:30 a.m. anymore. Instead, she woke up whenever her body felt like waking up. As she got up later and later, she naturally started going to sleep later. Her activity levels slowly started changing as well. She was no longer as active as she was when she had more responsibilities. She ate when she wanted, slept when she wanted, and did what she wanted, without discipline or self-governance.

Because she had access to money and could spend at will, she started to become impulsive, buying things when she felt bored and shopping to fill the time in her day. Sure, this brought an instant joy, but the immediate gratification started to become paper thin, each time creating a hole or an itch that couldn't be satisfied with scratching. Before long, her willpower wasn't being exercised whatsoever.

Food started to lose its flavor, so she ate at nicer and nicer places to satisfy her taste buds. The clothes she wore didn't bring that feeling of excitement like they used to, so she tried shopping more often. She worked harder and harder to get those immediate feelings of excitement (falsely mistaken as happiness) that things once brought her. Sleeping in was now the new everyday habit. Ironically, it started making her feel like shit because the day would pass her by, even though she had nothing to do. But that was the thing: SHE HAD NOTHING TO DO!

Sheila started to feel like her life was spiraling out of control. Empty. Like it had no purpose. Meanwhile, I was full of determination, dedication, routine, LIFE! We started to grow apart. Our frequencies were not aligned.

But she continued to live life on a day-by-day basis, swallowed by the heap of bad habits she'd formed by not maintaining her positive ones. More and more, her emptiness set in. One day, it all came crashing down on her. Things became too dark! Then she had an awakening. A breakthrough. But when she did, she realized she had gained more than thirty pounds, lost her sense of stick-to-itiveness, and was told by her doctor that she had high blood pressure. It was a moment of reckoning for her when she wondered how she had arrived there.

She then went through a heavy transformation period and reunited with herself. Discovered what was really important to her. Reconditioned herself. Realigned her resolve to find purpose. When she came out of her dark period, she had a whole new perception about what she wanted to do with her life.

The Muse Speaks

Somehow God spoke to her through art, and the canvas was her universe. She found self-therapy through painting, and this became her place of peace. And she didn't stop there. She dedicated herself to create a full-fledged nonprofit organization. By losing herself and finding her way through darkness, she ignited a fiery passion and purpose in two places!

With her charitable organization, we've found ways to give back to the same communities we grew up in, including feeding over 600 families every week, giving kids from our neighborhood scholarships for college, providing emergency housing to those who are homeless, and holding drives and initiatives of countless public acts of service. To date, we've given over $2 million to those who need it most from our own pockets and our corporations through our philanthropic efforts!

We have found a balance.

It's a beautiful synergy. I strategize on investments and how to make more. She figures out how to give more. As far as money goes, I figure out a way to make it, while she figures out a way to donate it to those in need. To me, that's a perfect balance of growth and contribution. And I'm not really a church person, but in my own spiritual way, this is my own way of tithing.

She also serves on the board of several other nonprofits in our local community, mentors younger female entrepreneurs, and provides financial education programs to help strengthen the skill set that most of our folks in poverty need. She has found a way to work that is fulfilling to her.

The Beauty of Delayed Gratification

Let's take a quick second to analyze this. There are a few valuable takeaways from Sheila's story. See, without devoting your life every day to a purpose, working toward a goal, turning imperfection into perfection, and striving to be the best version of yourself, you create a void. We all think we want to get rich and just sit around all day, right? But the irony is, that is *exactly* the opposite of what we truly want. It's a trick of the mind versus the spirit. Our subconscious self versus our conscious self. Our impulsive self versus our true north. The kid in us versus the adult in us. A paradox and a mirage of the fake oasis in the desert. A crackhead, for example, would like nothing more than a mountain of crack at his disposal. The problem is, he'd overdose before the week was out if he were granted such a wish.

The point is, overindulging in your vices and giving in to your impulses just because you can creates emptiness and becomes detrimental to the mind, body, and spirit if not controlled. Happiness is truly rooted in delaying gratification, disciplining yourself, and serving the universe and God by always evolving toward the best version of yourself. Don't believe me? Just try it with a few simple things. I tell people that I help guide in health and fitness all the time, especially when I first start working with them, to stop eating sugar for one month. Besides the serious health benefits and fat loss (which is highly rewarding in itself) of that decision, when they allow themselves to have a cheat meal and eat those Cinnabons, they taste amazing. Serotonin is released in your brain when you delay gratification and discipline yourself to wait for something. When you finally reward yourself, the effects of serotonin mixed with anticipation are damn near *euphoric*! I kid you not.

This thinking applies to life and success, as with fitness and health. Continue to work to build your mind and spirit the same as you would to build your body to never let it get frail and weak. So a word to the wise: even when you have it at your disposal, do everything in moderation. Be your own enforcer to keep from getting out of control and potentially losing yourself. This is a priceless lesson that should be internalized in your personal book of wisdom.

Lack of discipline leads to lack of purpose, which leads to emptiness, which inevitably leads to depression. It's true that the lack of money can be the root of evil. But it's also true that having money can open the same door from the opposite end of the hallway.

We can all learn from Sheila's story here. The principles she birthed from her journey leave great wisdom for us to pocket. Just because you *can* doesn't always mean that you *should*!

Here's a jewel for you: self-discipline is the path to enlightenment.

35

My Reason Will Always Be My Girls

Me and my daughters, more than ten years ago.

I STARTED MY story off by telling you about the day I found out I was losing my place to stay and my girlfriend was pregnant. What a ride it's been! Like I've said so many times already, my two kids will always be the most beautiful things in my life. They're also the catalysts for nearly all of my internal changes that came after they were born. I'd like to end this book by talking to my daughters, Kai and Ree: I hope by the time

I finally allow you to read this, you'll have seen all sides of me and can appreciate the changes you made in my life. I hope you'll also understand the sacrifices I made to help get you where you are today.

Now it's on you! As I told you both before, I want you to be better than me and do more than me. I promise, my perfect dream is to compete with you guys in business and battle to see who can be the most successful while we evolve into the best possible version of ourselves. God blessed us with one another's existence, and I am grateful for this every day. I hope that I have shown you guys the very best that life has to offer in terms of being a great role model, teacher, and coach to you.

Ree and Kai during our trip to Africa.

Ree: My Beautiful Firstborn

My beautiful firstborn. The one thing I know about this child is that she has certain qualities that I have myself. And she will be a true beast once she develops them properly. Fruit becomes sweeter the more it ripens. I believe that's true of the still-developing traits that this young one possesses, even as I write this book.

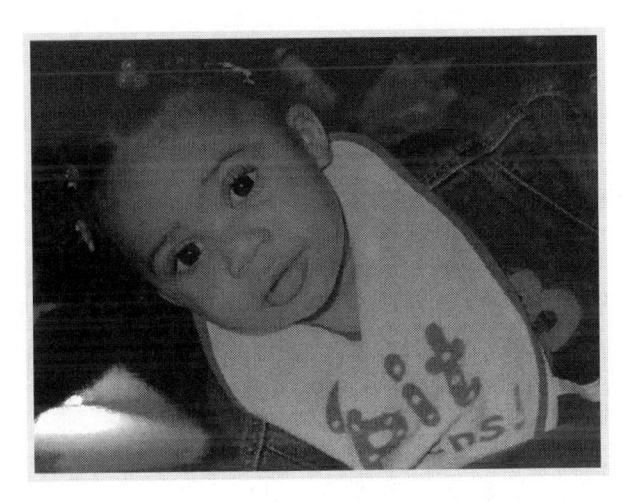

Ree as a baby.

When I was younger, I didn't know my strengths. But now I see that they were the same qualities that push me to be the high-achieving, highly ambitious person I am today. My goal as a parent and coach is one that should be shared by all parents: to help develop habits in my children that will allow them to unlock their potential.

Ree was born on January 22, 1998. That makes her birthday just twelve days before mine, so we share the zodiac sign of Aquarius. Aquarians are known to be thinkers, philosophers, against-the-grainers, innovators, inventors, and creators. We are very free-spirited, determined creatures who bring extreme passion to anything we truly care about. Because we get bored easily and lose interest, the true test of an Aquarian is to channel this explosive drive, using our discipline to maintain our passion. Once we've mastered that, the Aquarian can be an unstoppable monster, capable of near-superhuman focus.

I believe Ree will face the same challenges I've had to face and continue to face, minus the struggles of growing up as I did. I think she'll also deal with the social challenges I've had, including those around forming the right friendships. Through the years, I've grown to be a social butterfly. I can keep a million associates but have very few *true* friends. That comes from a combination of my abandonment issues, the struggles I've had with friends, and my inability to fully trust people (the result of spending so many years in the streets, no doubt). The closer someone is to you, the more vulnerable you are to them, opening yourself to possible hurt. I know Ree struggles with this because I have and still do, only at a different and more advanced level.

In attempting to ensure that my kids never had to grow up the way I did, I've come to understand that there are certain truths they *have* to learn on their own and can't be shielded from. For parents, this is the toughest lesson to learn. As a father, especially, you want to protect them from all harm. And this is an impossible mission because God and the universe did not design life that way. The more you attempt to shield them after a certain point, the more you hinder their personal growth and interfere with their journey. Some of the most important lessons in life *must* be walked alone.

Ree as a teenager.

Because Ree is my firstborn, most of my experiences and challenges with being a father were introduced with her. In short, you can say she is still forcing me out of my comfort zone to continue this thing called evolution.

Kai: From Fragile to Fierce

Kai's team of doctors had no problem showering us with negativity. They consistently hit us with statistics, constantly told us of how bad she was doing, and regularly reminded us of how short her life would be. They were never positive. There were times when she wasn't even that sick and they would still admit her to the hospital for two months. Fuck her social life; they were stealing her childhood. It was hard for her to make friends at school, and she always talked about how she felt like she stood out. Kids were mean, and she feared that they would tease her because of her condition or, better yet, avoid her because they thought that they could catch it. Ignorance.

I felt her pain. I comforted her as much as possible and protected her when I could. She didn't ask for CF. One thing I admired about her, though, was how strong she stood in the face of adversity. Actually, as she grew older, she became fearless. And an adrenaline junkie. And I think that happened because of her condition and the hospital stays. She became numb to the constant IVs, the poking and prodding, the multiple needle intrusions every week, the drawing of blood, and the new meds, and wouldn't complain. I promise you, that girl has more heart than half the grown men I know. Most people couldn't go through what she did and keep a great attitude.

By the time she went to middle school, she was already defying the odds. I attribute that to her spirit, though. She is a fucking fighter. A warrior. The doctors told us to have patience with her as she could fall behind in school because her mental processing speed might be slower than the other kids. She didn't listen to that! Hell no! Kai still managed to be number one in all her classes, from first grade on up.

Kai with her medals of honor.

    She won every award possible. She always made straight As. Never made Bs. If she even thought she was going to make anything less than an A, she considered that failing. She entered spelling bees and won her district. She was often the youngest kid on the stage and would only lose to the older kids. Yes, her social life suffered, but her accomplishments were incredible. You couldn't hold this kid down. She was the epitome of "No matter how life comes at you, persevere." I think she probably secretly competed with every kid in her class to show them that they would never be better than her, regardless of her condition.

    When Kai was in sixth grade, we were told she had a crooked spine. The condition was unrelated to her CF. She successfully went through back surgery and still didn't miss a beat with school.

    That song I wrote for her? I wrote it right around this time. Here's how it ends:

> WITHOUT A DOUBT, I'LL HURT ANY THAT OPPOSE YOU,
> AND CROSS ANY OBSTACLE JUST TO HOLD *you*,
> IT'S A BLESSING, WORD THE FUCK UP, TO KNOW YOU,
> SOMEHOW I'LL STRAIGHTEN ALL OF THIS,
> WATCH ME SHOW *you*.
>
> —EXCERPT FROM HIP-HOP SONG BY SHILOH JONES WRITTEN FOR KAI

I had no way of knowing it then, but my time to "show her" was coming. And it was amazing.

SHE WAS ONE OF THE 2 PERCENT!

When Kai was in seventh grade, I started to deal with my anger. And the more I released it, the more beautifully life responded to me. Let me show you how the universe works. We got a phone call from Kai's doctors, asking for a meeting. When we got together, they explained that donations to the Cystic Fibrosis Foundation were healthy, so there was a lot of research being done on CF.

A trial run was coming down the pipe on a new drug named Kalydeco. It would not be a cure, but it was a reversal drug that would stop the progression of the disease. "But," her doctors explained, "it's only going to be effective for people who have the specific CF mutated genes G551D, G1244E, G1349D, and S1255P. These genes are very rare in CF patients, so less than 2 percent of the CF population will qualify. We want to bring Kai in and do some blood work to see if she has one of these genes. Hey, it's worth a shot, right?"

I thought, *You damn skippy it's worth a shot. Do your thing, Doc!* But honestly, I didn't think much of it. A few months later, we got the phone call. SHE WAS ONE OF THE 2 PERCENT. Holy shit! You gotta be kidding me! I remember that day vividly. I screamed with joy. My eyes immediately filled with tears. This couldn't be happening. Out of all the years CF had existed, what were the chances that this would happen, at this very moment in time, at this point in her life? First of all, the chances were slim to none that she would even be born with CF. Then for a black girl to have it was even more rare. Then for a reversal drug to come out while she was still alive. And then for her to be in the 2 percent of the entire CF population? WOOOW! I distinctly remember feeling like the luckiest person on this planet.

Cheers to Being Fierce

Kai started being admitted to the hospital less and less and, by the middle of eighth grade, her life had stabilized enough that she could start making friends. She is in high school now, as I write this book, and I can't keep her away from friends. She has them over every weekend and still makes straight As in all of her classes, most of which are advanced level. She and her sister were both accepted into—take a guess—Richmond Community High School, the college prep school where I met Sheila. Ree successfully graduated from there and is now in Hampton University, part of a five-year MBA program.

As a father, I couldn't be more proud. They are such great kids. And I guess the sacrifices I made for them are paying off. Every chance I get, I try to help expand their horizons by taking them with me on business trips around the country and the world. I have been blessed enough to take them to Hawaii, Jamaica, Mexico, Amsterdam, and Africa, just to name a few places. I believe each trip will add to their outlook and world view.

And every time we go out of town, Kai wants to do the most insane shit (shit that I have to keep up with, by the way, 'cause as a father, I can't let her outdo me!). All kinds of shit, from hang-gliding to skydiving to ziplining—any extreme sport she sets her sights on. It's torturous, really! But I admire her courage, and the only reason I compete with her is because I don't ever want her to lose that quality. Cheers to being a fierce warrior!

Thanks for Being My Inspiration

Life will only continue to get better the more we strive to perfect ourselves, increase our capacity to love, and aim for more success. And when I say "success," I'm not just talking about business and financial freedom, although they're important. I'm talking about success in terms of accomplishing your goals in life, being who you want to be, doing what you want to do, and growing into the great beings that you are destined to become.

I love you more than life itself. It is you who truly inspired me to write this book. In fact, through most of it, I was speaking directly to you.

Me and my inspirations!

And Then It All Makes Sense...

Do you believe in destiny?

Do you believe God, The universe, or whatever you believe in spiritually, can lead you to your assignment?

Can your passion for the impacts that you want to make in this world, be traced back to the traumas and troubles you experienced psychologically as an adolescent growing up?

Will this inevitably become the force that drives you?

Did my current passions get birthed from my past traumas?

I don't know...

All I can tell you for certain is this; that all paths I traveled led to this moment.

And recently, I had the most powerful revelation!

And as I currently stoke these words on this page that I can with total certainty say, "that I am in my assignment!"

I repeat, I AM IN MY ASSIGNMENT!

Listen, what I went though, EVERYTHING I went though, was a testimony to make me not only qualified to do what I do now in my community, but serve as an influence. Ironically, to be the same influence that I never had, but always needed. I am now extremely grateful that I can be that for others. And maybe…

…just maybe…Their choices will be different; or they will be inspired to create greater options for themselves.

Let's recap and review and make some very potent connections.

Starting with my mom…

And me being completely traumatized by her mental health issues as a child. And not even knowing what it was, why it was or even how to identify with it. Even worse, seeing what it did to her. And how it was responsible for 3 major suicide attempts on her own life.

WATCH THIS: Look at what I do now. At the time of writing this, for over 15 years I've established a mental health organization that has helped thousands and thousands of individuals to better cope with their mental health issues.

I was doing this work BEFORE doing this work!

Now let's take the subject of drugs.

First, look at what drugs did to my family. Then, look at what drugs did to my environment. Not to mention I grew up in neighborhood that suffered from the direct effects of the War On Drugs (Initiated by President Nixon and still having its consequences to this day specifically on the black community). I was on every side of the fence with drugs. I was influenced by drugs, I sold drugs, I even used drugs.

NOW WATCH THIS: Now I run programs that assist people in completely getting drugs out of their life in every way possible.

Next, I was homeless twice in my life, one at 15 and one at 17. I truly know what it feels like to not have a safety net, or no one you can turn to, and what it feels like to sleep unprotected in the streets, trying to stay alert enough so no one will rob you or physically threaten you in any way.

WATCH THIS: now I run several housing programs that allow people to have the ability to have safe, secure housing from affordable housing models to brand new construction built single family homes with luxury. I also run an emergency housing program that helps get people off of the streets, and off of drugs.

And lastly, I know spoke in depth to how much I struggled in my teen years. It was times that it was such a battle and struggle to obtain resources within that day, that it was many times that I didn't know where my next meal was coming from. Thank God I had Sheila in my life! She worked at a place called Lees Chicken. Every night they would allow her to take whatever food they didn't sell to customers home. She would then bring that food to me. If it wasn't for those meals, on certain days I wouldn't have ate.

NOW WATCH THIS: Since then we've created a food pantry together where we donate and feed over a 40,000 families a year! We have a goal of doubling this in size, and then continuing to grow it from there.

What is interesting to note is, the very same elements that entrapped me, are the very same elements that now free me.

I used to hate others for what I went through;

…now the way I show love to others is by helping them to not go through what I had to go through.

I spent half of my life in the street;

…now I dedicate myself to keeping people out of the street!

So I ask you again…

Do you believe in destiny?

Do you believe that the Universe can align someone in their assignment?

I truly believe I am walking testimony that everything happens for a reason. Even though it's up to you to determine how YOUR story will end.

And therefore it is impossible for me not to believe that I am currently in my assignment, in this season of my life.

Every moment we breathe, we have a chance to affect our next chapter in our story.

The question is, what will you do with yours?

Part III

RESPECT

By now you understand my struggles
and what made me me,
How a fire started in me and what raised the heat!
How on one side, it made a nigga strong, that's confirmed,
But on the other side, a fire is flames,
and **FLAMES BURN**!
After a while all you see is the blaze and nothing else,
Until you get lost in it and parts of yourself melt,
I equate this to **ANGER** and the **PAIN** that I felt,
It came clear the biggest war I had to face was with myself

—Excerpt from hip-hop song by Shiloh Jones

My Dad: By Ree Jones, My Daughter

I KNOW EVERYONE isn't fortunate enough to have had a good dad, or even have a dad at all, but I'm fortunate enough to have the best dad. I've always tried my best to be just like my dad because I've never seen something he couldn't do, no goal he couldn't achieve, and no height he couldn't reach. I've had the best physical representation of what it means to be strong yet compassionate.

My little sister, Kai, was diagnosed with cystic fibrosis when she was very young. For as far back as I can remember, every holiday, birthday, and celebratory event was spent in her hospital room because she was always in and out. What was strange to me was that my dad normally wouldn't go see her in the hospital as much as my mom and I would. He would go, but he never stayed for long, and I always assumed it was because of work. I never asked because it wasn't my place.

My dad and Kai would frequently butt heads because she was young and she didn't place much value on taking her medication. She would come home, she wouldn't take her medicine, and as a result, she would end up right back in the hospital, which earned her a lecture from our dad every time. I was also very young at the time, so I thought maybe he was just doing what grown-ups do, annoying their kids on purpose.

One day, my mom went to the hospital before I got out of school so I couldn't go with her, but I know Kai was scheduled for some type of surgery. I got home and I knew Daddy was there, but I didn't make my presence known. I crept up our old wooden stairs and my parents' bedroom door was cracked open a little. I saw him sitting on the bed, hands on his head, crying. I couldn't believe my eyes. I had barely ever seen him sad before this.

I was like my dad in a lot of ways, so I didn't cry much either back then—not because I didn't want to but because he always taught us that if you fall and scrape your knee, you put a Band-Aid on it and keep working. I never said anything, but at that moment, seeing the strongest person I knew cry, I realized that being strong doesn't mean being careless. It means being strong enough to allow yourself to feel, to accept that things in life will happen that you have no control over.

The Continuing Success of Shiloh Jones:
By Bill Jones, My Father

I HAVE WITNESSED my son become successful and continue to build on his financial ventures and make them successful, one at a time. Having an analytical nature, I decided to put energy into trying to understand why he has had one project after another that is earning him and his family financial independence. I have narrowed it down to four areas: the way he treats his family, his employees, his customers, and his friends.

Firstly, beginning with his family, this is, in my opinion, the most important of all areas I studied. Shiloh has two girls, eighteen and sixteen. They are both tops in their schools. The oldest graduated from high school and received a scholarship to one of the top-rated HBICs in the country. The sixteen-year-old is studying at a college level, even though she just passed to the eleventh grade.

From the beginning, Shiloh has taught his girls to be financially independent by giving them their own ATM cards to use on expenses and recreational purposes. The oldest girl has worked since she became of legal age to work. This type of freedom had to be earned by the girls through good grades and good behavior.

Shiloh has also exposed the girls to other countries to learn that all people throughout the world are connected on a deep level. As a result, the girls have friends from every ethnic group—truly an amazing accomplishment. Furthermore, he has shown a deep love for his family and their continued well-being.

Secondly, Shiloh made a decision to concentrate on the well-being of others by creating a mental health and substance abuse agency to help give back to his community in ways he felt that he could contribute most and create the most impact. From the moment he started the business, he decided to hire the top counselors, mentors, therapists, and trained professionals in the area to provide his clients with expert service. On an ongoing basis, Shiloh monitors the progress of his clients to ensure that improvement is being made in their lives, once again endearing his clients, counselors, and himself to the business.

Shiloh and one of his corporate crews at a team-building event.

Thirdly, Shiloh treats his employees with the utmost respect and dignity. Shiloh just recently paid for all of his employees to take a cruise to the Bahamas—an example of how he is focused on fostering a harmonious work environment and beautiful culture.

Finally, Shiloh has friends who have privately told me that he has done things for them that have improved the quality of their lives, from helping friends get married to assisting some with starting their own businesses.

The above-mentioned areas are those that I believe have helped Shiloh gain and keep financial stability, and I am so proud of him. I love you, Shiloh!

What the Evolution of Shiloh Jones Means to Me: By B. J. Moore, My Friend

I KNOW THIS may sound strange, but Shiloh and I met twice. The first time we met, it was in Long Island through a mutual friend (HT) who was in a rap group with him. We met briefly but never really kept in touch. The second time we met or linked up, it was through another mutual friend (rest in peace, Kleph Dollaz) who was actually with me in Long Island the first time we met. My friend kept saying, "Man, you have to meet Shiloh. He is a real dude and reminds me a lot of you."

I had to remind him that I met Shiloh a while back in New York when he was with me, and he was shocked at how everything came back around full circle. He forgot all about the initial meeting. At that time, my friend and Shiloh had been doing music and building a strong friendship for a while. He used to talk about us to each other, so when Shiloh and I met again, it was like we had known each other for years.

The mutual respect was already there, and we had so many things in common. There was definitely a purpose for us getting reacquainted with each other. He has been literally a brother to me ever since. We made money together, lost money together, and learned from each other every step of the way. I witnessed his moves in the streets, music, and entrepreneurship. One thing that has always been a common denominator for him is he approaches everything strategically and with a business mindset, so it was only right for his business ventures to be successful.

One of the realest things he said to me that I carry with me today and share with everyone is, "Just because your plan didn't work successfully the first time, it doesn't mean that you have a bad idea. You have to be honest with yourself about your execution. Did you give it 100 percent? If so, come back to the drawing board and reassess some things. Refocus and restrategize." I think this piece of advice helps define who he is and how he is becoming more and more successful. He has always been a risk-taker and a realist. He knows how to define success and failure, and he could accept either one.

But the difference between him and most people is he would never get down about something that was unsuccessful. He would analyze what went wrong to see if there was any room for improvement or if it was just something that was out of his control or his field of expertise. If something wasn't successful, he wouldn't just give up on it without analyzing what went wrong or how it could be better. He's also honest enough with himself to accept that a certain venture or idea may not be the best move or may not be beneficial. Everything is a lesson learned, and experience is the best teacher. Another strong attribute of his is that most people lack his accountability. He holds himself accountable for the good and the bad, the gains and the losses. I watched him from up close and afar consistently grow in his entrepreneurial endeavors.

It amazes me how someone without a college degree or any kind of high-level professional certification builds businesses that are progressively moving in the black each year. He is living proof for anyone, no matter what your upbringing or ethnic background, that you can reach your goals if you only apply yourself. You have to have that burning desire, the discipline, the sacrifice, and the dedication to truly be successful. He embodies all of those characteristics. He is a role model that the average kid with his background needs to read about or know about, so they can be inspired to reach their goals, too, with no excuses or regrets. He is an inspiration for me. He has become my benchmark. He is at the level of success that I'm striving to get to, and I was the one who took the college route. His hunger for knowledge and inquisitive way of thinking are unparalleled.

The two best things about him, in my opinion, are that he's not selfish and that he's a teacher. He will give anyone the formula if they are willing to learn and put the work in. He wants to see everyone be successful and live out their dreams. Personally, I think this is the reason why he wrote this book: to be an inspiration to others or some kind of spark for change. The best of Shiloh is yet to come. He's just getting started.

Shiloh Jones: By Jetaune Bledsoe, My Friend

I GUESS IT sounds a bit rhetorical to say because he's my little brother, but I always knew Shiloh would excel and do great things. Let's go back to around the time I came into the Jones' life. Shiloh was in middle school, around twelve years old. His older sister (Brandi), his mother (Joan), and his mother's friend (Brenda) lived in the Northside of Richmond, off Brookland Park Boulevard. I always felt that he was initially struggling with some internal issues he wasn't sure how to express, or perhaps they were just normal puberty issues.

By the time he was in Richmond Community High School (RCHS) for the gifted and talented (also known as the high school for "smart smart" kids), things began to go downhill. Things were also becoming tense at home and, by the time Shiloh was fifteen years old, Mom had made a very difficult decision that if he couldn't live under her rules and give up selling marijuana in her house, he had to go. So go he did.

During this time, Shiloh was actually homeless. He hung out on the corner of Brookland Park Boulevard. I'm not quite sure why, but I think it was the consequences of him selling weed. He stayed out for nearly a year. He transferred from RCHS to George Wythe High School and kind of lost interest in school. During this time, he was in touch with his dad. Shiloh did finally complete high school. I say finally because my brother had the intellect to graduate early, ahead of his class, but he gave up along the way. After a couple of years, he got it together and got back on track.

In the years following, Shiloh dabbled in many endeavors, a few with his dad. He sold meats and ADT systems and became pretty good at his entrepreneurial skills, mostly selling marijuana. Shiloh went through a self-discovery period and met a beautiful queen who really got him and loved him. We talked about his dreams and visions. He started working with troubled kids and decided he would have his own business helping children. By now, he had two beautiful daughters and his own home and was doing pretty well, but he had visions and a passion to become financially successful. One of his princesses faced health issues that proved the strength, spiritual faith, and love of our family. This little girl is the strongest and bravest child I know. Today, she is well, and she and her sister are brilliant like their parents.

I remember an incident with this one cat, a guy my brother knew and looked out for many times. (You see, Shiloh has a heart of gold and will do anything for anyone, especially if he's down for you.) So this guy broke into his house when his girls were there alone and it really frightened them. The girls recognized him. Dear God, it took *every* angel in heaven and earth to keep my brother from going after this loser.

Mom intervened to keep Shiloh grounded, but he was so furious. We could see the rage of revenge in his eyes and felt it in his heart, not because the guy broke into his house but because his two babies—the loves of his life, the drive behind his ambition, the blood that pumps his heart—were in the house during the home invasion. He wanted that cat *dead*. Thanks be to God, he did not seek revenge. And after a long, *long* time, he moved past it. He was so angry at Mom and didn't speak to her for a minute. We understood the desire to retaliate but knew there were greater things in store, things that he would not accomplish from a life in prison. Nor did we want him to live with that in his soul. That one incident would have changed his entire life forever.

What I Know about Shiloh Jones: By George Copeland, My Friend and Mentee

SHILOH JONES IS my friend, my mentor. He's the big brother that I missed out on growing up. He cares so much about me that he refuses to give up on me, giving me countless hours of listening when I need an ear, wisdom when I need guidance, and heart when I need tough love. There are three things I can say for certain about Shiloh:

1. **He is always positive:** Whenever we've been faced with a problem together or I've brought one to him, he goes straight for the solution. Even if it's an unwinnable situation, he will still try to find a way. You either win or you learn and move on quickly. I've never seen Shiloh act out of regret either because he never doesn't act on his instincts (if that makes sense). It's like he's always on a mission and too busy to look back.

2. **He tells it to you straight:** There have been *so* many arguments over the past few years, but not one has ended on a genuinely negative note. Almost all of the arguments were toward the first few months, when I was working for him, and I would say they were a mixture of arrogance and lack of maturity on my end—something we all go through but sometimes never grow out of (not saying I'm there yet, haha). But Shiloh has never once given up on me. There were so many times when he could have said

"F" this and moved on (as opposed to taking a genuine interest in my future and success, which at his level of success isn't necessary for him). I remember one time, we were in the nightclub he used to own, sitting in the lobby with a bunch of our fellow employees. I straight up disrespected him with smart-ass comments and a really negative demeanor because I wasn't happy about a few things and I was a poor communicator at the time (another thing he has really helped me with). Instead of firing back, he waited until I was walking out and followed me out, which led to one of the most valuable conversations I've ever had. We ended up having a real heart-to-heart, with him laying down *mad* wisdom (not holding any punches) that still has an impact on my life today. There have been many scenarios like that and, honestly, I feel like every time I hang out with Shiloh, he's impacting me in a positive way. Another related example is when Shiloh went to Ireland for a few weeks, which meant we went over a month without talking (I feel like I'm in a relationship right now, haha) and I was really getting overwhelmed with my business and letting it get to me. I ended up meeting him at his gym at 7 a.m. and, by 8 a.m., dude, I was out that gym door with energy and motivation like no other.

3. **He is humble:** He might dress fly and wear some bling here and there, but one memory I'll never forget is when one of his employees (from one of his other businesses) walked out of the nightclub and saw him getting into his Lexus. She said, "Whose car is that?! That ain't yo' car!" because she had only seen Shiloh's humble-mobile, a 2000 Toyota Camry. That's true character!

In general, the first time I ever saw Shiloh, he was sitting in a nightclub he owned and was probably one of the most charismatic people I've ever met. He was completely embracing and extremely positive. We set up a second meeting with one of his business partners and they hired me on the spot. This was only two weeks after I had been fired from Clear Channel (iHeartMedia), so I was amazed at the timing (it kind of felt like fate). But ever since then, he picked me up and has been pushing me to grow. Honestly, I have no idea where I'd be right now without Shiloh. I know for certain I wouldn't be as wise or mentally tough, though.

The Evolution of Shiloh Jones: By Rocstagis

THERE IS INDEED a great benefit to having a mentor. One who comes from similar circumstances. One who has been resilient enough to transcend humble beginnings and develop the sort of confidence that can move a mountain. Shiloh's life is a testament to overcoming adversity. He proves that the harsh urban environment from which we came can either make you or break you, depending on your outlook in life. There is so much to say about this brother that I could literally write a short book from my own perspective. Instead, I'd rather focus on a few key elements:

- **Time management:** When I first met this brother, I was contracted to do photography at a nightclub that he had recently purchased. I admired his ability to multitask and delegate certain tasks to employees without missing a beat. I later learned that the nightclub was only a small part of the empire that he had managed to build. His ability to run multiple businesses, and still balance fatherhood and family, is nothing short of noteworthy.
- **The power of positive thinking and affirmations:** After building a rapport with Shiloh, I realized that he is one who truly uses the power of positive thinking and affirmations. Nearly 99 percent of the advice I receive from him starts with a command for me to utilize positive thinking. In the years I have known

him, I can't recall one time when I've witnessed him fall victim to negativity.

- **Discipline, the boss who is at work before his employees:** As a former employee and current gym partner, I can tell you that discipline is—or rather it should be—his middle name. To maintain many businesses and a family life and still make it to the gym at 5 a.m. five or six days a week is admirable, to say the least. Again, there is so much more I could say, but I'm sure after reading the contents of this book, you will know exactly what you *need* to know about the evolution of Shiloh Jones. I'm honored to sit front row with my popcorn and watch as this success story continues to unfold.

I am equally honored to consider him a friend and mentor.
Peace.

Epilogue

The Letter

This is a letter to my hustlers,
    Who hustle to their customers,
        Never hold your head down,
            We gotta keep the struggle up,
                Get in, get the fuck out!
            Stack it when you double up,
                Keep in mind the street's hot,
Like crack rocks when it bubble up,
            Know they trying to fuck with us,
        The inner city tough enough,
Then coppers, when they spot us
            trying to rock them handcuffs on us,
            Press to search your luggage up,
                Laugh when they busting us,
    While the government and judge-fucks,
            Love to lock us brothers up!

Knowing when we get time, or women lose their lust in us,
Ten years, time pass, out of jail, come home to what?
Real niggas don't snitch, I know it's just a couple 'us
That's why I keep a burnout,
It's hard to tap the touch with us,
Crazy, but this continent, they hate to see us coming up,
But rap is dominant, white America in love with us,
They hate it when we trouble them,
But love it when they trouble us,
But know what's up!
The system designed to keep them drugs in us!

—Excerpt from hip-hop song by Shiloh Jones

Made in the USA
Middletown, DE
07 October 2022